The
CRACKING
of the
BIBLE:

The Divine Pattern Revealed

THE FIRST EDITION

GEORGE KIDD, JR.

Table of Contents

📖 Preface

This book provides a clear pattern of the Divine via demonstrated and recorded examples. God's pattern of activities in the Bible and beyond has been analyzed in detail. Based on this analysis of what many believe, and after many years of research by others, a confirmation will be provided that the divine God does truly exist, and there is a Modus Operandi or pattern to what he does within the Bible and elsewhere.

For I am the LORD, I change not. (Malachi 3:6)

• Introduction

All scripture is given by inspiration of God.
(2 Timothy 3:16)

"The Cracking of the Bible: The Divine Pattern Revealed." WHAT A BOLD CLAIM TO MAKE! A claim that could not be made until now. There is stark evidence to prove and support it! There are those who have researched and provided various analyses of the Bible i.e. topical, literary, critical, biographical analysis, textual data analysis, correspondence analysis, and statistical analysis, etc. I have focused on some of the works of those who have searched the Bible for a secret code, hidden messages, or hidden information using scientific and mathematical skills such as Sir Isaac Newton. Some have done scientific research on the Bible and discovered what they claim to be the Bible Code. Jews, Christians, and others believe the scriptures were written by God, so did he place some secret code in the Bible? If the answer is yes, can it be proven?

This scientific research done on the Bible called the Bible Code was done by a group of researchers which entailed finding hidden messages in the Bible with something called Equidistant Letter Sequences (ELS) i.e. skipping a desired number of letters in the biblical text to come up with messages using computers. These scientific researchers of the Bible Code were Doron Witztum, Dr. Eliyahu Rips, and Yoav Rosenberg who published a paper called "Equidistant Letter Sequences in the Book of Genesis" in the American journal *Statistical Science*,[1] in August of 1994 presenting evidence that the book of Genesis contained encoded information. The article, the published paper, was the basis of a book that was published in 1997 called "The Bible Code" by Michael Drosnin who also wrote "The Bible Code II" in 2002, and "The Bible Code III" in 2007. So that there is no confusion this book does not endorse nor support the works of Mr. Drosnin. A different approach was taken by me to come up with a more accurate and definitive conclusion about the Bible. There are those who say "The Bible Code" is controversial in that it relies heavily on computers which were not invented during the time of the authors of the Bible. There are those who would say that these biblical authors were not adept in introducing hidden messages into the Bible to be found by computers in the future. The Bible code research being done today focuses on the Torah or the first five books of the Bible.

While others were looking at only part of the Bible as they searched for secret messages, I stepped back and looked at the entire Bible from another perspective. I felt there had to be something simpler which could be understood by all and on a much larger scale than the "Bible Code." I call it the "Bible Pattern." I considered what some call "The Law (or Rule) of Threes" in which things tend to happen in threes. The authors of the Bible used the number three and its derivatives at least 680 times. Some declare that the number three is the perfect number of divinity, that it is symbolic of something

---

[1] *Statistical Science,* Volume 9, Number 3 (1994), pp. 429-438. Source - Wikipedia, Bible Code, 2012, http://dx.doi.org/ 10.1214%2Fss%2F1177010393, Retrieved 12.30.2012

being complete as it relates to the divine. There are those who say that the number three relates to permanence. Until now I have never seen any documentation that proves three is the number of divine perfection. **If the number three is divine and the Bible is divinely inspired, then we should be able to reconcile these two statements.** The epiphany I had is that in the "Law of Threes" there exists a pattern. Two of the items are linked together in some fashion while the third item that is separate is still linked to the other two items in the context of the subject matter. It is as if the three items form a triangle. It might be said that this is God's true fingerprint.

They are events, symbols, subjects, and word patterns in threes unique in the Bible where this triangular pattern can be identified. Even in lists that were divinely defined, the pattern can be discerned based on the scriptural presentation, in some permutation of the first three or four items: 1st, 2nd, 3rd; 2nd, 3rd, 4th; 1st, 2nd, 4th; or 1st, 3rd, 4th. Based on what is presented in the biblical text, there were in some cases more items listed, but they also yielded the three pattern.

The documentary called "Encounters with the Unexplained - Secrets of the Bible Code," presented an experiment relating to the Bible Code/Torah Code. It was updated in the enlightening 1998 documentary called "Secrets of the Bible code Revealed." By using the word TORAH (TORH) via ELS it was found that the first two books, Genesis and Exodus, and the last two books, Numbers and Deuteronomy, point to the center, or third, book, Leviticus. The word TORH was shown to be going forward for the first two and backward for the last two pair of books. In the book of Leviticus, the name of God, YaHWeh (YHWH) is discovered by skipping 7 letters via ELS in the book. The message that I got from the experiment after viewing the video was, *I am God and I am three.* (Note: A snippet of the video demonstrating the experiment is located at http://www.youtube.com/watch?v=rcNrAZTQ45k)

It is said that the name of God YaHWeH (YHWH) is a ". . . **third person singular** imperfect form. . ." of a verb called *hayah* meaning "He is."[2] In looking at the structure of Lamentations, the 25th book of the Bible, it consists of five chapters where the first, second, fourth, and fifth chapters are all twenty-two verses in length. The third chapter however is sixty-six verses in length. This is triple the number of verses in each of the other four chapters—the two preceding and the two succeeding the third chapter. This made me think of the Bible code experiment having even more credence. Of the five chapters the ". . .first four are written as **acrostics** – chapters one, two, and four each have twenty-two verses, corresponding to the twenty-two letters of the Hebrew alphabet, the first lines beginning with the first letter of the alphabet, the second with the second letter, and so on. Chapter three has sixty-six verses, so that each letter begins three lines, and the fifth poem (chapter) is not acrostic but still has twenty-two lines. The purpose or function of this form is unknown."[3]

Note: "An **acrostic** is a **poem** or other form of writing in which the first letter, syllable or word of each line, **paragraph** or other recurring feature in the text spells out a word or a message."[4] In this case, the acrostic is in the fashion of the Hebrew alphabet from the first to the last letters, א (*aleph/Alef* or *El* in Ancient Hebrew) to ת (*tav/tau* or *waw* in Ancient Hebrew).

2   Source - Wikipedia, I am that I am, 2013, http://en.wikipedia.org/wiki/I_Am_that_I_Am, Retrieved 04.16.2013

3   **Source - Wikipedia, Book of Lamentations, 2014,** http://en.wikipedia.org/wiki/Book_of_Lamentations**, Retrieved 02.14.2014**

4   Source - Wikipedia, Acrostic, 2014, http://en.wikipedia.org/wiki/Acrostic, Retrieved 02.12.2014

Later I noticed also that in the book of Psalms, the 19th book, it is divided into five sections or volumes. The first section ranges from chapters one to forty-one. The second section is from chapters forty-two to seventy-two. The third is section from chapters seventy-three to eighty-nine. The fourth section is from chapters 90 to 106. The last section ranges from chapters 107 to 150. There are those who state that each of these five sections or volumes are representative of the themes of the first five books of the Bible, the Torah. I viewed the structure of the book of Psalms as being in line with the experiment that was performed also and as a confirmation of it. I found a picture of God and Jesus with God the Father, being depicted as having an equilateral triangle around his head which is supposed to be the equivalent of having a halo or nimbus that is normally seen as circular in shape. The picture is shown below:

Source of image: http://www.mgr.org/trinity.html

The Bible Code experiment and the picture confirmed my pattern analysis and helped me think of triangles going the directions of up or down, ▲▼△▽, for what I call the Bible Pattern. In the 1998 mentioned documentary Dr. Rips believes according to Michael Drosnin that with the ELS, ". . .we have found the first and simple level of a code that is far more complex and far beyond our reach . . . his assumption if we find this clear a pattern there is almost certainly a much larger pattern but we don't yet have the mathematical tools or perhaps the technology to see it." I would contend that you have to have some sense of faith that is strong in order to see that "much larger pattern," for nothing is impossible and God does not have limitations. I discovered that "much larger pattern" throughout the entire Bible. This pattern is NOT complex nor is it "far beyond our reach" as stated in the documentary. There are a number of books that demonstrate the versatility of God such as his character and nature, but none that demonstrate his consistency in my view. Nothing close to what is being present in this book.

The triangle is first and foremost associated with the divine number of three and the triangle is the symbol of God. It is said that the origins of the triangle is lost in time from a human perspective in my view. No one has ever linked actual biblical text to the triangle symbol until now. I looked at dissecting verses of events, objects, and phrases to find the pattern. I listed some of the major and significant highlights in and out of the Bible to demonstrate the findings by providing summarized examples in and of the Old Testament (O.T.), the New Testament (N.T.), between the Old and New Testaments, and outside the Bible also. In these summarized examples, triangles symbols are used before the paragraph/passage to denote the start or first divine directional triangle pattern within the example paragraph/passage. In some cases a few of the triangle symbols are shown at the beginning of an example paragraph/passages to indicate a number of triangles displayed within the example paragraph/passage. Triangle symbols were also used within the example paragraphs/passages in some cases after a list of three items were cited to show that those three items also displayed the triangle pattern. These are pointed out also.

IMPORTANT: WHEN YOU ARE READING ALL TRIANGLE SHAPES AND DIAGRAMS READ THEM FROM RIGHT TO LEFT! This is being done out of the respect for the work that was done. Besides I know that in Hebrew they are going to be depicted in this fashion. I wanted to be the first to demonstrate the triangles in this fashion. In the future they can be presented in a way accustomed to western standards. Again, note that before each example passage/paragraph a number of triangle symbols, △▽▲▼, have been placed. This is done to denote each of the divine triangles within the paragraphs/passage. Each denoted triangle symbol that is at the start of the paragraphs/passage will be pointed out within paragraphs/passage. Here are just some of those divine examples.

✡ Examples of the Divine Pattern in the Old Testament

Genesis, Days of Creation

To begin I see the triangle patterns in the six Days of Creation, the Greek term *Hexameron* and one could also say the Emanation of the world, as told in Genesis chapter 1.

The **first day,** "Light" for the earth which ". . .was without form, and void" and the **second day,** the "Firmament of Heaven" or the atmosphere for the earth are related or linked to creation in and of the heavens as established in verses 1-8.

The **third day** dealt with the "Seas" and "dry land" and the creation of plant life/vegetation in verses 9-13 or work that was done on the earth.

On the **fourth day,** there was a return back to doing work in the heavens again to deal with the "two great lights"— the Sun the greater light for the day and the moon the lesser light for the night. The stars are addressed also with the sun and the moon in verses 14-19.

The **fifth day** deals with the creation of other life in the seas and in the air, fish and birds respectively, in verses 20-23.

On the **sixth day** "beast of the earth after his kind. . ." and other life for the land along with man was created in verses 24-31.

Here are the patterns that I saw.

▽ **Day 1 and 2** were linked to doing work in the heavens with **Day 3** doing work on the earth—a triangle pointing downwards for those three days.

△ **Day 4** was dedicated to doing work in the heavens again with **Day 5 and 6** doing work relating to life on the earth—a triangle pointing upwards for those three days.

✿ Based on my analysis both triangles incorporate both activities of God's work in the heavens and on the earth being interwoven and creating the hexagram. I can say the hexameron can be combined with the hexagram. As I see the pattern of the days of Creation, days 1, 2, and 4 relate to the creation of and in the Heavens with Creation days 3, 5, and 6 relating to the Creation of Life. The summary of what God had done is stated in Genesis 2:1, "Thus the heavens and the earth were finished, and all the host of them." All six days of work was done in chapter 1 of Genesis. I noticed that the beasts were created to live in three areas—in the water and in the air on Day 5, and on land on Day 6 (Genesis 1:20-21, 24-25). Another identified triangle being viewed downward, ▽.

The precise origin of the Judaism hexagram symbol has now been revealed. Evolutionists question the six days of creation. Others argue the logical sequence of the days of creation should have been 1, 4, 2, 3, 5, and 6 which could fit the narrative of the Big Bang theory. It could have been done differently, but it was done the way it was for a reason. Exodus 20:11 states, "For in six days the LORD made heaven and earth, the sea, and all that in them is. . . ." Exodus 31:17 states, "for in six days the LORD made heaven and earth."

Below are the triangle diagrams depicting the Days of Creation:

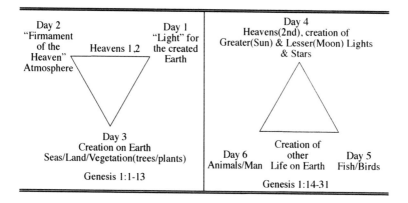

The two triangles combined in the following manner forms the symbol that is known as the hexagram the symbol of Judaism:

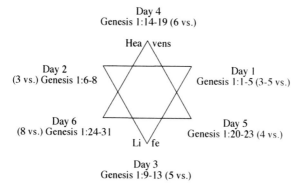

The Hexameron meets the Hexagram
New symbol for 21st century

"Thus the heavens and the earth were finished, and all the host of them."
(Genesis 2:1)

The phrase "God said" is stated ten times in this first chapter relating to creation (verses 3, 6, 9, 11, 14, 20, 24,

26, 28, and 29). I also noticed that on days three and four of Creation they needed further analysis. I viewed the information provided for those days and thought they could be turned each into separate triangles also based on the stated information.

The information pertaining to **Day 3** in Genesis 1:9-11 is, ". . .Let the waters under the heaven be gathered together unto one place, and let the dry land appear: [10]And God called the dry land Earth; and the gathering together of the waters called he Seas: [11] . . .Let the earth bring forth grass, the herb yielding seed, and the fruit tree yielding fruit after his kind, whose seed is in itself, upon the earth". The information pertaining to **Day 4** in Genesis 1:16 is, "God made two great lights; the greater light to rule the day, and the lesser light to rule the night: he made the stars also."

Here are the triangle diagrams for the two mentioned days:

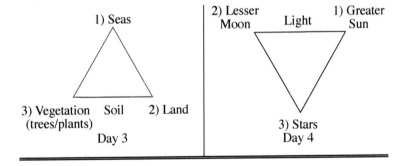

1) Seas

3) Vegetation   Soil   2) Land
(trees/plants)
Day 3

2) Lesser   Light   1) Greater
Moon   Sun

3) Stars
Day 4

Once the triangles were formed I thought that these two top and bottom points of the Star of David, or Magen David, had to be turned into each other. The image became three Xs aligned with the numbered days above and below the Xs. I had to wonder what is it that needed to be seen? Next I added the numbers assigned to the days together on top and bottom of the figure to get 2+4+1=7 on top and 6+3+5=14 on bottom for a total of 21. The diagram of the mentioned activities is below:

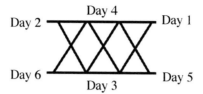

The top half of the symbol relates to work done
in the Heavens on Days 2+4+1 = 7
The bottom half of the symbol relates to work done on
the Earth pertaining to life on Days 6+3+5 = 14

After figuring out how the symbol calculates out to 21 or three sevens, 777, one on top and two on the bottom, this was a confirmation that I was correct. I noticed the date and time of this revelation occurred 09.29.2011 at around 3:30 a.m. Later I recalled the date of 09.29.2008 at 4 p.m. was the date the U.S. stock market Dow Jones industrial average was down 777.68 points or 777.7, which is equivalent to 7 percent. It was said that it was the biggest point drop in U.S. history at the time. The number 777 is stated one time in the Bible in Genesis 5:31, "And all the days of Lamech were seven hundred seventy and seven years." The ninth generation of man.

7

7△7

21 for 21ˢᵗ Century. Truly "Forever 21"

I viewed the various ways that the number 777 was expressed in Hebrew, Greek, and in Roman numerals. In Hebrew it can be expressed today as *ע=7, ז=70, ן=700.* In Greek as *Psi Ψ=700, omikron O=70,* and *zeta Z=7.* In Roman numerals as *DCC=700, LXX=70, VII=7.* Another way that the number was expressed in the same manner as the ones mentioned was in a book relating to Judaism called "777 and other Qabalistic Writings" by Aleister Crowely as $N=700$, $O=70$, $Z=7$."[5] In these instances the pattern was pretty much the same. Hebrew, Greek, and Roman were chosen because of the significant event in the New Testament that will be mentioned later.

Analyzing further I began to see diagonally and up and down sevens around the three Xs in that 1+6, 4+3, and 2+5 and vice versa. The number of sevens was six in all for a total of forty-two. There were three sevens on the top and on the bottom. A depiction of what was done can be viewed below. Also the alignment of the six sevens around the three Xs made me think of one of the symbol/Sigil/Seal that I saw from a book called "The Book of Raziel the Angel" (**Sefer Raziel HaMalakh** the Hebrew title)[6] which is another book related to Judaism. It is said that the term *sigil* meaning "seal" is derived from the Latin word *sigilum*. The seal is also shown below:

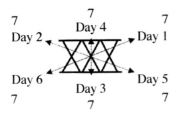

Source of Seal:
The Book of Raziel the Angel
(**Sefer Raziel HaMalakh**)

5   Crowley, Aleister, 777 and other Qabalistic writings of Aleister Crowley, page 4, York Beach, ME: Samuel Weiser, Inc. 1977. ISBN 0-87728-222-6.

6   Book of Raziel the Angel (Sefer Raziel HaMalakh, Amsterdam (1701) Chabad-Lubavitch Library. Full-text PDF version, in Hebrew, Page 88, from HebrewBooks.org (http://www.hebrewbooks.org/pdfpager.aspx?req=23968&st=&pgnum=1&hilite=)

One last thing that had to be addressed to confirm I was on the right path were the three Xs. The three Xs viewed as roman numerals are three tens converted to total thirty. But when the three Roman numeral 10s are viewed in binary 101010 the total is forty-two or six sevens. (Note: More information relating to the number 42 will be mentioned later.)

And what one nation in the earth is like thy people, even like Israel, whom God went to redeem for a people to himself. . ." (2 Samuel 7:23).

There are those who have stated over time that pagan gods and other occult practices that used the symbol were the basis for the Jewish symbol of ancient times. In one's view that notion has clearly been dispelled. There are those who may say that the hexagram symbol, relating to Jews, was not in existence in ancient times. I would point out there is the story or legend of King Solomon having a ring given to him that had the hexagram as a design in it. If this story is true then it was in use in ancient times by at least one person. As I trekked though the Bible I continued to find more evidence of the divine triangle pattern in the text.

Note: The works of Mr. Crowely and the reference to the Sefer Raziel HaMalakh should be noted as works that were done outside of the Bible and may or may not have validity relating to the Bible.

Adam and Eve

▽ **There are four rivers coming out of the Garden of Eden, "four heads" that effects three lands (Genesis 2:10-14).**
The first two lands which are "compasseth" by rivers are Havilah by the Pison river and Ethiopia by the Gishon river. The third land Assyria, is flanked by the Hiddekel (Tigris)

and Euphrates rivers which are east and west of it respectively, is not mentioned as being encompassed. This is the basis for the denoted triangle.

△/▽ **There are the three main corporeal characters in Genesis chapter 3—the Serpent, Adam, and Eve.**

The serpent enticed Eve to eat of the fruit of the tree that God did not want them to eat from. She did eat from that tree and then in turn ". . .gave also unto her husband with her; and he did eat" (3:6). The last two characters, Adam and Eve, are linked in that they are married and human. The first character is an animal. The first denoted triangle. In verses 1-6 the serpent and Eve are the only two characters of the three to have had a conversation about eating the fruit from the forbidden tree. Adam is not mentioned in the conversation nor does he have a conversation with the other two about the fruit of the three. The second denoted triangle. In verse six there are three things stated that Eve saw of the forbidden Tree: 1) "it was good for food," 2) "pleasant to the eyes," and 3) "to be desired to make one wise." Of these three the last item states the true nature of the tree. Another identified triangle, ▽.

△/▽ **God punishes all three characters for their acts pertaining to the eaten fruit of "the tree" in the midst of the Garden of Eden.**

1) For The serpent, ". . .thou art cursed above all cattle, and above every beast of the field; upon thy belly shalt thou go, and dust shalt thou eat all the days of thy life:" (Genesis 3:14)
2) For Eve, ". . .I will greatly multiply thy sorrow and thy conception; in sorrow thou shalt bring forth children; and thy desire shall be to thy husband, and he shall rule over thee." (Genesis 3:16)

3) For Adam, "Because thou hast hearkened unto the voice of thy wife, and hast eaten of the tree, of which I commanded thee, saying, Thou shalt not eat of it: cursed is the ground for thy sake; in sorrow shalt thou eat of it all the days of thy life;" (Genesis 3:17)

Of the three stated verses for the three characters the last two verses establishes the link between the last two characters where they are "husband" and "wife" and are the two characters of the three that ate the forbidden fruit. The first denoted triangle. From another perspective the word "cursed" and the phrase ". . .shalt thou eat all the days of thy life. . ." is used by God against the serpent and Adam but not Eve. The second denoted triangle.

▽ **The first two of the three named sons of Adam and Eve, Cain and Abel, were born close in age (Genesis 4:2).**
These two made offerings to God, but Cain's offering was not accepted by God while Abel's was by God (Genesis 4:3-4). The third son, Seth, 130 years later, there is no mentioning of a job or any sacrificing of his own to God (Genesis 4:25, 5:3). The first two sons were linked to their offerings to God and there is an introduction and conclusion for the first two sons, but not the third son. This is the basis for the denoted triangle. There is nothing relating to Seth's activities, not even in the book of Jasher which is mentioned in Joshua 10:13 and 2 Samuel 1:18), other than having offspring. Genesis 4:25 indicates that Seth was the replacement son for Abel who was killed by Cain his brother. It is said according to other ancient texts that Seth was also favored by God like his brother Abel. With that being said, I viewed another identified triangle where the first son Cain is not favored by God while the last two sons are, Abel and Seth,△.

▽/△ **Read of Enoch, 7th generation from Adam, and his three heavenly encounters.**

These encounters are in the third chapter of the book of Jasher. Again, a book that is referenced in Joshua 10:13 and 2 Samuel 1:18. Here are those encounters:

1) An "angel of the Lord called to him from Heaven", in verse 3, and told him "Rise, go forth from thy house and from the place where thou dost hide thyself, and appear to the sons of men, in order that thou mayest teach them the way in which they should go and the work which they must accomplish to enter in the ways of God", in verse 4. Enoch had been in seclusion.

2) "27And at that time the sons of men were with Enoch, and Enoch was speaking to them, and they lifted up their eyes and the likeness of a great horse descended from heaven, and the horse paced in the air; 28 And they told Enoch what they had seen, and Enoch said to them, On my account does this horse descend upon earth; . . . 29 And the horse descended at that time and stood before Enoch, and all the sons of men that were with Enoch saw him."

3) Enoch ascends into heaven, "36And when the kings returned they caused a census to be taken, in order to know the number of remaining men that went with Enoch; and it was upon the seventh day that Enoch ascended into heaven in a whirlwind, with horses and chariots of fire." This is also alluded to in Genesis 5:24 of the Bible, "And Enoch walked with God: and he was not; for God took him."

Of these three encounters the first two are coming down from heaven of the three. The first denoted triangle. Of the three encounters the last two of the three involved horses. The second denoted triangle. I think it can be safe to say that the horse that came down from heaven for Enoch also ascended back up into heaven with him. Note that is stated in Jasher 3:13 "And these are the generations of Enoch, Methuselah, Elisha, and Elimelech, three sons; and their sisters were Melca and Nahmah,". Of Enoch's three sons his first son Methuselah is where his genealogy continues on from. Another identified triangle,△. This is also stated in Genesis 5:25-26.

Noah and the Ark

▽/△ **In Genesis 8:6-12 after forty days in the ark, a raven and a dove were sent out by Noah as way to check the conditions**: ". . .to see if the waters were abated from off the face of the ground" (verse 8).

The raven is mentioned once but the dove is released three times. They both come back after being released together the first time in verses seven and eight. The dove comes back to Noah, but it is not stated where the raven goes after its release. It can be assume that it comes back to the Ark and lands on it somewhere since the waters were not abated. The raven is not mentioned again as being used in checking on the condition of the waters. Seven days later a dove is sent again, a second time, and it comes back with evidence of plant life in its beak (verses 10-11). Seven days later the dove again is sent forth the third time, but does not come back to Ark. In focusing on the actions of the dove, it was released three times by Noah coming back twice but not the third time it is released. This is the basis for the first denoted triangle. From another perspective it seems that the raven and the dove come back, once for the raven and twice for a dove. This is the second denoted triangle.

▽ **Genesis 9:1 states, "And God blessed Noah and his sons, and said unto them**: "Be fruitful, and multiply, and replenish the earth." Of the three items mentioned at the end of the verse, the objective of God is the third item ". . .and replenish the earth." This is the basis for the denoted triangle.

△ **Genesis 9:22 states, "And Ham, the father of Canaan, saw the nakedness of his father, and told his two brethren without" (Shem and Japheth).**

This was considered an evil act that was done by Ham to see the "nakedness" of his parent. The other two sons went and they covered him up by walking backwards toward him, "And Shem and Japheth took a garment, and laid it upon both their shoulders, and went backward, and covered the nakedness of their father; and their faces were backward, and they saw not their father's nakedness" in verse 9:23. One brother did an evil act, Ham, and the other two brothers addressed the issue, Shem and Japheth. This is the basis for the denoted triangle. Because of Ham's evil act he was cursed by his father Noah. (Genesis 9:24-27).

Abram/Abraham

△ **Abram is listed as the first of three sons of his father:** "And Terah lived seventy years, and begat Abram, Nahor, and Haran."(Genesis 11:26). Later Abram is told by the LORD to "Get thee out of thy country, and from thy kindred, and from thy father's house, unto a land that I will shew thee" in Genesis 12:1. Of the three sons born to Terah, Abram, the first of the three, is chosen of God. The basis for the denoted triangle is where in this instance God chose the first son Abram and not one of the other two of the three.

▽/△ **Genesis 15:9 states, "And he said unto him, Take me an heifer of three years old, and a she goat of three years old, and a ram of three years old."**

The first two beasts that are to be sacrificed are female animals and the last a male animal of the three pertaining to the offering. This is the first denoted triangle. All three beasts are part of the Bovidae family of animals, but the goat and the ram are part of the same subfamily, the Caprinae. The heifer is a part of the Bovinae subfamily. This is the second denoted triangle. All three of these animals are land animal, three of five or three fifths. The other two animals that are sacrificed with the three mentioned in the verse are birds, "and a turtledove and a young pigeon." The three land animals were divided for the sacrifice, but not the birds in verse 15:10. Five is the third prime number behind the numbers two and three which is ironic in that is it the numerical breakdown of the five animals sacrificed. I think of the number of the books of the Torah / Pentateuch. The two triangle diagrams of the three three-year-old beasts are shown below:

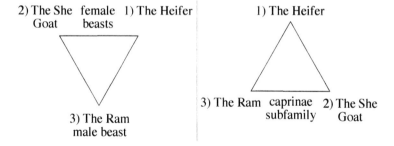

△**There were three altars built by Abram before his name was changed, and one as Abraham:**

1) He builds the first at Shechem on the plain of Moreh in Genesis 12:6-7.
2) The second is between Bethel and Hai in Genesis 12:8 near Bethel east and of the city.

3) The third was on the Plain of Mamre in Hebron in Genesis 13:15-18.
4) As Abraham in Moriah where he was about to sacrifice his son Isaac in Genesis 22:9-17.

I see the triangle pattern in the first, third, and fourth built altars where the land is stated to be given to Abram's seed for those altars while nothing is mentioned concerning getting something from God in the second altar. In the three built altars where something is stated to be given, in altars three and four the land, inferred in the fourth, and the innumerable seed is promised to be given. Innumerable seed is not mentioned for the first altar just ". . .thy seed. . .". This is the basis for the denoted triangle. Again, of the four altars one, three, and four it is stated that Abram/Abraham is going to be given something from God. One can conclude that God promised Abram/Abraham the following:

1) ". . .make of thee a great nation"
2) ". . .and make thy name great" (Genesis 12:2)
3) The Land of Canaan (Genesis 17:8)
4) Innumerable seed/offspring (Genesis 13:16; 22:17)

△/▽ **Abram/Abraham is told from heaven that "thy seed" will be multiplied based on three analogies:**

1) "the dust of the earth" in Genesis 13:16
2) "the stars of the heaven" in Genesis 22:17 and 15:5
3) "the sand which is upon the sea shore" in Genesis 22:17

Of the three analogies the second and the third are both mentioned in the same verse Genesis 22:17. This is the first denoted triangle. From another perspective the "dust of the earth" and "the sand which is upon the sea shore" are on the earth while the "stars of the heaven" is not. This is the basis for the second denoted triangle.

△/▽ **There are three verses relating to the laughing of Abraham and Sarah regarding having and the birth of their son Isaac in their old age.**

Abraham laughs in the first verse, Genesis. 17:17, and Sarah laughs in the last two verses, Genesis 18:12 and 21:6. The basis for the first denoted triangle. Also one can view that there was laughter twice before the birth by Abraham and Sarah, and once after Isaac's birth by Sarah. This is the second denoted triangle. Here are the verses:

1) Genesis 17:17 "Then Abraham fell upon his face, and laughed, and said in his heart, Shall a child be born unto him that is an hundred years old? and shall Sarah, that is ninety years old, bear?"

2) Genesis 18:12 "Therefore Sarah laughed within herself, saying, After I am waxed old shall I have pleasure, my lord being old also?"

3) Genesis 21:6 "And Sarah said, God hath made me to laugh, so that all that hear will laugh with me."

△ **The Divine Triangle Pattern is presented to Abraham**: "¹And the LORD appeared unto him in the plains of Mamre: and he sat in the tent door in the heat of the day; ²And he lift up his eyes and looked, and, lo, three men stood by him: and when he saw them, he ran to meet them from the tent door, and bowed himself toward the ground" (Genesis 18:1-2). The Lord physically appeared unto Abraham and he is accompanied by two other companions in the plains of Mamre. The three men visiting him is the clear example of the triangle pattern and the basis for the denoted triangle.

△ **Lot, Abraham's nephew, and his two daughters**: They are recorded as the only three people who ultimately survived the destruction of the cities Sodom and Gomorrah. This is the basis for the denoted triangle. (Genesis 19:16-26 and Book of Jasher 19:51-55).

△ **Abraham is called from heaven three times.**

The first time is by God when he tells him to sacrifice his son Isaac. Later on a third day, he finds a place to do it in Moriah in Genesis 22:1-4. The second time he is called from heaven by an angel of the Lord when he is about to slay his son on the altar. The angel tells him not to slay Isaac in Genesis 22:11-13. The third time the angel of the Lord tells him that he is blessed for his sacrifice in Genesis 15-19. Of the three times Abraham is called from heaven, once is by God and twice by "the angel of the LORD." This is the basis for the denoted triangle. Out of heaven Abraham's name is mentioned four times once by God and three times by the "angel of the LORD." Of the three times the angel called Abraham's name in verses 22:11 and 15, the first time he says his name twice in verse 11, and later once in verse 15. Another identified triangle, ▽.

▽ **Notice Abraham says, "Here am I" three times in Genesis 22:1, 7, and 11.**

The first two times he says these words it is in connection to the mentioning of the "burnt offing" for God. To God first before it is stated by God ". . .and offer him there for a burnt offering . . ." referring to his son Isaac. He says the phrase to his son Isaac in the second verse, seventh, the second time, before his son asks the question, "Behold the fire and the wood: but where is the lamb for a burnt offering?" The third time he says the phrase it is said to the "angel of the Lord" after he calls Abraham. The "burnt" offering is not mentioned. This is the basis for denoted triangle.

▽/▽ Abraham had children by three women.

1) Concubine Hagar in Genesis 16 who bore Ishmael
2) His Wife Sarah in Genesis 21 who bore Isaac
3) The Wife/Concubine Keturah in Genesis 25:1-2 who had Zimran, Jokshan, Medan, Midian, Ishbak, and Shuah.

Of the three women the first two women each had one child and the third had six. The first denoted triangle. Of the three women the first two lived together with each other. Hagar was servant to Sarah. The second denoted triangle. From another perspective the women of Abraham were Sarah his wife, and Hagar and Keturah were concubines. Another identified triangle,△. According to 1 Chronicles 1:32 Keturah is considered a concubine. The verse states, "Now the sons of Keturah, Abraham's concubine". Note, while watching the show "The King is Coming" on the Trinity Broadcasting Network one Sunday, the host of the show Dr. Ed Hindson stated that these three women were mothers of the Middle East. Sarah is the mother of those of Jewish descent, with Hagar and Keturah considered the mothers of those of Arab descent and "Middle Easterners."

▽/△ Three times the clause "She is my sister" was used. Twice by Abram/Abraham and once by his son Isaac regarding their wives.

Abram said it about Sarai to Pharaoh of Egypt in Genesis 12:11-19 and again to King Abimelech of Gerar in Genesis 20:2-14. Third, Isaac said it to Abimelech king of the Philistines unto Gerar about Rebekah in Genesis 26:6-12. The first denoted triangle is based on Abraham saying it twice and his son Isaac once. The second denoted triangle is based on how is said to Pharaoh of Egypt once and King Abimelech of Gerar twice.

▽/▽ **A confluence of major threes that are associated with Abram/Abraham:**

1) Abram is listed as the first of three sons of his father, "And Terah lived seventy years, and begat Abram, Nahor, and Haran" in Genesis 11:26. Abram is chosen by the LORD and he is told by the LORD "Get thee out of thy country, and from thy kindred, and from thy father's house, unto a land that I will shew thee" in Genesis 12:1.

2) Abram is told by the LORD to sacrifice three three-year-old animals to him, "And he said unto him, Take me an heifer of three years old, and a she goat of three years old, and a ram of three years old" in Genesis 15:9.

3) The Divine Triangle Pattern is presented to Abraham, "And the LORD appeared unto him in the plains of Mamre: and he sat in the tent door in the heat of the day; And he lift up his eyes and looked, and, lo, three men stood by him: and when he saw them, he ran to meet them from the tent door, and bowed himself toward the ground" in Genesis 18:1-2.

Of these three that are stated the third item is the greatest because "the LORD" had physical contact with Abraham. This is the basis for the first denoted triangle. Of these three the first two instances pertain to "the LORD" telling him to do something. The second denoted triangle.

Jacob

▽ **Reviewed the first three to four sons Jacob had by his wife Leah and how they were named.**

Notice the third son Levi was not named as stated as the other three. Levi, the patriarch of God's chosen group for the future priesthood. The verses are as follows:

1) Genesis 29:32 "And Leah conceived, and bare a son, and she called his name Reuben."
2) Genesis 29:33 "And she conceived again, and bare a son; . . . and she called his name Simeon."
3) Genesis 29:34 "And she conceived again, and bare a son; . . . I have born him three sons: therefore was his name called Levi."
4) Genesis 29:35 "And she conceived again, and bare a son: . . . therefore she called his name Judah."

The denoted triangle is based on the birth of the first three sons where the third son is recorded differently than the first two sons and the fourth son. Notice also that all twelve sons of Jacob are stated as being born across three chapters of the book of Genesis. In chapter 29 the birth of the first four sons as mentioned above. In Genesis chapter 30 the birth of the next seven sons are mentioned in verses 6, 8, 11, 13, 18, 20, and 24 referring to Dan, Naphtali, Gad, Asher, Issachar, Zebulun, and Joseph respectively. The last son is stated to have been born in Genesis 35:18, Benjamin. The first two chapters mentioned states multiple births with the last chapter mentioned stating only one. This is another identified triangle,▽. From another perspective Leah and her servant Zilpah had eight or two-thirds of the sons while Rachel and her servant Bilhah had four or one-third of the sons. Another identified triangle,▽. Three of the women had two sons each, Rachel, Zilpah, and Bilhah. Of these three women the

35

last two are servants. Another identified triangle,△. Also of the three women Rachael and Bilhah are linked as mistress and servant. Another identified triangle,▽.

▽ Jacob was involved in three recorded detailed narrative deceptions:

1) He got his brother Esau to "sell" him his birthright with some "red pottage" while Esau was "faint" in Genesis 25:29-34.
2) He tricked his father stating he was Esau and took the blessing his father had meant for Esau in Genesis 27:18-29.
3) Jacob was tricked into being married to Leah instead of Rachael as he had hoped in Genesis 29:21-27.

The first two of these three deceptions Jacob was the one who deceived others while the third states that he himself was deceived by Laban his uncle. This is the basis for the denoted triangle In Genesis 31:4-16 Jacob states how his uncle Laban, from Jacob's point of view, has deceived him as it relates to the cattle and their attributes, "speckled" and/ or "ringstraked" relating to his wages which he says was changed ten times. There is no detailed narrative of this deception like the other three, but it is a recorded discussion between Jacob and his two wives Rachel and Leah, Laban's daughters, the three of them. This is another identified triangle,△.

▽ Jacob worked for his two wives fourteen years, seven years each, and six years for his cattle which equaled twenty years in all.

"Thus have I been twenty years in thy house; I served thee fourteen years for thy two daughters, and six years for thy cattle: and thou hast changed my wages ten times"

(Genesis 31:41). Jacob worked twenty years for three things: his two his wives who were sisters and the cattle. This is the basis for the denoted triangle.

△/▽ **In Genesis 33:1-7, Jacob had three groups of his people bow down before his bother Esau as they greeted him.**

1) In verse 6, "Then the handmaidens came near, they and their children, and they bowed themselves."
2) In verse 7, "Leah also with her children came near, and bowed themselves."
3) In verse 7, "After came Joseph and Rachel and they bowed themselves."

Notice that the last two groups who bowed before Esau are linked in that they are the wives with their children and are sisters. The first denoted triangle. From another perspective Jacob cared more about Rachel and Joseph than the other two groups that bowed before Esau before they bowed. The second denoted triangle. Of the three groups the last two groups who bow are stated in the same seventh verse. Another identified triangle, △.

▽ **God changed the names of three people in the book of Genesis.**
The first two are in Genesis 17 with Abram being called Abraham and Sarai being called Sarah. The third person who had his name changed was Jacob in Genesis 32:28 by an angel and it is told to him again by God in Genesis 35:10. The name change for him was from Jacob to Israel. The first two people are married and the third their grandson. This is the basis for the denoted triangle.

▽/△ **There were three built named pillars/altars of remembrance relating to Jacob.**

1) In Genesis 31:47, 51 Galeed pillar where he and Laban, his father-in-law, made a pact.
2) In Genesis 33:20 where he named the altar Elelohe-Israel that was built after the purchase of land in Shalem.
3) In Genesis 35:7 where the place of the altar Elbethel is called because God told him to go to Bethel.

Of these three mentioned pillars/altars that are built the most sacred is the third because God told him to build it, "And God said unto Jacob, Arise, go up to Bethel, and dwell there: and make there an altar unto God, that appeared unto thee when thou fleddest from the face of Esau thy brother." (Genesis 35:1) This is the basis for the first denoted triangle. Also of these three others assisted in the making of the pillar, in verse 31:46, while the last two, altars, are built by him only. The second denoted triangle. There are other pillars of remembrance by Jacob. In Genesis 28:18 and restated by God in Genesis 31:13 as the unnamed pillar of Bethel and in Genesis 35:14 another unnamed pillar in Bethel after God appeared unto him again and he poured a drink offering and oil on it. Note that between he and his grandfather Abraham four pillars/altars were built near or around Bethel. He did three and one was done by his grandfather Abram in Genesis 12:8.

▽/△/△ **Read of the three instances where angels are mentioned as it relates to Jacob:**

1) In Genesis 28:12 it states how Jacob had a dream of a host of angels "ascending and descending" on a ladder.
2) In Genesis 32:1-2 it states that "And Jacob went on his way, and the angels of God met him."

3) In Genesis 32:24-29 is when Jacob wrestled with an angel ". . .until the breaking of the day."

The first two instances recorded relate to a host of "angels" and the third instance had only one angel. The first denoted triangle. The first instance is somewhat referenced in Genesis 35:7, "there God appeared unto him, when he fled from the face of his brother," and the third instance is referenced in Hosea 12:4, "he had power over the angel, and prevailed: he wept, and made supplication unto him: he found him in Bethel." From another perspective the first instance is in a dream while the next two instances the angels appear in reality. The second denoted triangle. Note that Jacob names the last two of the three places where angels are mentioned. In Genesis 32:2, "and he called the name of that place Mahanaim," and Genesis 32:30, "And Jacob called the name of the place Peniel." The third denoted triangle.

▽ A confluence of major threes that are associated with Jacob:

1) Jacob worked for his two wives fourteen years, seven years each, and six years for his cattle which equaled twenty years in all in Genesis 31:41
2) Read of the three instances where angels are mentioned as it relates to Jacob in Genesis 28:12, 32:1-2, 32:24-29,
3) God changed the names of three people in the book of Genesis in Genesis chapter 17, 32:28, and stated again in 35:10

Of these three that are stated the third angelic encounter leads to him being the third person whose name is changed. This is the basis for the denoted triangle.

Abraham, Isaac, and Jacob

△ **God "appeared" to the three Hebrew patriarchs—Abraham, Isaac, and Jacob**:

1) To Abram/Abraham in Genesis 12:7, 17:1, 18:1
2) To Isaac in Genesis 26:2, 24
3) To Jacob in Genesis 35:1, 9

For the last two men it is recorded and stated that God "appeared" to them twice, and to the first person, Abram/Abraham, God "appeared" to him three times. This is the basis for the denoted triangle. God "appeared" seven times amongst the three men. Note in Genesis 35:1 it is stated that God references the dream Jacob had in 28:12, and stated in Genesis 35:7, as an appearance to him. With that being the case, it can be said that God appeared to Jacob three times also as it was done to his grandfather, Abraham. That would then mean God "appeared" to Abraham three times, Jacob three times, and Issac twice. Another identified triangle,▽. Of these appearances to the three men, God never tells the three men his name.

▽/▽ **Genesis 38:2-10 states Judah, the fourth son of Israel, had three sons by Shuah, a Canaanite woman.**

His three sons' names were Er, Onan, and Shelah. His first two sons Er and Onan were "slew" by God for their wicked acts. The third son was left alive. This is the basis for the first denoted triangle. The widow Tamar had married Er and Onan one after the other and was supposed to marry Shelah also, Judah's third son when he grew up as Judah had promised her. That did not happen. The basis for the second denoted triangle.

▽ **Abram, Isaac, and Jacob each had to deal with a "famine in the Land."**

For Abram it is stated in Genesis 12:10-11. For Isaac it is stated in Genesis 26:1, and for Jacob it is stated in Genesis 41:56 and 43:1. There is no record of activities of how Abram and Isaac survived the "famine in the land" other than going to another place. As for Jacob, there is a detailed account of how he addressed and survived the act of God from Genesis 42-47. Jacob tells his sons, "I have heard that there is corn in Egypt: get you down thither, and buy for us from thence; that we may live, and not die" in Genesis 42:2. This account is also stated in Acts 7:11-12. Of the three men there is a detailed account of how Jacob addresses the issue but there is no record as such for Abram and Isaac. This is the basis for the denoted triangle. Note that of the three men, Abraham and Jacob went to Egypt. Isaac was told not to go there in Genesis 26:2.

▽ **The ages of the three Patriarchs and their deaths.**

Abraham was 175 years old, and Isaac was 180 years old when they each "gave up the ghost" in Genesis 25:7-8 and 35:28-29 respectively. Jacob "yielded up the ghost" at his death in Genesis 49:33. Jacob's age when he died was given in Genesis 47:28, ". . .the whole age of Jacob was an hundred forty and seven years." Abraham and Isaac are recorded to have "gave up" and Jacob "yielded up" "the ghost". This is the basis for the denoted triangle. Note Jacob died younger that the first two men. Notice also that the first two patriarchs, Abraham and Isaac, were buried by their first two sons in Genesis 25:9 and 35:29 respectively. Jacob was buried by his twelve sons in Genesis 50:13. Another identified triangle,▽. All three patriarchs were buried in the "cave of Machpelah" as stated in Genesis 25:9, 49:31, and 50:13. The cave was purchased by Abraham in Genesis 23:3-9. Each were buried there with their first wives—Sarah,

Rebekah, and Leah respectively. Note that when Jacob's wife Rachel died in Genesis 35:18-19, he was left with Leah and the servant women Zilpah and Bilhah who were the three mothers of his other children. Another identified triangle, △.

Joseph

▽ **Joseph interpreted the dreams of three Egyptians.**
The first two of them, while he was in prison with them, was Pharaoh's chief of the butlers, and chief of the bakers in Genesis 40:2. Each of these two men told Joseph of the three things in their dreams. For the chief butler it was three branches and for the chief baker it was three baskets. Joseph told them each what the three things represented in their dreams meant. Within three days something would happen. The chief butler was restored to his position and the chief baker was hanged in Genesis 40:21-22. Lastly Joseph interpreted the dreams of Pharaoh himself with him having two dreams being linked to a seven year famine in the land that he ruled as recorded in Genesis 41. The dreams of the three men is the basis for the denoted triangle with the first two men being in prison and Pharaoh's.

▽ **Joseph held three positions:**

1) Hebrew servant to "Potiphar, an officer of Pharaoh, captain of the guard, an Egyptian" in Genesis 39:1,17
2) Hebrew Prisoner/servant to the "keeper of the prison" in Genesis 39:22-23
3) Governor of Egypt in Genesis 40:40-41, 42:6.

The first two positions are linked to being a servant while the third as a governor. This is the basis for the denoted triangle. Genesis 50:23 states how long Joseph's life continued, "And Joseph saw Ephraim's children of the third generation: the children also of Machir the son of Manasseh were brought up upon Joseph's knees."

△ The confluence of threes that are associated with Joseph:

1) The third son of his mother Rachael (note the first two sons she claimed are by her servant Bilhah in Genesis 30:5-8.
2) The third person's dreams he interpreted was Pharaoh's.
3) His third job was governor of Egypt given to him by Pharaoh after being a Hebrew servant twice to someone else.

The last two items of the three are linked to Pharaoh since the interpretation of his dreams lead to Joseph's third position. The basis for the denoted triangle.

▽/△ Three men had a pair of dreams recorded in the book of Genesis:

1) Jacob in Genesis 28:12-15 of the angels on stairs, and in 31:10-13 the conceiving of cattle.
2) Joseph in Genesis 37:5-6 of eleven sheaves bowing to his sheaf, and in 37:9-10 sun, moon, and eleven stars bowing to him.
3) Pharaoh of Egypt in Genesis 41:1-4 of the seven well favored and seven ill favored, and 41:5 seven ears of good and seven ears thin corn thin.

The first two men are of a father and son, linked as family, then Pharaoh later. The first denoted triangle. The last two pair of dreams to two of the three men are linked to the destiny of Joseph being governor of Egypt. The second denoted triangle. The first men's dreams were over some time while the last man's dreams were in one night. Another identified triangle,▽. Note that last man can be considered a monarch of the three. Another identified triangle,▽.

▽ Joseph's brothers bowed to him only in three instances.

1) The first time is in a dream Joseph had in Genesis 37:7 where only his brothers are depicted as the sheaves bowing to him.
2) The second time is in a dream Joseph has in Genesis 37:9 includes "the sun and the moon" which is interpreted as being his father and mother along with eleven stars which was a depiction of his brothers also. The focus was only on the brothers.
3) In Genesis 44:14 and 50:18 they bow to him in reality.

The last verse of the three is what is stated that happened in reality. This is the basis for the denoted triangle. Note Hebrews 11:21 could be viewed in that Jacob bowed to Joseph, "By faith Jacob, when he was a dying, blessed both the sons of Joseph; and worshipped, leaning upon the top of his staff."

Exodus, Moses the chosen leader of a nation that followed

▽ Moses is the third child of the Hebrew couple Amram and Jochebed who was chosen by God. Moses being the third child is indicated in Exodus 6:20 and 15:20.

The first two children were Miriam, seven years older according to some sources, and Aaron, three years older as indicated in the verse of Exodus 7:7. This is the basis for the denoted triangle. Moses was also raised as an Egyptian according to the narrative of his story, while the other two children as Hebrews. Another identified triangle,▽.

△/△ The three men whose future wife was met at a well:

1) Isaac in Genesis 24:13-14 where Abraham's eldest servant of his house met the damsel Rebekah at the well who later became the wife of Abraham's son Isaac. Her father is Bethuel.
2) Jacob in Genesis 29:9-10 the second son of Isaac met his second future wife Rachel as she came to water the sheep of her father's, Laban.
3) Moses in Exodus 2:15-17 met his future first wife, it is said, Zipporah and helped her with the watering at the well of her father's flock, Jethro.

Of the three men the last two men met their future wife personally and helped them with the animals also at the well while for the first man his wife was met by his father's servant. The basis for the first denoted triangle. The last two men of the three were fleeing for their lives before they got to the wells. Jacob because he deceived his brother Esau and Moses because he killed an Egyptian. This is the basis for the second denoted triangle. Note, Rebekah offered to give water to the ten camels of Abraham's servant in 24:14 and 19.

▽ **In Exodus 3:14 God showed his divine pattern to Moses, "I AM THAT I AM**:
. . .and he said, Thus shalt thou say unto the children of Israel, I AM hath sent me unto you." "I AM" is stated three times. He says it two times where it is separated or connected by the word "THAT" and then later alone. In my view this is genius. The triangle diagram is below:

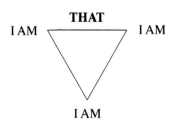

45

△ **There were three wonders Moses encountered when he was in the presence of God:**

1) In Exodus 3:2 he saw the burning bush that was not consumed
2) In Exodus 4:3 his rod/staff turns into a snake and back into a rod/staff
3) In Exodus 4:6 his hand is turned leprous as snow and returns to normal

The last two wonders of the three are linked to Moses himself. The first one is not. This is the basis for the denoted triangle.

The Ten Plagues of Egypt

▽ **The ten plagues of Egypt brought upon the Egyptians for refusing to let the children of Israel go are listed in Exodus 7:19- 11:5.**

The first two plagues are linked to water and the third is linked to the land. Of these first three plagues they are activated, technically, by Aaron. This is the basis for the denoted triangle. The other seven plagues are air/heaven based plagues. In looking at the first three plagues the stated phrase "The LORD spake unto Moses, **Say unto Aaron. . .**" is prefaced before the plague was activated. The first three plagues are performed with the rod/staff of Moses used by the hand of Aaron, Moses' brother or perhaps his own staff/rod. Also note the last two plagues of the first three plagues are recorded in the same chapter. Another identified triangle,△. **Note** the plagues are also mentioned in Psalm 105:28-36.

The Plagues of Egypt are as follows:

1. **Water to Blood** – Exodus 7:19 - water based. "And the LORD spake unto Moses, **Say unto Aaron**, Take thy rod, and stretch out thine hand upon the waters of Egypt, upon their streams, upon their rivers, and upon their ponds, and upon all their pools of water, that they may become blood." In further focusing on the details, notice that the third and fourth items mentioned are standing waters. The first two instances of the waters mentioned by Moses are flowing waters. Another identified triangle is the first two flowing waters and the first standing water mentioned, $\triangledown$. Seven days passed before the water returned to normal in Exodus 7:25.

2. **Frogs** – Exodus 8:2-5 - water based. Exodus 8:5 states, "And the LORD spake unto Moses, **Say unto Aaron**, Stretch forth thine hand with thy rod over the streams, over the rivers, and over the ponds, and cause frogs to come up upon the land of Egypt." Again in further focusing on the details, notice that the third item mentioned is standing water. Again the first two instances of the waters mentioned are flowing waters. This is another identified triangle, $\triangledown$. Exodus 8:13 states, "and the frogs died out of the houses, out of the villages, and out of the fields."

3. **Lice** – Exodus 8:16-17 - Land based. "And the LORD said unto Moses, **Say unto Aaron**, Stretch out thy rod, and smite the dust of the land. . .[17]. . .for Aaron . . .smote the dust of the earth and it became lice in man, and in beast; all the dust of the land became lice throughout all the land of Egypt."

47

Of these three plagues there is no mention of how the lice are dispelled from the land as opposed to the first two of these three plagues. Another identified triangle, ▽.

▽ The next three plagues can be viewed as displaying the pattern where Moses is told to go see Pharaoh by God in the fourth and fifth plagues. For the sixth plague both Moses and Aaron have ashes in their hands, but Moses was the one to "sprinkle" the ashes in the air for the activation of the plague. The basis for the denoted triangle. Moses is involved with the activation of these three plagues with Aaron apart of the sixth plague.

4. **Swarms of Flies** – Exodus 8:20-31 - Air/Heaven Based. Activated by the word of the Lord via Moses in verse 8:20, "**And the LORD said unto Moses, Rise up early in the morning, and stand before Pharaoh.**" In Exodus 8:24 it states, ". . .there came a grievous swarm of flies into the house of Pharaoh, and into his servants' houses, and into all the land of Egypt." And in Exodus 8:29 it adds, "I will intreat the LORD that the swarms of flies may depart from Pharaoh, from his servants, and from his people." Exodus 8:31 states the LORD, "he removed the swarms of flies from Pharaoh, from his servants, and from his people."

5. **Livestock/Animals Diseased** – Exodus 9:1-3 - Air/ Heaven based. Activated by the word of the Lord via Moses in verse 9:1, "**Then the LORD said unto Moses, Go in unto Pharaoh, and tell him,** Thus saith the LORD God of the Hebrews. . ." In Exodus 9:3 it states, "Behold, the hand of the LORD is upon thy cattle which is in the field, upon the horses, upon

the asses, upon the camels, upon the oxen, and upon the sheep: there shall be a very grievous murrain."

6. **Boils** – Exodus 9:8-9 - Air/Heaven based. Activated with ashes in the air, "**And the LORD said unto Moses and unto Aaron, Take to you handfuls of ashes of the furnace, and let Moses sprinkle it toward the heaven. . .** [9] And it shall become small dust in all the land of Egypt, and shall be a boil breaking forth with blains upon man, and upon beast, throughout all the land of Egypt."

Notice that it is mentioned of how the flies are dispelled from the Egyptians but nothing relating to how the last two plagues are stopped of the three. This is another identified triangle,△. Also note that of these three plagues the last two are mentioned in the same chapter. Another identified triangle,△.

▽ Moses was told by God to "Stretch forth thine hand. . ." three times to activate the next three plagues. In plagues seven and eight, he does not do that but instead he "stretched forth his rod" for the start of the plagues. He does use his hand as he is told in the ninth plague. The basis for the denoted triangle.

7. **Thunder and Fire Hail/Rain** – Exodus 9:18-24, 33-34 - Air/Heaven based. In Exodus 9:22 it states, "**And the LORD said unto Moses, Stretch forth thine hand** toward heaven, that there may be hail in all the land of Egypt, upon man, and upon beast, and upon every herb of the field." In Exodus 9:23 it states, "And Moses stretched forth his rod toward heaven: and the LORD sent thunder and hail, and the fire ran

along upon the ground." In Exodus 9:25 it states, "And the hail smote throughout all the land of Egypt all that was in the field, both man and beast; and the hail smote every herb of the field." In Exodus 9:33 it states, "And Moses . . . spread abroad his hands unto the LORD: and the thunders and hail ceased, and the rain was not poured upon the earth." Then in Exodus 9:34 it states, "And when Pharaoh saw that the rain and the hail and the thunders were ceased."

8. **Locusts** – Exodus 10:4-6, 12-13, 19 - Air/Heaven based. In Exodus 10:6 it states, "And they shall fill thy houses, and the houses of all thy servants, and the houses of all the Egyptians," and in Exodus 10:12 it states, **"And the LORD said unto Moses, Stretch out thine hand** over the land of Egypt for the locusts." In Exodus 10:13 it states, "Moses stretched forth his rod over the land of Egypt, and the LORD brought an east wind upon the land all that day, and all that night; and when it was morning, the east wind brought the locusts." In Exodus 10:19 it states, "And the LORD turned a mighty strong west wind, which took away the locusts, and cast them into the Red sea; there remained not one locust in all the coasts of Egypt." This was done because Moses ". . .intreated the LORD" on Pharaoh's behalf in verse 10:18.

9. **Darkness** – Exodus 10:21-22 - Air/Heaven based. In Exodus 10:21 it states, **"And the LORD said unto Moses, Stretch out thine hand** toward heaven, that there may be darkness over the land of Egypt. . .And Moses stretched forth his hand toward heaven; and there was a thick darkness in all the land of Egypt three days."

Of these three plagues the cessation of the first two plagues, seven and eight, is stated with some involvement by Moses but not for the third plague the cessation was done by God alone. Another identified triangle,▽. Note that of these three plagues Moses uses his hands as part of the cessation of the seventh plague and not for the other two. Another identified triangle,△. Also note that of these three plagues the last two are mentioned in the same chapter. Another identified triangle,△.

10. **Death of First Born** – Exodus 11: 4-5 - Air/Heaven based. Activated by the word of the Lord to Moses in Exodus 11:5, "And all the firstborn in the land of Egypt shall die, from the firstborn of Pharaoh that sitteth upon his throne, even unto the firstborn of the maidservant that is behind the mill; and all the firstborn of beasts." Also stated in Exodus 12:29 ". . .at midnight the LORD smote all the firstborn in the land of Egypt, from the firstborn of Pharaoh that sat on his throne unto the firstborn of the captive that was in the dungeon; and all the firstborn of cattle."

This tenth and last plague established the monumental event in Judaism called the Passover. Note that in Genesis 12:17 it states that there were plagues in Egypt before, "And the LORD plagued Pharaoh and his house with great plagues because of Sarai Abram's wife."

▽ **Exodus 12:7 tells how the children of Israel were to put or "strike" the blood of the lamb or goat on "the two side posts and on the upper door post of the houses" so that their houses would be passed over as the tenth plague commenced.** The denoted triangle is based on the order of the three stated places the blood had to be placed on the houses. After the blood had been stuck three times on the doorway, in a sense a physical upward triangle was composed in my view.

▽/△/△/▽ Some further analysis of the Ten Plagues.

Notice that plagues four, five, and ten were executed by the word of God. The fourth and fifth plagues were to Pharaoh via Moses and the word of God to Moses only for plague ten. The basis for the first denoted triangle. The plagues of lice, flies, and locusts, the third, fourth and eighth respectively, pertain to the use of insects. The last two plagues of these three are air based. The second denoted triangle. Also of these three plagues Aaron handled the first one and Moses the last two. The third denoted triangle. The fifth, sixth, and tenth plagues can be viewed as the use of some airborne pathogen. The fifth plague effected beasts only. The sixth plague effected men and beasts. Both of these plagues were recorded as non lethal. The tenth being unique effected only the "firstborn" of all men and beasts in Egypt killing them. The fourth denoted triangle. From another perspective the last two plagues of the three effected men and beasts together. Another identified triangle, △.

▲**Commentary**: I noticed that Moses was told by God to use the "rod" in the first three plagues via Aaron (Exodus 7:19, 8:5, and 8:16). In the seventh, eighth, and ninth plagues, Moses was told to use his hand but instead he used the "rod" himself in the Fire/Hail and Locusts plagues. The "rod" was used in five plagues: the first, second, third, seventh, and eighth. The first three by Aaron and the last two by Moses. I can make a correlation with the number of animals that was sacrificed by Abram to God in Genesis 15:9 and the number of times the "rod" was used by Moses and Aaron where in both instances it is the number five. The third prime number.

I also noticed that over a good number of many years there have been many skeptics from various disciplines who have stated that the ten plagues could be explained by some naturally occurring phenomena in an event sequence. There is a segment in the 2007 movie called "The Reaping" that depicts this thinking by the actress Hilary Swank. It seems there was a focus on the all of the acts that were done. I have found no one who has ever viewed the ten plagues in this fashion to show the probability of these plagues being of the divine. That probability is now very high to a certainty based on a pattern, the triangle/three pattern. A quick review of the first nine plagues. Aaron handled the first three technically. Moses handled the next three with a little help on the sixth plague from Aaron, and Moses handled the last three of the nine alone. This is also a triangle pattern of its own,△.

▽ Three times Moses used the rod as part of a miracle of God against the Egyptians:

1) The seventh plague of Thunder and Fire Hail/Rain in Exodus 9:18-24
2) The eighth plague of Locusts in Exodus 10:12-13
3) God said in Exodus 14:16, "But lift thou up thy rod, and stretch out thine hand over the sea, and divide it: and the children of Israel shall go on dry ground through the midst of the sea" for the parting of the Red Sea.

The first two times he used the "rod" it pertains to the plagues against Egypt. The third it is not part of the plagues. The basis for the denoted triangle. In the third instance, another miracle, the children of Israel escape from the Egyptians. Note in Exodus 14:26 it states, "And the LORD said unto Moses, Stretch out thine hand over the sea, that the waters may come again upon the Egyptians, upon their chariots, and upon their horsemen." This is the fifth time God tells Moses to stretch out his hand as part of his work against the Egyptians. In Exodus 14:27 it states, "Moses stretched forth his hand over the sea and the sea returned to his strength when the morning appeared." Six times the hand of Moses was involved or requested to be involved with an action against the Egyptians—plagues 6, 7, 8, and 9, the parting of the Red Sea to allow the children of Israel to escape from them, and the coming together again of the Red Sea. Of these six times his hand is used two-thirds of those times. The sixth and ninth plagues, and the two times relating to the Red Sea. Another identified triangle,▽.

▽ Reviewed the three times water was used against the Egyptians as a miracle of God:

1) The first plague of Water being turned into Blood in Exodus 7:19;
2) The second plague of Frogs coming from the water in Exodus 8:2-5; and
3) When the waters of the Red Sea came back together again and drown the pursuing Egyptians in Exodus 14:26.

Of the three mentioned the first two are of the ten plagues where none of the Egyptians died. In the third instance many of the Egyptians died along with their horses. This is the basis for the denoted triangle.

△ Review of the three actions God did for the children of Israel when they were at the Red Sea in Exodus 14:19-28.

1) He caused a pillar of the cloud used for light for Israel turned to fire for the Egyptians to halt their advance (Exodus14:19-20, 24).

2) He command Moses to stretch out his hands with rod to cause the Red Sea to part (Exodus 14:16, 21-22).

3) He caused the Red Sea to come together again to drown the advancing Egyptians (Exodus 14:26-28).

The last two actions of the three relate to the activities of the Red Sea. This is the basis for the denoted triangle.

▽ **Ramses I and Seti I were the first two Pharaohs with Ramses II as the third Pharaoh of the 19th Dynasty of Ancient Egypt.**

Ramses II has been traditionally viewed as the Pharaoh of the Hebrew slaves of the Exodus, 1:8-11, during the time of the plagues. He could be viewed as the Pharaoh who released the Jewish slaves of the three in the dynasty. This is the basis for the denoted triangle.

△ **The first three recorded miracles God did for the children of Israel relating to sustenance while they were in the wilderness:**

1) In Exodus 15:24-25 the waters turned sweet via a tree

2) In Exodus 16:13 they were given quail from heaven

3) In Exodus 16:14 they were given manna from heaven

Of the three miracles the last two are linked to being sent from heaven, quail and manna. The denoted triangle is form based on how God provided. Also of these three the last two are in the same chapter. Another identified triangle,△. Note that the last two items of the three are mentioned in Psalms 105:40. Another identified triangle,△.

▽ **Exodus 19:1 states, "In the third month, when the children of Israel were gone forth out of the land of Egypt, the same day [suggested by some the third day]**

came they into the wilderness of Sinai." This suggests that it took two months of traveling to arrive there in the "third month." This is the basis for the denoted triangle.

▽ **Exodus 19:11 states, "And be ready against the third day: for the third day the LORD will come down in the sight of all the people upon Mount Sinai."** This suggests that nothing was going to be done the first two days by the LORD. This is the basis for the denoted triangle.

The Ten Commandments

▽ **The Ten Commandments or the Decalogue is in Exodus 20:3-17 and Deuteronomy 5:6-21.**
The first three commandments pertain to God and his divinity and deity with the first and second being linked relating to other "gods." The third item is the most sacred to him, HIS NAME. This is the basis for the denoted triangle. The other seven Commandments are designated specifically to the actions of men.

The Commandments are:

1. "Thou shalt have no other gods before me."
2. "Thou shalt not make unto thee any graven image." (idol)
3. **"Thou shalt not take the name of the Lord thy God in vain**." Since the third commandment is the most sacred to God one reviewed other scriptures relating to the use of a "name" in the footnote below.[7] This is

---

7   Proverbs 22:1 - "A good name is rather to be chosen than great riches, and loving favour rather than silver and gold." Ecclesiastes 7:1 - "A good name is better than precious ointment." I think of what is stated in the Lord's prayer of Matt. 6:9 and Luke 11:2 in the second phrase: "Hallowed be thy name." Read the 10 scriptures

the commandment that should be most reverenced as it relates to the Divine because this is something that belongs to Him and it is **personal to Him. It is the reason it is listed as the third commandment!**

4. "Remember the sabbath day, to keep it holy." (Man should not work, day of rest)
5. "Honour thy father and thy mother."
6. "Thou shalt not kill."
7. "Thou shalt not commit adultery."
8. "Thou shalt not steal."
9. "Thou shalt not bear false witness against thy neighbor."
10. "Thou shalt not covet."

△/▽ As I reviewed the three Xs or three Roman numeral 10s after the collapsing of the Jewish symbol relating to creation, it was pointed out to me that there are three groups of ten that are significant and important within the first two books of the Bible, Genesis and Exodus. They are the ten times that the phrase "God said" is stated and the words uttered afterwards as it pertains to creation. The second and third tens are the ten plagues of Egypt that led to the freedom of the children of Israel, and the Ten Commandments God gave to the children of Israel at Mount Sinai/Horeb. Of these three important and significant tens the last two tens that are

relating to God and "my holy name" in Lev. 20:3, 22:2,32, Eze. 20:39, 36:20, 39:7, 25, 43:7-8, Amos 2:7. Read other scriptures as Romans 2:24 - "For the name of God is blasphemed among the Gentiles through you, as it is written", and 1 Timothy 6:1 - "Let as many servants as are under the yoke count their own masters worthy of all honour, that the name of God and his doctrine be not blasphemed," and lastly Revelation 16:9 "And men were scorched with great heat, and blasphemed the name of God, which hath power over these plagues: and they repented not to give him glory." ". . .Lord, how excellent is thy name in all the earth!" (Psa. 8:1,9) in the same book Exodus relate to the children of Israel. This is the basis for the denoted triangle. Of the three tens the first two tens relates to what God did in his acts and the last ten as to what God wrote. This is the basis for the denoted second triangle.

The Priest office, The Tabernacle, and ordinances

△/▽ In Exodus 29:1-37 and Leviticus 8:1-36 states the use of three animals as sacrifices relating to the Consecration of Aaron and his sons into the office of the priesthood. Those animals are a bullock and two rams.

This is the basis for the first denoted triangle. The stated use for the animals is as follows:

1) The young bullock "is a sin offering" in Exodus 29:14 and Leviticus 8:14
2) One ram "is a burnt offering unto the LORD" in Exodus 29:18 and Leviticus 8:18
3) The other ram "is a ram of consecration" in Exodus 29:22 and Leviticus 8:22. Notice that the third animal was also a ram in thinking of the sacrificial animals in Genesis 15:9.

Of the three animals the first two are related to an "offering". The second denoted triangle. In Exodus 29:13, 22 and Leviticus 8:16, 25 these verses mention three internal body parts of the first and third animals that are burned "upon the altar" "the caul that is above the liver, and the two kidneys". The caul is stated to be by some the large lobe or the liver's flap. Another identified triangle based on the internal animal parts, △. These three animals are mentioned again in Leviticus 23:18, "and one young bullock, and two rams: they shall be for a burnt offering unto the LORD, with their meat offering, and their drink offerings, even an offering made by fire, of sweet savour unto the LORD."

△ **In Exodus 29:19-20 and Leviticus 8:22-23 the second ram, and third animal, is used as part of the consecration for the priesthood.**
The blood of this killed animal is supposed to be put on Aaron and his son's three body parts:

1) "the tip of the right ear,"
2) "upon the thumb of their right hand,"
3) "and upon the great toe of their right foot."

The last two body parts of the three are linked to being called a digit of the hand and foot. This is the basis for the denoted triangle. Note that these three body parts are mentioned again four times in Leviticus 14:14, 17, 25, and 28 as it relates to a trespass offering.

△ **The three materials used from three animals for the coverings of the Tabernacle of the Congregation:** goat's hair, ram's skins, and badger's skins (Exodus 26:7, 36:14, 19). The last two of the three coverings state "skins" and are stated to be the last two coverings for the Tabernacle of the three. The basis for the denoted triangle.

▽/△ **The three entrances for the Tabernacle of the congregation:**

1) The gate to the Outer Court in Exodus 27:16-19.
2) The door to the Holy Place in Exodus 26:36-37 and 36:37-38.
3) The veil to the Holy of Holies in Exodus 26:31-33.

Of these three entrances the most sacred is the veil. The first denoted triangle . Also notice that the last entrances of the three are linked to the same structure, the tent. The second denoted triangle.

▽/△/▽/△ The Jewish High Priest Hoshen/Breastplate.

There are twelve stones where the layout of four rows should be seen logically and theoretically as forming two Stars of David.

The rows of the stones are as follows:

Row 1 – "a sardius, a topaz, and a carbuncle"
Row 2 – "an emerald, a sapphire, and a diamond"
Row 3 – "a ligure, an agate, and an amethyst"
Row 4 – "a beryl, an onyx, and a jasper"

Based on the verses of Exodus 28:21 and 29 the stones are representative of each of the tribes of Israel with each of the names of the patriarchs of the tribes of Israel being inscribed in a stone. The order of the inscriptions is based on the birth of each of the twelve patriarchs of the tribes as stated in the book of Genesis 29, 30, and 35. Exodus 28:21 states, "And the stones shall be with the names of the children of Israel, twelve, according to their names, like the engravings of a signet." Exodus 28:29 states, "And Aaron shall bear the names of the children of Israel in the breast-plate of judgment upon his heart, when he goeth in unto the holy place, for a memorial before the LORD continually." The following shows the twelve names arranged in threes in order of birth and are arranged in rows the same way the stones are arranged in the breastplate:

Row 1: 1-Reuben, 2-Simeon, and 3-Levi. All three sons are born to Leah noting that Levi's name was recorded uniquely of the three ▽.

Row 2: 4-Judah, 5-Dan, and 6-Naphtali. The first of these sons is born to Leah and the other two sons to Bilhah Rachael's servant △.

Row 3: 7-Gad, 8-Asher, and 9-Issachar. The first two sons are born to Zilpah Leah's servant and the third son is born to Leah▽.

Row 4: 10-Zebulun, 11-Joseph, and 12-Benjamin. The first son is born to Leah and the last two sons are born to Rachael △.

This most likely is an accurate assessment of the configuration of the stones since the triangle patterns mimic the ones of Genesis chapter 1 twice. The four denoted triangles are the rows for the names of the sons. The diagram of the triangles for the Stars of David is shown below:

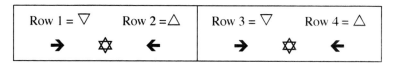

Row 1 = ▽ Row 2 =△	Row 3 = ▽ Row 4 = △
→ ✡ ←	→ ✡ ←

△ In Leviticus 11:4-6 and Deuteronomy 14:7 it states the first three animals that should not be eaten:

1) the Camel
2) the coney (cooney)
3) the hare.

The last two of these three animals are defined as pertaining to rabbits. The basis for the denoted triangle.

△ Deuteronomy 14:4 states the first three animals which could be eaten by the people: "the ox, the sheep, and the goat." All three are of the Bovidae family of animals, but the ox is of bovinae subfamily and the sheep and goat are of the caprinae subfamily. This is the basis for the denoted triangle.

▽/▽ **God ordered the men of Israel to appear before the Lord three times within a year as indicated in the following three verses:**

1) Exodus 23:17 states, "Three times in the year all thy males shall appear before the LORD God."
2) Exodus 34:23 states, "Thrice in the year shall all your men children appear before the Lord GOD, the God of Israel."
3) Deuteronomy 16:16 states, "Three times in a year shall all thy males appear before the LORD thy God in the place which he shall choose; in the feast of unleavened bread, and in the feast of weeks, and in the feast of tabernacles: and they shall not appear before the LORD empty:"

The first two of verses are in the same book, as well as being very similar without any other added verbiage as the third. The first denoted triangle. The third verse is similar to the others in the beginning, but there is also the mention of the three major feasts with the men's appearance before the "God of Israel" which the other two verses do not mention. The second denoted triangle.

The three major Feasts

▽ **The first Passover is recorded in Exodus 12:8 where the children of Israel are the coming out of Egypt.**
The items on the menu were lamb or goat, flesh/meat, with " unleavened bread; and with bitter herbs." The second, and perhaps, the third Passovers are recorded in Numbers 9:1-11 where the children of Israel are in the "Wilderness

of Sinai" and they ate manna, bread from heaven, as part of Passover. The third Passover being held as make-up in Numbers 9:11. In this verse it is stated that for some reason if it cannot be done the first month then, "The fourteenth day of the second month at even they shall keep it, and eat it with unleavened bread and bitter herbs." Some may view what I call the third Passover as part of the second Passover. The next recorded Passover is stated in Joshua 5:10-12 where the children of Israel are encamped in a place called Gilgal. This is the last time they ate manna as part of the Passover before going into Promised Land. Exodus 16:35 states how long the children of Israel ate manna, "And the children of Israel did eat manna forty years, until they came to a land inhabited; they did eat manna, until they came unto the borders of the land of Canaan." The last three Passovers are linked to the people having and eating the manna with the second and third almost together being held a month apart. The basis for the denoted triangle.

▽ **The three major feasts/festivals that were to be held each year known as Shalosh Regalim i.e. the three pilgrimage festivals. They are as follows:**

1) Passover, unleavened bread, feast defined in Leviticus 23:5-6.[8]

2) Feast of the weeks/harvest defined in Leviticus 23:10-15.

3) Feast of the tabernacles defined in Leviticus 23:34-43 and mentioned in Deuteronomy 31:10.

---

[8] Note: Think of the scriptures of how Passover has been mentioned in Exo. 12:18, Num. 9:5, 28:16, 2 Chr. 35:17, Eze. 45:21, and Luke 22:1

In Deuteronomy 16:16 the three major festivals are stated together, ". . .in the feast of unleavened bread, and in the feast of weeks, and in the feast of tabernacles." The feasts of weeks (Shavuot) was observed seven weeks from the second day of Passover, feast of Unleavened Bread, as stated in Leviticus 23:15, and the feast of Tabernacles (Sukkot) the fifteenth day of the seventh month as stated in Leviticus 23:34. The first two feasts are linked by the time of seven weeks. The third feast that is stated has no time linkage as the first two feasts have. This is the basis for the triangle. Note that all three feasts are also mentioned in 2 Chronicles 8:13, "on the solemn feasts, three times in the year, even in the feast of unleavened bread, and in the feast of weeks, and in the feast of tabernacles." Notice also that two of the feasts/festivals are seven days long, Unleavened Bread and Tabernacles, and the other is one day. Another identified triangle,▽. The triangle diagram is shown below of the Feasts:

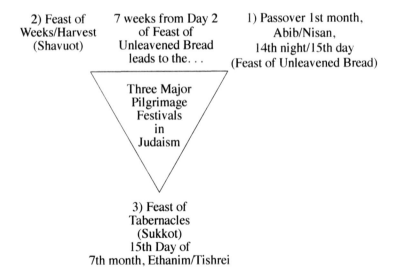

2) Feast of
Weeks/Harvest
(Shavuot)

7 weeks from Day 2
of Feast of
Unleavened Bread
leads to the. . .

1) Passover 1st month,
Abib/Nisan,
14th night/15th day
(Feast of Unleavened Bread)

Three Major
Pilgrimage
Festivals
in
Judaism

3) Feast of
Tabernacles
(Sukkot)
15th Day of
7th month, Ethanim/Tishrei

The book of Numbers

▽ **Numbers 7:7-8 lists the Levites in three groups in the order of the Gershonites, Kohathites, and Merarites as they were given the Lord's offerings from the other tribes.**

"Two wagons and four oxen he gave unto the sons of Gershon, according to their service: and four wagons and eight oxen he gave unto the sons of Merari, according unto their service, under the hand of Ithamar the son of Aaron the priest." Noticed how one third of the wagons (two wagons and four oxen), were given unto the sons of Gershon and two thirds (four wagons and eight oxen) were given to the sons of Merari. The second group, "Kohath he gave none because the service of the sanctuary belonging unto them." This is the basis for the denoted triangle. The triangle diagram is as follows:

2) Merarites(3rd)   1) Gershonites(1st)
4 wagons/ 8 oxen   LORD's   2 wagons/4 oxen
2/3rd   offering   1/3rd

3) Kohathites(2nd)
Nothing

△ **The First Census of Israel excluding the Levites:** 603,550 men twenty years old and upward as stated in Exodus 38:26, Numbers 1:46, and 2:32. The same number is stated in all three verses. The last two times it is stated is in the book of Numbers. The basis for the denoted triangle.

△/△ **The most rebellious three men who antagonized/ opposed Moses among the people are mentioned in Numbers 16:1, 4-24, and 27.**

"Now Korah, the son of Izhar, the son of Kohath, the son of Levi,. . . and Dathan and Abiram, the sons of Eliab." The last two men of the three mentioned are linked as brothers which is the basis for the first denoted triangle. In Numbers 16:24, 27 it states, "Speak unto the congregation, saying, Get you up from about the tabernacle of Korah, Dathan, and Abiram. . . . . [27]So they gat up from the tabernacle of Korah, Dathan, and Abiram, on every side: and Dathan and Abiram came out, and stood in the door of their tents, and their wives, and their sons, and their little children."

Note the three sons of Eliab in Numbers 26:9, "And the sons of Eliab; Nemuel, and Dathan, and Abiram. This is that Dathan and Abiram, which were famous in the congregation, who strove against Moses and against Aaron in the company of Korah, when they strove against the LORD:" Of the three sons listed of Eliab, the last two of them are part of "the company of Korah." The basis for the second denoted triangle. Kohath, Dathan, and Abiram, along with others, were destroyed when "the earth opened her mouth, and swallowed them up together with Korah" in Numbers 26:10. This event is also recorded in Deuteronomy 11:6. Korah is also mentioned in the Book of Jasher 84:1-2 as the ring leader of the group that opposed Moses and Aaron.

▽/△ **The three instances of the wrath of God in Numbers 16:28-49:**

1) Korah, Dathan, and Abiram and some of those that were part of their conspiracy against Moses were "swallowed" up by the earth in verse 32 (also mentioned in Psalm 106:17)

2) Later fire came down from heaven and consumed "two hundred and fifty men" that were in league with them, the three, in verse 35

3) The next day the people "murmured against Moses and Aaron, saying, Ye have killed the people of the LORD." God sent a plague among the people as a response, "they that died in the plague were fourteen thousand and seven hundred" along with the others the previous day in verse 49.

The first two instances of the three are linked as happening on the same day. The first denoted triangle. The last two instances of the three are related to God's wrath coming out of heaven, fire and the plague. The first is related to the earth. The second denoted triangle.

△/▽ **In Numbers 22:22-28 (and 2 Peter 2:16) Balaam, a prophet, the son of Beor to Pethor, "Now he was riding upon his ass, and his two servants were with him." He smote his "ass" twice and later a third time "he smote the ass with a staff."**

The "ass" was trying to get out of the way of the angel all three times. "And the LORD opened the mouth of the ass. . .What have I done unto thee, that thou hast smitten me these three times?" (verse 28). Notice the three men of the prophet's party. The first denoted triangle. Three times Balaam hit "his ass" with the third time using his staff. The first two times of the three it is not recorded how he hit the animal. The second denoted triangle.

▽ **Balaam, the prophet was asked by King Balak of Moab to curse Israel three times in three different places:**

Place 1 – "the high places of Baal" in Numbers 22:41-23:3, seven altars are built with a bullock and a ram put on each and they both made the burnt offerings then Balaam went and met God by himself.

Place 2 – "the field of Zophim, to the top of Pisgah," seven altars are built with a bullock and a ram put on each in Numbers 23:14-15. The burnt offerings are made and Balaam went and met God by himself.

Place 3 – "the top of Peor, that looketh toward Jeshimon." Seven altars are built with a bullock and ram put on each in Numbers 23:28-30. The burnt offerings are made and Balaam "went not, as at other times, to seek for enchantments, but he set his face toward the wilderness" (Numbers 24:1).

Balaam went the first two times to meet God but the third time he did not. This is the basis for the denoted triangle. ". . .Balak said unto Balaam, I called thee to curse mine enemies, and, behold, thou hast altogether blessed them these three times" (Numbers 24:10)

▽ List of the first three High Priests (Kohen Gadol) of Israel:

1) Aaron, during the Exodus from Egypt (First High Priest of Israel) in Leviticus 8.
2) Eleazar, the third son of Aaron in Numbers 20:22-29.[9]
3) Phinehas, the son of Eleazar, who is stated as High priest in Joshua 22:13, 30, 32.

---

[9] Note the first two sons of Aaron, Nadab and Abihu, died because they "offered strange fire before the LORD" as stated in Lev. 10:1-2 and Num. 3:4.

All three were involved with Moses in some capacity, but Aaron and Eleazer were both appointed into the high priesthood office by Moses/God. God via Moses made a Peace covenant with Phinehas separately in Numbers 25:11-13. Phinehas is not recorded as being appointed by God via Moses as the new High Priest. This is the basis for the denoted triangle. The descendants of Levi, the third son of Jacob and patriarch of the Israelite tribe Levites, were destined for the Priesthood of all the Israelites. Note the third son of Aaron and his son's position as the new Priest at that time. The first two older sons of Aaron died. Another identified triangle, ▽.

Three Biblical Covenants

△ **The three named biblical covenants where an everlasting token/sign was given by God**:

1) "The Noahic Covenant" in Genesis 9:11 applicable to all of humankind and all living creatures on the earth in that God promises that HE will "never again destroy all life on earth by a flood, and creates the rainbow."[10] Or as stated in scripture a "bow" as "a token of a covenant between me and the earth" and "for an everlasting covenant" and "for perpetual generations" in Genesis 9:12-13,16.

2) The Abrahamic Covenant" is "the covenant which was for Abraham and his seed, or offspring, both of natural birth and adoption." The act of circumcision "is to be the permanent sign/[token] of this everlasting covenant with Abraham and his male descendants," and is known as the "covenant of circumcision" as

---

10   Source - Wikipedia, Noahic covenant, 2011, http://en.wikipedia.org/wiki/Covenant_(biblical)#Noahic_covenant, Retrieved 11.25.11

described in Genesis 17:9-14.[11] "He that is born in thy house, and he that is bought with thy money, must needs be circumcised: and my covenant shall be in your flesh for an everlasting covenant" (Genesis 17:13). Abraham was told by God, "a token of the covenant betwixt me and you" in Genesis 17:11.

3) "The Mosaic Covenant" where God promises to make the children of Israel His, "if ye will obey my voice indeed, and keep my covenant, then ye shall be a peculiar treasure unto me above all people" in Exodus 19:5, and to make the children of Israel "a kingdom of priests and a holy nation" in Exodus 19:6. The Sabbath was given to the children of Israel by God as the permanent sign of His covenant with them, "Verily my sabbaths ye shall keep: for it is a sign between me and you throughout your generations" in Exodus 31:13, and "It is a sign between me and the children of Israel forever" in Exodus 31:17.[12] Note also what is stated in Leviticus 24:8, "Every sabbath he shall set it in order before the LORD continually, being taken from the children of Israel by an everlasting covenant," and in Ezekiel 20:12 it states, "Moreover also I gave them my sabbaths, to be a sign between me and them."

Of these three covenants the last two covenants, The Abrahamic and The Mosaic, are linked to or pertains to the children of Israel specifically while the first covenant is applicable to all life. This is the basis for the denoted triangle. The first two covenants mention "token" in the book of Genesis, and the third mentions a "sign" in the book of

---

11   Source - Wikipedia, Abrahamic covenant, 2011, http://en.wikipedia.org/wiki/Covenant_(biblical)#Abrahamic_covenant, Retrieved 11.25.11

12   Source - Wikipedia, Mosaic Covenant, 2011, http://en.wikipedia.org/wiki/Covenant_(biblical)#Mosaic_covenant, Retrieved 11.25.11

Exodus. The most sacred of the three in my view is keeping the Sabbath. Another identified triangle,▽.

▽ **Based on the three everlasting covenants with each having a sign or token, I think of what is called the Three Oaths.**

"The Three Oaths is the popular name for a Midrash found in the Talmud, which relates that God adjured three oaths upon the world. Two of the oaths pertain to the Jewish people, and one of the oaths pertains to the other nations of the world."[13] This is the basis for the denoted triangle. It is said that the Talmud is another sacred text, as the Torah, in Judaism. Note: "Midrash is a Hebrew term for the body of homiletic stories told by Jewish rabbinic sages to explain passages in the Tanakh."[14]

▽ **There are three verses where God states ". . .I will . . . make of thee a great nation."**

The first time it is to Abram. The second time it is to Israel/Jacob, and the third time is to Moses. The first two are linked as grandfather and grandson, and they are two of the three patriarchs. The third person that God said this to was Moses his chosen leader. This is the basis for the denoted triangle. When God said this to Moses he was anger with his chosen people and he was looking to begin a new with Moses because of them. God makes his promise to the first two men in a serene mood of the three. Another identified triangle,▽. (Note: Abraham and Hagar are told of Ishmael, "I will make him a great nation" in Genesis 17:20 and 21:18.) . Here are the verses:

---

[13] Source - Wikipedia,The Three Oaths, 2013, http://en.wikipedia.org/wiki/Three_Oaths, Retrieved 05.24.2013

[14] Source - Wikipedia, Midrash, 2013, http://en.wikipedia.org/wiki/Midrash, Retrieved 05.24.2013

To Abram in Genesis 12:2 "And **I will make of thee a great nation**, and I will bless thee, and make thy name great; and thou shalt be a blessing."

To Israel/Jacob in Genesis 46:3 "And he said, I am God, the God of thy father: fear not to go down into Egypt; for **I will there make of thee a great nation.**"

To Moses in Exodus 32:10, "Now therefore let me alone, that my wrath may wax hot against them, and that I may consume them: and **I will make of thee a great nation.**" (also in Deuteronomy 9:14)

△/▽ **There were three times Moses "smote" a rock for water for the people to drink with his rod.**

1) In Exodus 17:5-6 ". . .and thy rod, wherewith thou smotest the river, take in thine hand, and go. [6]Behold, I will stand before thee there upon the rock in Horeb; and thou shalt smite the rock, and there shall come water out of it, that the people may drink. And Moses did so in the sight of the elders of Israel."

2 & 3) In Numbers 20:11 "And Moses lifted up his hand, and with his rod he smote the **rock twice**: and the water came out abundantly, and the congregation drank, and their beasts also".

The three times he "smote" the rock is the basis for the first denoted triangle with the last two times being linked. The first place is "in Rephidim" and when Moses had acted "And he called the name of the place Massah, and Meribah," in Exodus 17:7. The second stated place is in the "desert of Zin" and it was stated that "This is the water of Meribah" in Numbers 20:9-13. Notice the name "Meribah" is used in both places along with a second name "Massah." The first place two names are given and in the second place one name is given The second denoted triangle. This activity is also mentioned in Psalms 105:41 and Isaiah 48:21.

△ **There were three recorded times God provided the children of Israel water for sustenance while they were in the wilderness.**

1) In Exodus 15:24-25, "the people murmured against Moses, saying, What shall we drink?" In verse 25 it states, "And he cried unto the LORD; and the LORD shewed him a tree, which when he had cast into the waters."

2) In Exodus 17:6, "I will stand before thee there upon the rock in Horeb; and thou shalt smite the rock, and there shall come water out of it, that the people may drink. . . ."

3) In Numbers 20:11, "And Moses lifted up his hand, and with his rod he smote the rock twice: and the water came out abundantly, and the congregation drank."

The last two times, of the three, relate to Moses hitting a rock for the water. The basis for the denoted triangle.

△ **There were three instances where a pair of sons are punished by God for acts that were wicked in God's view**:

1) The first pair is in Genesis 38:2-10 the two sons of Judah who are Er and Onan.

2) The next pair are "Nadab and Abihu, the sons of Aaron" who "offered strange fire before the LORD" in Leviticus 10:1-2.

3) The third pair are the sons of Eliab, Dathan and Abiram, who opposed Moses and Aaron in the

wilderness and "the earth opened her mouth, and swallowed them up together" in Numbers 26:9-10.

The last two pair of the three were punished together at once. The first pair are punished separately. This is the basis for the denoted triangle. There are two other recorded instances where a pair of sons died but it is not stated that God was involved with the deaths. The first pair are in Ruth 1:5 with the two sons of Naomi, Mahlon and Chilion. The second is the pair of sons of the priest Eli in 1 Samuel 4:17, Hophni and Phinehas, who died on the field of battle against the Philistines where the "Ark of the God" was taken.

▽ **The first three groups to get their inheritance, the allotment of land that was given on the East side of Jordan.**

"The Reubenites, and to the Gadites, and to half the tribe of Manasseh, . . ." is in Joshua 1:12. In Joshua 1:14 it states, "Your wives, your little ones, and your cattle, shall remain in the land which Moses gave you on this side Jordan." It is also mentioned in Numbers 32:31-33, Deuteronomy 3:12-13, and 29:8. The first two groups mentioned are linked to being whole groups. The third is not. The basis for the denoted triangle.

▽ **It is said by some that in the Talmud Moses asked of God three things:**

1) The divine presence, the Shechinah, "might rest on Israel."
2) "That it might rest on none but Israel."
3) "That God's ways might be known to him (Beracheth, fol. 7, col. 1)."[15]

---

[15] Source - The Meaning of in the Bible # 3, 2012, http://www.Biblestudy.org/Bibleref/meaning-of-numbers-in-Bible/3.html, Retrieved 12.28.2012

The first two requests of the three are linked in this case relating to the "divine presence" on Israel. The basis for the denoted triangle. Based on this information Moses seems to have known of the divine pattern. In Exodus 33:13 Moses asked, ". . .shew me now thy way. . ." and in Psalms 103:7 it states, "He made known his ways unto Moses." The way the ten plagues were enacted by Moses this would seem to support this fact.

△ **Moses' life could be divided into three forty year periods. In order to determine if this was the case, various scriptures were reviewed starting with his death.**

1) In Deuteronomy 34:7 states that ". . .Moses was an hundred and twenty years old when he died."
2) In Exodus 7:7 states "Moses was fourscore years old [80]" when he and his brother Aaron "spake unto Pharaoh."
3) In Deuteronomy 2:7, 8:2, 29:5, and Joshua 5:6 suggest that the children of Israel were in the wilderness for forty years with Moses as their leader. I would say as a shepherd.

Based on this information, I can say that the third forty year period of Moses' life was dedicated to being God's servant and leader of the freed people of Israel. In Exodus 2:11-22 Moses fled to the land of Midian after he killed an Egyptian while in Egypt. In Acts 7:29-30 it suggests that Moses lived in the land of Midian/Madian for forty years. Since Moses married one of the seven daughters of a man, Reuel, who had flock that were cared for by the man's daughters, one would think that Moses also became a shepherd of those flock also. This is the basis for Moses' second forty year period dedicated to being a shepherd of sheep. In Exodus 2:5-10 states that Moses was a baby when he was noticed by "the daughter of Pharaoh. . .at the river" and considered him her own since she ". . .drew him out of the water." Acts 7:22-23 states that "Moses was learned in all the wisdom of the Egyptians, and was mighty in words and in deeds. And when he was full forty years old, it came into his heart to visit his brethren the children of Israel." This suggests that Moses was considered Egyptian royalty, a prince perhaps, during his first forty year period of his life. Moses three forty year periods can be shown as follows:

1) Moses first forty years of life was lived as royalty.
2) The second forty year period he could be considered a shepherd.
3) The third forty year period he was a leader, and shepherd over God's chosen people the Israelites leading them to freedom.

Of the three forty year periods of Moses' life, the second and the third are linked to being a shepherd of sorts. This is the basis for the denoted triangle. Genesis 6:3 states, "And the Lord said, My spirit shall not always strive with man, for that he also is flesh: yet his days shall be an hundred and twenty years."

The Book of Joshua

△ The first three battles Joshua led after entering the Promised Land:

1) The destruction of Jericho in Joshua 6:1-25.
2) The first battle with the city of Ai which was a failure in Joshua 7:1-5 because of the trespass of Achan, the son of Carmi who took some silver and gold from Jericho. In this fight thirty-six men of Israel were killed out of 3,000.

3) The successful second battle at Ai in Joshua 8:1-:29 after the trespass of Achan was resolved in Joshua 7:25-26.

The last two battles are linked to fighting the same foe twice of the three. The basis for the denoted triangle. Note the next foe(s) are stated in Joshua 9:1-3, "And it came to pass, when all the kings which were on this side Jordan, in the hills, and in the valleys, and in all the coasts of the great sea over against Lebanon, the Hittite, and the Amorite, the Canaanite, the Perizzite, the Hivite, and the Jebusite, heard thereof; ²That they gathered themselves together, to fight with Joshua and with Israel, with one accord. ³And when the inhabitants of Gibeon heard what Joshua had done unto Jericho and to Ai."

▽ **Joshua 12:9-10 gives the names of the first three kings and cities taken after the children of Israel entered the Promised Land "Jericho, and Ai, and Jerusalem."**
Jerusalem or *Yerushalayim* in Hebrew is listed as the third city. There should not be any other conclusion other than it was the third city taken by the children of Israel based on this listing. The first two cities of the three mentioned are recorded in detail in how they were taken in Joshua 6:1-27 and 7:2-8:29 respectively, but there is no record in the Bible of how Jerusalem was taken, the third city. This is the basis for the denoted triangle. Jerusalem is the most holy city in the Jewish tradition.

▽/△ **There are three verses where it is stated that God ". . .is a jealous God."**
The first two verses pertain to Moses and the third verse pertains to Joshua. The first denoted triangle. In the first verse God tells Moses and in the last two verses Moses and

Joshua, servants/leaders of God, respectively are telling the people. The second denoted triangle. Here are the verses:

1) Exodus 34:14 states, "For thou shalt worship no other god: for the Lord, whose name is Jealous, is a jealous God:"
2) Deuteronomy 6:15 states, "(For the Lord thy God is a jealous God among you) lest the anger of the Lord thy God be kindled against thee, and destroy thee from off the face of the earth."
3) Joshua 24:19 states, "And Joshua said unto the people, Ye cannot serve the Lord: for he is an holy God; he is a jealous God; he will not forgive your transgressions nor your sins."

The Book of Judges

▽ **The first three Judges of Israel are listed in Judges 3:1-31.**

1) Othniel, "the son of Kenaz, Caleb's younger brother," in verses 7-11 and mentioned as part of the tribe of Judah.
2) Ehud, "the son of Gera, a Benjamite" mentioned in verses 12-30.
3) Shamgar, "the son of Anath " in verse 31.

The first two are considered major judges in that there is a beginning and an end provided in the scriptures. Before the first Judge, Othniel, eight years the children of Israel were being oppressed. After being oppressed they had forty years of rest. Before the second judge, Ehud, eighteen years the children of Israel were being oppressed. After being oppressed they had eighty years of rest. Shamgar, the third judge, is considered a minor judge because there is no stated beginning or any conclusion relating to him. There is no time mentioned of how long the children of Israel are oppressed or any subsequent rest after being oppressed. He is only mentioned in verse 31 of the chapter. This is the basis for the denoted triangle. The first two are stated as being a "deliverer" in the scriptures and the third is not. Another identified triangle, ▽.

△ **There are three instances where the name of God, Jehovah, is used in connection with an altar.**

1) Abraham used Jehovah Jireh (the Lord will provide) in Genesis 22:9-14 pertaining to the sacrifice of his son Isaac.
2) Moses used Jehovah Nissi (the Lord is my banner) in Exodus 17:13-16 after the battle with Amalek/Amalekites.
3) Gideon used Jehovah Shalom (the Lord is Peace) in Judges 6:16-24 after he heard from God.

The last two altars of the three are built as part of the context of a battle. This is the basis for the denoted triangle.

△ **In Judges 6:11-21 and 6:36-40 Gideon ask for three signs.**

1) The first is from the angel who was on earth and Gideon asking the angel "[17]. . .shew me a sign that thou talkest with me" and to wait for him as he went to go get food for the angel. "[21]Then the angel of the LORD put forth the end of the staff that was in his hand, and touched the flesh and the unleavened cakes; and there rose up fire out of the rock, and consumed the flesh and the unleavened cakes."

2) Gideon asked God to cause only the fleece to become wet with dew in verse 37.

3) He asked God that the fleece be dry and dew to lie everywhere except on the fleece in verse 39.

The last two signs of the three are linked to a request to God in heaven and the fleece. The basis for the denoted triangle.

▽/△ **There were three Judges who lead the children of Israel to forty years of "rest/quietness" after overcoming from being oppressed:**

1) Othniel in Judges 3:7-11 "And the land had rest. . ." (verse 11).

2) Deborah w/ Barak, a military leader, in Judges 4-5:31 "And the land had rest. . ." (verse 5:31).

3) Gideon in Judges 6-8:28 "And the country was in quietness. . ." (verse 8:28).

The word "rest" is associated with the first two Judges while "quietness" is associated with the third Judge, Gideon. The first denoted triangle. The last two Judges have chapters devoted to their activities while the first just has a few verses associated to him. The second denoted triangle.

▽ **Judges 16:7-17 tells of how Samson "mocked" Delilah three times regarding the secret to his strength:**
"Thou hast mocked me these three times, and hast not told me wherein thy great strength lieth" (verse 15).

The first two times he told her to get "seven green withs" and "new ropes" to bind him in verse 7 and verse 12 respectively which were ineffective. The third time he told her that weaving his hair into a weaving apparatus in verse 14 was the secret to his strength. This third time was very close to his secret. The first two times are linked to Samson being bound and the third time he is not. This is the basis for the denoted triangle. Note the fourth time she asked of him he told her, the truth, in cutting his hair he would "become weak, and be like any other man" in verse 17.

▽ In Judges 20:18-35 three times the "children of Israel" fought against the "children of Benjamin" in Gibeah on three separate days.

"The children of Israel arose, and went up to the house of God, and asked counsel of God and said, Which of us shall go up first to the battle against the children of Benjamin? And the LORD said, Judah shall go up first" (verse 18).

Day 1: The ". . .men of Israel went out to battle against Benjamin. . ." and the "men of Israel" lost 22,000 men (verses 20-22).

Day 2: The "children of Israel. . .asked counsel of the LORD, saying, Shall I go up again to battle against the children of Benjamin my brother? And the LORD said, Go up against him". On this second day the "children of Israel" lost 18,000 men (verses 23-25).

Day 3: "The children of Israel enquired of the LORD . . . And Phinehas, the son of Eleazar, the son of Aaron, stood before it in those days,) saying, Shall I yet again go out to battle against the children of Benjamin my brother, or shall I cease? And the LORD said, Go up; for tomorrow I will deliver them into thine hand." On the third of battle day, "And the LORD smote Benjamin before Israel: and the children of Israel destroyed of the Benjamites that day twenty and five thousand and an hundred men: all these drew the sword" (verses 28-35).

In summary, notice they sought the LORD for guidance all three times, but were not told they were going to be victorious until the third request to God when the "ark of the covenant of God" and the priest Phinehas is mentioned relating to the third request. This is the basis for the denoted triangle. The first request to God was who would be first to fight. The response was Judah, but they did not ask whether they should fight them as they did the next two times. Another identified triangle, △.

Notice that the first two stated days of battle the "men of Israel" lost but were victorious on the third day of battle. Another identified triangle, ▽.

Also noticed that the "men of Israel" "went up" and "wept" after the first two battles which were losses, in verses 23 and 26, but not the third. Another identified triangle,▽.

The number of men lost by the "men of Israel" is stated for the first two battles in the thousands, but not for the third battle which in verse 31 it is stated to be 30 men. Another identified triangle,▽.

The number of men the Benjamites lost is stated for the third day of battle but not the first two days of battles. Another identified triangle,▽.

Ruth

△ There were three men who died that were related to Naomi.

In Ruth 1:3 it states, "Elimelech Naomi's husband died." Then in verse 5 her two sons died about ten years later, "Mahlon and Chilion died also both of them." Her husband died first then her two sons. This is the basis for the denoted triangle.

1 & 2 Samuel, 1 &2 Kings, and 1 & 2 Chronicles

▽/△ Three biblical women, Sarah, Rachel, and Hannah were upset because they were barren at a point in time:

1) In Genesis 16:2, Sarah – who gives her servant Hagar as a surrogate, who has one child Ishmael,
2) In Genesis 30:1-3, Rachel – who gives her servant Bilhah as a surrogate, who has two children Dan and Naphtali,
3) In 1 Samuel 1:5-8, Hannah.

Notice the first two women of the three are recorded in the book of Genesis. The first denoted triangle. The last two women of the three are depicted as weeping in the scriptures because of their situation. The second denoted triangle. The first two women of the three offer their servant women as surrogates for them. Another identified triangle, ▽. The last two women of the three had sons of their own who became great in statue in the eyes of God and men: Rachel who had Joseph who became governor of Egypt and Hannah who had Samuel who became a priest/prophet/Judge of Israel, Another identified triangle, △. Two of the women of the three are wives to the Patriarchs, Sarah to Abraham and Rachel to Jacob. Another identified triangle,▽. (Note: In Judges 13:3 Samson's mother was barren and there is no record of her showing emotion relating to her barrenness. In 2 Kings 4:8-37 there was a Shunammite woman who took care of the Prophet Elisha who was barren and later bared a son based on the word of the Prophet, but there is not record of her displaying any emotions regarding her situation. There is one other woman who was stated to be barren in Luke 1:7 and 1:36. This was Elizabeth the mother of John the Baptist. Of these last three women mentioned the first two are in the Old Testament and the last in the New Testament. An identified triangle, ▽.) It seems that God likes to display his divinity via the use of barren women.

△/△ In 1 Samuel 1:24-25 there were items that were presented to the Priest Eli along with the boy Samuel:
". . .three bullocks, and one ephah of flour, and a bottle of wine." Of the three bullocks one is slain in verse 25. There is no mention of what happened to the other two at all. The first denoted triangle. What was brought can also be viewed as three separate things. The first is the three bullocks, the second is the flour, and the third is a bottle of wine with the first thing having multiple items. The second denoted triangle.

▽ Three times Samuel is called of God thinking it is Eli who calling him in 1 Samuel 3:5-9.
The first two times God calls Samuel, as Samuel goes to Eli, Eli does not perceive that it is God calling Samuel. After the third time Eli gets that God is calling Samuel and tells Samuel what to say, "Speak, LORD; for thy servant heareth" in verse 9. This is the basis for the denoted triangle.

▽/△ There were three Philistine controlled places the Ark of the Covenant was taken after they captured it from Israel in battle as recorded in 1 Samuel 4:10-11.

1) They took it to Ashdod which was destroyed by God with "emerods"/boils because they had the Ark, "But the **hand of the LORD** was heavy upon them of Ashdod, and he destroyed them, and smote them with emerods, even Ashdod and the coasts thereof." (1 Samuel 5:6)

2) It was decided next to send the "Ark of the God of Israel" to the Philistine controlled city of Gath. That city was also hit by God ". . .with a very great

destruction: and he smote the men of the city, both small and great, and they had emerods. . .", boils. "And it was so, that, after they had carried it about, the **hand of the LORD** was against the city with a very great destruction: and he smote the men of the city, both small and great, and they had emerods in their secret parts." (1 Samuel 5:9).

3) Next "the ark" was being sent to the city of Ekron, but "[10]. . .the Ekronites cried out, saying, They have brought about the ark of the God of Israel to us, to slay us and our people so it was decided by all the lords of the Philistines to send away the ark of the God of Israel, and let it go again to his own place, that it slay us not, and our people . . . [11]for there was a deadly destruction throughout all the city; the **hand of God** was very heavy there. " (1 Samuel 5:10-11).

Notice that verses 5:6 and 5:9 for Ashdod and Gath stated that it was "the hand of the Lord," and for Ekron in verse 11 is was "the hand of God" as the source of the "deadly destruction." This is the basis for the first denoted triangle. It is also mentioned twice, for the last two cities of the three, as to where the "Ark of the God of Israel" would reside by ". . .all the lords of the Philistines . . ." of the three places. There is no mention in scripture who made the decision for the Ark to go to Ashdod the first place but the same group of men should be suspected. The second denoted triangle. The Philistines held the "Ark of the Lord . . . seven months" in their country called the "pentapolis" (1 Samuel 6:1), five cities they controlled. The other two areas in this "pentapolis" that were not affected by God were Gaza and Ashkelon.

△ **Three times the Lord used thunder at the behest of his servant:** Moses once and Samuel twice. This is the basis for the denoted triangle.

1) The first was for Moses relating to the seventh plague along with fire and hail against Egypt in Exodus 9:18-24, 33-34.

2) The second was for Samuel as he ". . .cried unto the LORD for Israel; and the LORD heard him" (1 Samuel 7:9) and while making a sacrifice to God with the Philistines coming to attack and ". . .the LORD thundered with a great thunder on that day upon the Philistines, and discomfited them; and they were smitten before Israel" (1 Samuel 7:10).

3) The third was for Samuel again, along with rain, this time it was requested to show the people the evil they did in asking for a king in 1 Samuel 12:18-19. "So Samuel called unto the LORD; and the LORD sent thunder and rain that day: and all the people greatly feared the LORD and Samuel."

▽/▽ **Three signs were told to Saul by Samuel the prophet as confirmation, after he is anointed, that he is the King of Israel in 1 Samuel 10:**

1) **The first sign** is that two men "². . .by Rachel's sepulcher in the border of Benjamin at Zelzah" will tell him that "The asses which thou wentest to seek are found".

2) **The second sign**, "³ . . .thou shalt come to the plain of Tabor, and there shall meet thee three men going up to God to Bethel, one carrying three kids, and another carrying three loaves of bread, and another carrying a bottle of wine". "⁴And they will salute thee, and give thee two loaves of bread; which thou shalt receive of their hands".

3) **The third sign**, "⁵After that thou shalt come to the hill of God, where is the garrison of the Philistines: and it shall come to pass, when thou art come

thither to the city, that thou shalt meet a company of prophets coming down from the high place with a psaltery, and a tabret, and a pipe, and a harp, before them; and they shall prophesy". "⁶And the Spirit of the LORD will come upon thee, and thou shalt prophesy with them, and shalt be turned into another man".

Of the three signs the first two mention animals in them while the third does not. The first denoted triangle. Note also that in the second sign three items are mentioned being with two of the three men. One man with three kids and another man with three loaves of bread. The third man has one item. The second denoted triangle. Saul is given two of the three loaves of bread from the man who has them in the second sign. Another identified triangle, ▽.

▽/△ In 1 Samuel 17:17-18 David's father Jesse instructs him to take three items to the battlefield to his brothers:

1) "an ephah of this parched corn"
2) "these ten loaves"
3) "these ten cheeses".

The first listed item, "an ephah of . . .parched corn" and the group of items of loaves are to go to his brethren and the third group of items, cheeses, are to go to "the captain of their thousand." The first denoted triangle. Of the three listed things, the last two are linked to the same number "ten." The second denoted triangle. It is recorded in 1 Samuel 17:13 that three of David's brothers are part of Saul's army, "And the three eldest sons of Jesse went and followed Saul to the battle."

▽ **In 1 Samuel 17:34-52 David was involved with the killing of three living things as a young man:**

He killed two animals, a lion and a bear, in regards to protecting his father's sheep, and he killed Goliath. In 1 Samuel 17:36 it states, "Thy servant slew both the lion and the bear: and this uncircumcised Philistine shall be as one of them, seeing he hath defied the armies of the living God." This is the basis for the denoted triangle.

▽/▽ **In 1 Samuel 25:13 and 30:9-10, 400 or two-thirds of David's men were going out with him among 600.**

In the first instance, first verse, one-third or "two hundred abode by the stuff" in 25:13 of the 600. The first denoted triangle. In the second instance 400 or two-thirds continued the pursuit of the invaders who took their "stuff" while 200 of them or one-third did not because they were exhausted to cross "The brook of Besor" in 30:9-10 of the 600. The second denoted triangle.

▽ **Read the three verses that states a woman ". . .lighted off her/the ass. . ."**

The first two verses are stated similarly and relate to the daughter of Caleb a leader under Moses. Her name was Achsah. The third verse relates to Abigail the wife to Nabal. Nabal was an enemy of David. Abigail later became the wife of David after the death of Nabal. This is the basis for the denoted triangle. Here are the verses:

1) Joshua 15:18 "And it came to pass, as she came unto him, that she moved him to ask of her father a field: and she lighted off her ass; and Caleb said unto her, What wouldest thou?"
2) Judges 1:14 "And it came to pass, when she came to him, that she moved him to ask of her father a field: and she lighted from off her ass; and Caleb said unto her, What wilt thou?"

3) 1 Samuel 25:23 "And when Abigail saw David, she hasted, and lighted off the ass, and fell before David on her face, and bowed herself to the ground."

▽ **The first three anointed kings of Israel, Saul, David and Solomon, who reigned over an undivided kingdom.**

1) Saul in 1 Samuel 10:1 and 15:1, "Samuel also said unto Saul, The LORD sent me to anoint thee to be king over his people, over Israel."

2) David in 1 Samuel 16:1 and 13, "Then Samuel took the horn of oil, and anointed him in the midst of his brethren: and the Spirit of the LORD came upon David from that day forward." In 2 Samuel 2:4 David was also ". . .anointed king over the house of Judah" and again king over Israel in 2 Samuel 5:3 and 1 Chronicles 11:3. Thus David was anointed three times, once as young man and twice as an older man to be king.

3) Solomon was anointed in 1 Kings 1:39, "Zadok the priest took an horn of oil out of the tabernacle, and anointed Solomon". This is also stated in 1 Chronicles 29:22.

The first and second kings were anointed with oil by Samuel, the prophet. The third king was not. This is the basis for the denoted triangle. The second and third kings were more favored by God than the first. Another identified triangle,△. The second and third kings are related as father and son of the three. Another identified triangle,△. The Third king was given wisdom, wealth, and power like no other king of the children of Israel and was more prosperous than the first two kings. Another identified triangle, ▽. King Solomon was also charged with building the Temple of God. The first Temple.

EEach of the three kings reigned for forty years as stated in Acts 13:21 for King Saul, 2 Samuel 5:4 and 1 Kings 2:11 for King David, and 1 Kings 11:42 for King Solomon. Note, before King Saul the priest Eli also judged Israel for forty years in 1 Samuel 4:18. There is no record of how long Samuel, after Eli, judged Israel.

Of the three kings mentioned two of them had recorded prophets to assist them. Samuel to King Saul in 1 Samuel 3:20, 10:1, 15:1. Gad was "David's seer" in 1 Samuel 22:5, 2 Samuel 24:11, 1 Chronicles 21:9, 2 Chronicles 29:25 and Nathan in 2 Samuel 7:2 assisted King David. "Now the acts of David the king, first and last, behold, they are written in the book of Samuel the seer, and in the book of Nathan the prophet, and in the book of Gad the seer" (1 Chronicles 29:29). The third king had no record of a prophet in the Bible that gave him advice. He had the gift of wisdom from God. This is another identified triangle,△.

Also it is stated for the first two kings, Saul and David, after they were anointed the "Spirit of the LORD" came upon them as stated in 1 Samuel 10:6 and 16:13 respectively of the three kings. Another identified triangle, ▽. It is stated in 1 Kings 3:5, 9:2, 11:9, and 2 Chronicles 1:7 ". . .the LORD appeared to Solomon in a dream by night" (1 Kings 3:5), a firsthand account, unto Solomon the third king, twice. There is no firsthand record of this activity happening for the first two kings. Another identified triangle,▽. Note that 2 Chronicles 3:1 mentions an appearance of God to David, but nothing from David himself in the scriptures.

Saul got three signs as a confirmation that he was king. David was anointed three times relating to being king. King Solomon three gifts from God were given to him wisdom, riches, and honor. Saul was given signs and the other two kings something else relating to being king. Another identified triangle,△.

Relating to the number of wives and concubines each of the first three Kings of Israel had: Saul had one wife and one concubine (1 Samuel 14:50 and 2 Samuel 3:7), David had at least eight wives and at least ten concubines (2 Samuel 5:13). 700 wives and 300 concubines for Solomon as stated in 1 Kings 11:3. The last two kings of the three had many of each. Another identified, △.

(Note: The verse of 2 Samuel 2:10 states "Ishbosheth Saul's son was forty years old when he began to reign over Israel, and reigned two years. But the house of Judah followed David." Based on this scripture, in my view, Saul's son did not rule over a united kingdom nor is there any record that he was anointed to be a king. It is stated in 2 Samuel 2:8-9 that "8. . .Abner the son of Ner, captain of Saul's host, . . . took Ishbosheth the son of Saul, . . . 9And made him king ". Nothing is stated factually that he was anointed but it could be assumed that it was done.)

Of the three kings, King Solomon is the only one who asked what he wanted from God that is recorded. Another identified triangle, ▽. Also of the three kings the last two are involved with the house of God. King David had the idea (2 Samuel 7:7-16, 1 Chronicles 17: 2-15), but King Solomon built the house of God (1 Chronicles 22:6-17) being charged with the task by his father David, This is another identified triangle, △.

△/△/△ The three anointings of David by prominent individuals:

1) In 1 Samuel 16:13, David is anointed by Samuel and is not a leader at this time.
2) In 2 Samuel 2:4 David is anointed King ". . .over the house of Judah" by "the men of Judah".
3) In 2 Samuel 5:3 David is anointed King over Israel by "the elders of Israel".

Of the three verses David is a leader of men in the last two verses. This is the basis for first denoted triangle. Of the three verses David is a young man in the first verse while in the next two scriptures he is an older man. The basis for the second denoted triangle. Of the three verses the last two are in the same book. The basis for the third denoted triangle. Also note the scriptures of 2 Samuel 23:1, "David the son of Jesse said, and the man who was raised up on high, the anointed of the God of Jacob." Psalm 89:20 states, "I have found David my servant; with my holy oil have I anointed him."

▽ **Read of the first three battles King David encountered in which all three were with the Philistines after being made king over all Israel.**

1) In 2 Samuel 5:17-21 and 1 Chronicles 14:8-12
2) In 2 Samuel 5:22-25 and 1 Chronicles 14:13-17
3) In 2 Samuel 8:1 and 1 Chronicles 18:1

The first two battles King David "enquired of the Lord.". There is no record of him enquiring of God the third time. The basis for the denoted triangle. Note that The fourth battle was with the Moabites in 2 Samuel 8:2 and 1 Chronicles 18:2.

▽ **David's first three sons are as follows:**

1) Amnon by Ahinoam, the Jezreelitess (2 Samuel 3:3, 1 Chronicles 3:1). He was killed on orders by Absalom (2 Samuel 13:28-29).
2) Chileab/Daniel by Abigail, the former wife of Nabal the Carmelitess (2 Samuel 3:3 and 1 Chronicles 3:1).
3) Absalom by Maacah/Maachah, the daughter of Talmai King of Geshur (2 Samuel 3:3 and 1 Chronicles 3:2).

Absalom rebelled against his father David as recorded in 2 Samuel 14:25–18:18. Absalom actions are in a result of David's involvement with Bathsheba the wife of Uriah, "Now therefore the sword shall never depart from thine house; because thou hast despised me, and hast taken the wife of Uriah the Hittite to be thy wife" (2 Samuel 12:10). The first two sons of the three did not cause David any problems as Absalom the third son. The basis for the denoted triangle.

△/△ **There are three women who are named Tamar:**

1) In Genesis 38:6 the first is the daughter-in-law of Jacob's son Judah.
2) In 2 Samuel 13:1 the second is the sister of Absalom and David's Daughter. "Absalom the son of David had a fair sister"
3) In 2 Samuel 14:27 the third is Absalom's daughter and David's granddaughter, "she was a woman of a fair countenance."

Of the three the last two are a close relation to David's son Absalom. The first denoted triangle. Also of the three women the last two are stated to be "fair". The second denoted triangle. Note, Ruth 4:12 states, "And let thy house be like the house of Pharez, whom Tamar bare unto Judah, of the seed which the LORD shall give thee of this young woman."

▽ **In 2 Samuel 18:2 King David is dealing with the trouble of his third son Absalom.**

As Absalom rebelled against King David his father, the King sought to break up those that he had with him into three groups. One third would go with Joab and one third with Abishai, the sons of Zeruiah. Ittai the Gittite lead the third group. This is the basis for the denoted triangle. The idea was rejected in verse three by the people.

▽ **One of David's men "Benaiah the son of Jehoiada" is recorded twice to have ". . .slew two lion like men of Moab" and ". . .slew a lion."**

Two men and an animal relating to a "lion" is the basis for the denoted triangle. The verses are as follows:

> 2 Samuel 23:20 it states, "And Benaiah the son of Jehoiada, the son of a valiant man, of Kabzeel, who had done many acts, he slew two lionlike men of Moab: he went down also and slew a lion in the midst of a pit in time of snow:"

> 1 Chronicles 11:22 states also, "Benaiah the son of Jehoiada, the son of a valiant man of Kabzeel, who had done many acts; he slew two lionlike men of Moab: also he went down and slew a lion in a pit in a snowy day."

△ **Three recorded verses where an Egyptian is slain by a person:** in Exodus 2:12, 2 Samuel 23:21, and 1 Chronicles 11:23. Exodus 2:12 relates to Moses slaying an Egyptian. 2 Samuel 23:21 and 1 Chronicles 11:23 relate to one of King David's men, Benaiah the son of Jehoiada, slaying an Egyptian ". . .with his own spear." This is the basis for the denoted triangle. The verses are as follows:

1) Exodus 2:12, "And he looked this way and that way, and when he saw that there was no man, he slew the Egyptian, and hid him in the sand."

2) 2 Samuel 23:21, "And he slew an Egyptian, a goodly man: and the Egyptian had a spear in his hand; but he went down to him with a staff, and plucked the spear out of the Egyptian's hand, and slew him with his own spear."

3) 1 Chronicles 11:23, "And he slew an Egyptian, a man of great stature, five cubits high; and in the Egyptian's hand was a spear like a weaver's beam; and he went down to him with a staff, and plucked the spear out of the Egyptian's hand, and slew him with his own spear."

△/△ There are three men who fought and killed lions and lived.

1) Samson in Judges 14:5-9
2) David in 1 Samuel 17:34-37
3) David's mighty man Benaiah in 2 Samuel 23:20 and recorded again in 1 Chronicles 11:22

Samson is the only one of the three recorded killing the lion with his hands. The other two seemed to have used a weapon. The first denoted triangle. The last two of these three men are connected. The second denoted triangle. Also read in 1 Kings 13:23-24 of how a prophet of God was disobedient to God and was later killed by a lion. His "ass" and the lion stood by the dead man. The three in one place, the two beasts alive and the dead man. Another identified triangle,▽.

△ Three things God told Solomon he would give him in 1 Kings 3:5, 12-13:

1) He requested of God, "Behold, I have done according to thy words: lo, I have given thee a wise and an understanding heart" (1 Kings 3:12).
2 & 3) God also gave him two things he did not ask for, "And I have also given thee that which thou hast not asked, both riches, and honour" (1 Kings 3:13). He got his request and two other added items by God

which he did not request. This is the basis for the denoted triangle. What God gave him is also mentioned in 2 Chronicles 1:12.

△/▽ **King Solomon built three houses designated for someone**:

1) The House of the Lord (1 Kings 3:1, 6:2,14, 38, 9:15; 1 Chronicles 6:32, 2 Chronicles 2:1, 7:11, 8:1; and Acts 7:27). The dimensions of the house of the Lord are given in 1 Kings 6:2. The house of the Lord was built in seven years (1Kings 6:38).
2) Solomon's own house (1 Kings 7:1-2, 9:10, 15; 2 Chronicles 2:1, 7:11, and 8:1). The dimensions of the house, and material used for Solomon's house is stated in 1 Kings 7:2. It took 13 years (1 Kings 7:1). "And it came to pass at the end of twenty years, wherein Solomon had built the house of the LORD, and his own house". (2 Chronicles 8:1)
3) King Solomon built the house for the Daughter of Pharaoh, Solomon's wife (1 Kings 7:8, 9:24; 2 Chronicles 8:11). No other information is provided other than it was built for her.

Of these three houses built the first is the most significant of the three. The first denoted triangle. The time it took to build the houses is stated for two of the three houses. The second denoted triangle. I noticed the phrase, "the house of the forest of Lebanon" which could be interpreted as either the use of the wood material used for the houses or the mentioning of another "house" that Solomon built. In 1 Kings 10:17 and Chronicles 9:16 it states, ". . .he made three hundred shields of beaten gold; three pound of gold went to one shield. And the king put them in the house." In 1 Kings 10:21 and 2 Chronicles 9:20 it states, ". . .king

Solomon's drinking vessels were of gold, and all the vessels of the house" suggesting this house could have been used as a storage facility for King Solomon. There was no recorded individual mentioned being designated for this house, but it can be implied that it is King Solomon's if it is a "house" that had been built or just a reference to the trees of the "forest of Lebanon."

△/△ **There are three men considered monarchs who had a pair of dreams that are recorded:**

1) Pharaoh of Egypt dreamed in Genesis. 41:1-4 of the seven well favored kine and seven ill favored, and then in Genesis 41:5 the seven ears of corn that are good and the seven ears of corn that are thin.
2) Solomon the third king of Israel and his two dreams as stated in 1 Kings 3:5 and 9:2.
3) Nebuchadnezzar King of Babylon in Daniel 2:1-45 and 4:5-18.

The last two men are linked as being stated kings while the first has the title of Pharaoh. The first denoted triangle. The first man's two dreams were in one night while the last two men's dreams were over some time. The second denoted triangle. Also the last two men were kings over the land of Judah in a way of the three. Another identified triangle,△.

△ **Read of how the three anointed kings of an undivided Israel died.**

King Saul committed suicide while on the battlefield fighting the Philistines and was later cremated and buried in a place called Jabash. King David and King Solomon both died of natural causes and were buried in the "city of David" a.k.a. Jerusalem.

Here are the three verses for the formed denoted triangle:

1) 1 Samuel 31:4, "Then said Saul unto his armour bearer, Draw thy sword, and thrust me through therewith; lest these uncircumcised come and thrust me through, and abuse me. But his armour bearer would not; for he was sore afraid."

2) 1 Kings 2:10, "So David slept with his fathers, and was buried in the city of David."

3) 1 Kings 11:43, "And Solomon slept with his fathers, and was buried in the city of David his father:"

△ **Read of how Jeroboam, a servant of Solomon, is told by a prophet of God, Ahijah the Shilonite, that he will be king.**

"I will rend the kingdom out of the hand of Solomon, and will give ten tribes to thee" (1 Kings 11:31). This will be the Northern kingdom of Israel. The prophecy comes true and is recorded in 1 Kings 12:20. This action was being done because Solomon had ". . .forsaken me [God], and have worshipped Ashtoreth the goddess of the Zidonians, Chemosh the god of the Moabites, and Milcom the god of the children of Ammon, and have not walked in my ways, to do that which is right in mine eyes, and to keep my statutes and my judgments, as did David his father." (1 Kings 11:33)

Of the three gods mentioned in the verse, the goddess Ashtoreth, the god Chemish, and the god Milcom the first is feminine and the last two are masculine. This is the basis for the denoted triangle. Solomon's son Rehoboam becomes the first king of Judah in the south as recorded in 1 Kings 14:21, "And Rehoboam the son of Solomon reigned in Judah" and also in 2 Chronicles 10:17. This action, the kingdom of Israel being divided, was done shortly after the death of Solomon, the third king of Israel. The ten tribes of Israel forming the Northern Kingdom, called Israel, under Jeroboam and tribes of Judah and Benjamin forming the Southern Kingdom called Judah under Rehoboam.

▽ **Three verses state the first kings of Israel and Judah (Rehoboam, Solomon's son, and Jeroboam Solomon's former servant) were at war with each other constantly. The kingdom has been is divided at this time.**

1) In 1 Kings 14:30 "And there was war between Rehoboam and Jeroboam all their days."
2) In 1 Kings 15:6 "And there was war between Rehoboam and Jeroboam all the days of his life."
3) In 2 Chronicles 12:15 "Now the acts of Rehoboam, first and last, are they not written in the book of Shemaiah the prophet, and of Iddo the seer concerning genealogies? And there were wars between Rehoboam and Jeroboam continually."

The first verse states that ". . .there was war between Rehoboam and Jeroboam. . ." with the third verse stating ". . .there were wars between Rehoboam and Jeroboam. . .". The first two verses are in the same book and state "was war" while the third verse states "were wars." This is the basis for the denoted triangle.

▽ **Three people erected altars in and/or around Bethel:**

1) Abraham's altar between Bethel and Hai in Genesis 12:8.
2) Jacob's s two to three altars at Bethel one after his dream of angels and the stairs in Genesis 28:18 and the second when he returned to the land where he created his first altar in Genesis 35:7 and another in Genesis 35:14.
3) King Jeroboam had an altar erected at Bethel with the golden calf in 1 Kings 12:28 because he thought he was going to lose the people.

King Jeroboam's altar was the only one with an idol. This is the basis for the denoted triangle. Two of the three men were closely related, Abraham and Jacob. Another identified triangle, ▽.

△ Three "acts of God" were shown to the prophet Elijah in 1 Kings 19:11-12: wind, earthquake, and fire.

"And he said, Go forth, and stand upon the mount before the LORD. And, behold, the LORD passed by, and a great and strong wind rent the mountains, and brake in pieces the rocks before the LORD; but the LORD was not in the wind: and after the wind an earthquake; but the LORD was not in the earthquake: And after the earthquake a fire; but the LORD was not in the fire: and after the fire a still small voice."

Of the three acts where God was not, the effects of the wind is describe in detail while there is nothing stating what the destructive effects were of the earthquake and the fire. This is the basis for the denoted triangle. The effects of the earthquake should have produced some of the same results as the wind but it is not recorded.

▽/△ Read three verses where God "opened the eyes" of someone:

1) Hagar in the desert, "And God opened her eyes, and she saw a well of water" in Genesis 21:19.

2) The prophet Balaam and the angel in front of him, "Then the LORD opened the eyes of Balaam, and he saw the angel of the LORD standing in the way. . ." in Numbers 22:31.

3) The servant of the prophet Elisha who saw host of angels around them, "And Elisha prayed, and said, LORD, I pray thee, open his eyes, that he may see. And the LORD opened the eyes of the young man; and he saw" in 2 Kings 6:17.

The first two people eyes were just opened by God. The third person eyes were opened because of a prayer unto God so that he could see. This is the basis for the first denoted triangle. Also of these three the last two people saw angels, Balaam and Elisha's servant. The second denoted triangle.

△ **A host of angels were seen by three people on earth in reality:**

1) In Genesis 32:1-2 "And Jacob went on his way, and the angels of God met him and when Jacob saw them, he said, This is God's host."

2) In 2 Kings 6:15-18 how Elisha saw a host of angels on chariots of fire.

3) The servant of Elisha who saw because of a prayer unto God for him to have the sight to see them, "I pray thee, open his eyes, that he may see. And the LORD opened the eyes of the young man; and he saw" in 2 Kings 6:17.

Jacob is the first person. Elisha and his servant together are the next two men. This is the basis for the denoted triangle.

▽ **The three miracles that involved widows that are stated in the Old Testament:**

1) In 1 Kings 17:10-16 where Elijah and a "handful of meal in a barrel and a little oil in a cruse" were increased that kept widow and her son alive along with the prophet Elijah.

2) In 1 Kings 17:17-21 Elijah prays for the life of the same widow's son to come back to life after boy got sick and died.

3) In 2 Kings 4:1-7 where the prophet Elisha tells a widow to borrow all vessels she can so that she can

fill them up with a little "pot of oil" so that she can pay her debts.

The first two are related to the Prophet Elijah and the third relating to the Prophet Elisha. This is the basis for the denoted triangle. Of the three miracles the first two are in the same book and chapter. Another identified triangle, ▽.

△ Three calves of gold were made by the Children of Israel.

1) The first in Exodus 32:3-6/Deuteronomy. 9:16 when they were out of Egypt near Mount Sinai.

2 & 3) The second and third in 1 Kings 12:28-29 in the Northern Kingdom of Israel where King Jeroboam had two calves built in the cities of Bethel and Dan out of fear the people would leave him.

This is the basis for the denoted triangle where the last two calves are linked. After the three calves were built it was stated that ". . . thy gods, O Israel, which brought thee up out of the land of Egypt." The last two calves are linked by person, area, and time. The first created calf is also mentioned in Psalm 106:19, Nehemiah 9:18, and Acts 7:41. Of these three mentioned verses, the first two verses are in the Old Testament and one in New Testament. Another identified triangle, ▽.

▽/△ There were three people who were raised from the dead in the Old Testament:

1) In 1 Kings 17:8-23 the Prophet Elijah raised the son of a "widow woman" of Zarephath in verses. 21-22 ". . .he stretched himself upon the child three times,

and cried unto the LORD,. . .and the soul of the child came into him again, and he revived".

2) In 2 Kings 4:8-37 the Prophet Elisha raised the son of the "Shunammite woman" after he pronounces that she would have one being barren, "[32]. . .when Elisha was come into the house, behold, the child was dead, and laid upon his bed [34]. . .he went up, and lay upon the child, and put his mouth upon his mouth, and his eyes upon his eyes, and his hands upon his hands: and he stretched himself upon the child; . . .[35] . . .he returned, and walked in the house to and fro; and went up, and stretched himself upon him: and the child sneezed seven times, and the child opened his eyes."

3) In 2 Kings 13:20-21 a dead man is being placed into a grave/tomb of Elisha and the man's body ". . . .touched the bones of Elisha, he revived, and stood up on his feet."

The first two of the three resurrections relate to boys/ sons being revived in the similar manner with the Prophets stretching themselves over the boys. The first denoted triangle. The last two of the three resurrections pertains to the Prophet Elisha. The second denoted triangle. Of the three, the resurrections the first two people, children, were not buried but the third man was in the midst of being buried. Another identified triangle, ∇.

∇/$\triangle$ There are three miracles relating to the Prophet Elijah that were done on the ground in 1 Kings chapter 17:2-24:

1) He was fed by ravens with ". . .bread and flesh in the morning, and bread and flesh in the evening; and he drank of the brook" in verse 17:6 as spoken to him

by God. The brook called Cherith is mentioned in verses 17:3, 5.

2) God told him to go to Zarephath where he "commanded" ". . .a widow woman there to sustain thee" in verses 17:8-16. There all the widow had was ". . .but an handful of meal in a barrel, and a little oil in a cruse" in verse 12. When he met her he asked her "make me thereof a little cake first. . ." in verse 13. "For thus saith the LORD God of Israel, The barrel of meal shall not waste, neither shall the cruse of oil fail, until the day that the LORD sendeth rain upon the earth" in verse 14.

3) He was involved in the resurrection of the widow's son from the dead in verses 17-24 in which "[21]. . .he stretched himself upon the child three times, and cried unto the LORD, . . .[22] . . .and the soul of the child came into him again, and he revived."

The first two miracles of the three are linked where he was being sustained because there had been no ". . .rain these years. . ." as stated in verse 1. The first denoted triangle. The last two miracles of the three relate are linked to the widow of Zarephath, the food, and her son. The second denoted triangle. (Note: In verse one which was the calling for ". . .not be dew nor rain. . ." can be consider the first miracle but I focused on miracles 2,3 and 4 within the chapter due to the fact that they provided the stronger evidence of the pattern based on the number of verses recorded for each with 5, 9, and 8 respectively and they are done on the earth. The first miracle done, as stated in verse 1, is heaven based.)

△ Three times fire was sent from God in heaven on behalf and at the request of the Prophet Elijah:

1) In 1 Kings 18:17-40 the contest at Mount Carmel between Elijah the Prophet of the Lord and 450 prophets of Baal in verses 19 and 22. When it was Elijah's turn to call on the Lord he had them, "Fill four barrels with water, and pour it on the burnt sacrifice, and on the wood" three times in verses 33-34. He then called on the Lord and "Then the fire of the LORD fell, and consumed the burnt sacrifice, and the wood, and the stones, and the dust, and licked up the water that was in the trench" in verse 38.

2) In 2 Kings 1:9-10 the first group of "a captain of fifty with his fifty" when Elijah stated to them in verse 10, "If I be a man of God, then let fire come down from heaven, and consume thee and thy fifty. And there came down fire from heaven, and consumed him and his fifty."

3) In 2 Kings 1:11-12 the second group of "another captain of fifty with his fifty" when Elijah stated to them in verse 12, "If I be a man of God, let fire come down from heaven, and consume thee and thy fifty. And the fire of God came down from heaven, and consumed him and his fifty."

The two groups of fifty-one men were sent by King Ahaziah for Elijah so that they could take him to the king. Fire came down for the sacrifice at Mount Carmel and against the two military companies. This is basis for the denoted triangle.

▽/△/▽ **In 2 Kings 1:9-14 it states King Ahaziah sent three army companies "a captain of fifty with his fifty" to get the Prophet Elijah.**

The first two of those companies were consumed by fire and the third one was spared. This is the basis for the first denoted triangle. Each of the three captains of fifty addressed Elijah:

1) "Thou man of God" in verse 9.
2) "O man of God" in verse 11.
3) "O man of God" in verse 13.

In the last two mentioned verses the captains address Elijah in the same manner. This is the second denoted triangle. Also the first two captains told him to "Come down" as per the command of the King while the third did not command him to "come down," but an "angel of the Lord" stated to him to "Go down." This is basis of the third denoted triangle. Note that the event of the actions against the first two companies is also referred to in Luke 9:54.

▽/△ **Four times the Prophet Elijah had contact with an angel in 1 Kings 19:5,7, 2 Kings 1:3 and 1:15.**

1) In 1 Kings 19:5 "And as he lay and slept under a juniper tree, behold, then an angel touched him, and said unto him, Arise and eat."
2) In 1 Kings 19:7 "And the angel of the LORD came again the second time, and touched him, and said, Arise and eat; because the journey is too great for thee."
3) In 2 Kings 1:3 "But the angel of the LORD said to Elijah the Tishbite, Arise, go up to meet the messengers of the king of Samaria, and say unto them, Is it not because there is not a God in Israel, that ye go to enquire of Baalzebub the god of Ekron?"
4) In 2 Kings 1:15 "And the angel of the LORD said unto Elijah, Go down with him: be not afraid of him. And he arose, and went down with him unto the king."

Of the first three instances he is told by the angel to "Arise" with the first two verses of these three verses to also "eat." The third instance he is told to go meet the king's messengers. The first denoted triangle. Of the last three scriptures it is stated "the angel of the LORD" tells him what to do, with the last two verses of these three relating to the king. The second denoted triangle.

△ **The Jordan River was parted three times.**

1) The first time was with Joshua and the Priests carrying the Ark of the Covenant in front of the congregation in Joshua 3:7-4:18.

2 & 3) The next two times it was parted was with the prophets Elijah and Elisha as they were departing each other. The prophet Elijah is going to heaven while the Prophet Elisha was staying on earth.

The parting of the river the second and third times is linked to the mantle/cloak of Elijah in 2 Kings 2:8, 14. As Elijah is about to leave he parts the Jordan with his cloak/mantle to get to the other side with Elisha. When he is leaving he leaves his cloak/mantle behind where Elisha uses it to part the Jordan again. This is the basis for the denoted triangle.

△ **There are three miracles of Elisha in 2 Kings 4 that relate to women:**

1) The first in verses 1-7 is the miracle of the woman whose two sons were going to be taken away from her ". . .to be bondmen" to pay ". . .the creditor. . .". Elisha asks her what did she have in her house ". . .save a pot of oil." He told her to ". . .Go, borrow thee vessels abroad of all thy neighbours, even empty vessels; borrow not a few." He told her to use

the oil that she had and ". . .pour out into all those vessels. . .". He told her later to ". . .Go, sell the oil, and pay thy debt, and live thou and thy children of the rest" in verse 7.

2) The second miracle is recorded in verses 8-17 when a Shunammite woman showed kindness to Elisha where she one day ". . .constrained him to eat bread. . ." at her place. On another day she and her husband made a "little chamber" for him and "he turned into the chamber, and lay there." For her generosity he prophesied that, "About this season, according to the time of life, thou shalt embrace a son" in verse 16. In verse 17 the prophecy is stated as coming to pass.

3) The third miracle involved the same Shunammite woman again in verses 18-37 where her son fell sick and while on his mother's knees ". . .and then died" in verse 20. "And she went up, and laid him on the bed of the man of God, and shut the door upon him, and went out." She then went to go find Elisha and found him at Mount Carmel. She then convinced Elisha to come back to her house and went to where the child was laid. "And he went up, and lay upon the child, and put his mouth upon his mouth, and his eyes upon his eyes, and his hands upon his hands: and he stretched himself upon the child; and the flesh of the child waxed warm. Then he returned, and walked in the house to and fro; and went up, and stretched himself upon him: and the child sneezed seven times, and the child opened his eyes" (verses 34-35) thus reviving the child.

The last two miracles of the three relate to the same Shunammite woman. The basis for the denoted triangle. Also note the fourth miracle of this chapter in verse 38-44 where Elisha miraculously used a "pot of pottage" and fed ". . .the sons of the prophets. . ." that was thought to contain "death in the pot" in verse 40. He put some "meal" in the pot that made it harmless.

▽ **God tells King Hezekiah how to survive, via the prophet Isaiah, the threat/siege of Sennacherib the king of Assyria (2 Kings 19:29).**

1 & 2) The first two years they did not work and were to eat that which "grows" of itself the first year and ". . . in the second year that which springeth of the same"

3) The third year they were to consume the fruits of their labor base on their own agricultural activities.

Of the three years the first two they are not to labor to grow their food but in the third year they are to do so. This is the basis for the denoted triangle. In Isaiah 37:30 the verse is stated the same but from the prophet's perspective, "And this shall be a sign unto thee, Ye shall eat this year such as groweth of itself; and the second year that which springeth of the same: and in the third year sow ye, and reap, and plant vineyards, and eat the fruit thereof." Note this was done during the time when the king of Assyria sent a "great host" against King Hezekiah and Jerusalem as recorded in 2 Kings 18:17-37.

▽/△**Three biblical or mentioned related source, the book of Jasher, where "chariot(s) of fire" is mentioned:**

1) In Genesis 5:22-24 relating to Enoch and how he ascended up into heaven, Book of Jasher 3:36, ". . .and it was upon the seventh day that Enoch

ascended into heaven in a whirlwind, with horses
and chariots of fire."

2) In 2 Kings 2:11 with the Prophet Elijah and him
ascending into heaven, "And it came to pass, as they
still went on, and talked, that, behold, there appeared
a chariot of fire, and horses of fire, and parted them
both asunder; and Elijah went up by a whirlwind
into heaven."

3) In 2 Kings 6:17 with the Prophet Elisha and them
being around him with angels, "And Elisha prayed,
and said, LORD, I pray thee, open his eyes, that he
may see. And the LORD opened the eyes of the young
man; and he saw: and, behold, the mountain was full
of horses and chariots of fire round about Elisha."

The first two verses relate to men going to heaven on
them and the third verse the chariots of fire being on the
ground. The first denoted triangle. The first one is not mentioned in the Bible, but from another source linked to the
Bible while the last two are in the Bible. The second denoted
triangle. Note the verse of Isaiah 66:15," For, behold, the
LORD will come with fire, and with his chariots like a
whirlwind, to render his anger with fury, and his rebuke with
flames of fire."

▽ **In 1 Chronicles 7:24 a woman by the name of Sherah,
an Ephraim descendant, founded/built three places**:
". . .Bethhoron the nether, and the upper, and Uzzensherah."
The first two places of the three pertain to Bethhoron. This is
the basis for the denoted triangle.

△ **In 1 Chronicles 21:12-14 King David was asked to
choose one of three punishment options from the Lord
for the evil he had done in the sight of the Lord.**

The choices were three years famine, three months of "the sword" from his enemies, or three days the "sword of the Lord" which is pestilence. He decided to let God choose the punishment. God chose option number three to punish him for his disobedience for numbering the people or for taking a census, ". . . and there fell of Israel seventy thousand men" (1 Chronicles 21:14). The last two choices of the three relate to "the sword". This is the basis for the denoted triangle. The story is also stated in 2 Samuel 24:12-15 with some variation.

▽/△/▽/▽ **There are three instances where an angel is seen with his sword.**

1) By the prophet Balaam in Numbers 22:31 "Then the LORD opened the eyes of Balaam, and he saw the angel of the LORD standing in the way, and **his sword drawn in his hand**."

2) By Joshua in Joshua 5:13,15 ". . Joshua was by Jericho, that he lifted up his eyes and looked, and, behold, there stood a man over against him with **his sword drawn in his hand**" (verse 13), ". . .the captain of the LORD'S host said unto Joshua, Loose thy shoe from off thy foot; for the place whereon thou standest is holy" (verse 15).

3) By King David and "the elders of Israel" in 1 Chronicles 21:16 "And David lifted up his eyes, and saw the angel of the LORD stand between the earth and the heaven, **having a drawn sword in his hand** stretched out over Jerusalem. Then David and the elders of Israel, who were clothed in sackcloth, fell upon their faces."

Of the three instances the first two only one man saw the angel. In the third a group of men saw the angel. The first denoted triangle. The first man had to have his eyes opened before he saw the angel. In the other two sighting this was not done. This is the basis for the second denoted triangle. In the first two instances the angel is on the ground and no one is injured. In the third instance the angel is in the air and 70,000 men die relating to his presence in 2 Chronicles 21:14. This is the basis for the third denoted triangle.

Note also the phrase ". . .his sword drawn in his hand" is stated in the first two instances but not in the third. The fourth denoted triangle. Also the first two instances are connected to the Exodus of the children of Israel from Egypt some time afterwards, the third is not. Another identified triangle,▽. Of the three instances the last one does something else also as recorded in 1 Chronicles 21:27, "And the LORD commanded the angel; and he put up his sword again into the sheath thereof". Another identified triangle, ▽.

Note: Genesis 3:24 states, ". . .he placed at the east of the garden of Eden Cherubim, and a flaming sword which turned every way, to keep the way of the tree of life". There is no mention or record of anyone seeing them. Also note in Psalm 104:4 it states, "Who maketh his angels spirits; his ministers a flaming fire."

Esther

▽/▽ Three women who are described as being "fair. . .to look upon/on:"

1) In Genesis 12:11 Sarai Abram's wife,
2) In Genesis 24:16 and 26:7 Rebekah wife of Isaac
3) In Esther 1:11 Vashti queen of Persia to King Ahasuerus.

Of the three women, the first two are wives to the patriarchs of Abram/Abraham and Isaac. The basis for the first denoted triangle. Also note that of the three descriptions recorded in Genesis, two scriptures describe Rebekah. Of the three women the third woman was put away and dethroned for her arrogance against her husband a king. This is the basis for the second denoted triangle. Of the three women it is stated for the first two women that they were "fair. . . to look upon" while for the third woman it is stated that she was "fair to look on". Another identified triangle, ∇.

∇ In the book of Esther there are three named men who were hung for being involved in an evil plot against others:

1 & 2) Bigthan and Teresh, "two of the king's chamberlains" who "sought to lay hand on the king Ahasuerus" in Esther 2:21. They were overheard by Mordecai, queen Esther's relative, who then told the queen Esther who in turn told the king. "And when inquisition was made of the matter, it was found out; therefore they were both hanged on a tree" (Esther 2:23).

3) Haman was a very close trusted advisor to the king who wanted to kill all the Jews in the Persian empire. When his evil plot was truly revealed ". . . they hanged Haman on the gallows that he had prepared for Mordecai" in Esther 7:10.

The first two men were hung on tree and the third man on his own "gallows." This is the basis for the denoted triangle. In Esther 9:13 Haman's ten sons were hung also but it was at the request of queen Esther, "Then said Esther, If it please the king, let it be granted to the Jews which are in Shushan to do to morrow also according unto this day's decree, and let Haman's ten sons be hanged upon the gallows." There is no record of the sons being involved in their father's evil plot.

▽/△ **In the last three chapters, 8-10, of the book of Esther the new power structure for the Persian Empire is established, the top three people.**

1) The first person is King Ahasuerus.
2) The second person is Queen Esther.
3) The third person is Mordecai a trusted advisor.

Of three the first two are linked by marriage. The first denoted triangle. Of the three the second and third persons are linked by kinship. The second denoted triangle. Mordecai, the cousin of Queen Esther, became the close trusted advisor to them, some say the new prime minister, taking Haman's place.

△/▽ **Four times the first month of the Jewish Calendar is mentioned as "month . . .Abib."**

1) In Exodus 13:4 "This day came ye out in the month Abib."
2) In Exodus 23:15 "Thou shalt keep the feast of unleavened bread: (thou shalt eat unleavened bread seven days, as I commanded thee, in the time appointed of the month Abib; for in it thou camest out from Egypt: and none shall appear before me empty)."
3) In Exodus 34:18 "The feast of unleavened bread shalt thou keep. Seven days thou shalt eat unleavened bread, as I commanded thee, in the time of the month Abib: for in the month Abib thou camest out from Egypt."
4) In Deuteronomy 16:1 "Observe the month of Abib, and keep the Passover unto the Lord thy God: for in the month of Abib the Lord thy God brought thee forth out of Egypt by night."

The first three verses are all in the same book and of these first three the last two also mention "the feast of unleavened bread" while the first verse does not. This is the basis of the first denoted triangle. In looking at the last three of the four verses the first two of the three are in the same book and state "feast of unleavened bread" and "month Abib" while the last scripture states "the month of Abib" and "Passover" which is viewed as the same festival. The second denoted triangle.

△/△ **Also read of three other scriptures relating to the first month of the Jewish Calendar:**

1) In Exodus 12:2 "This month shall be unto you the beginning of months: it shall be the first month of the year to you."

2) In Nehemiah 2:1 "And it came to pass in the month Nisan, in the twentieth year of Artaxerxes the king, that wine was before him: and I took up the wine, and gave it unto the king. Now I had not been beforetime sad in his presence."

3) In Esther 3:7 "In the first month, that is, the month Nisan, in the twelfth year of king Ahasuerus, they cast Pur, that is, the lot, before Haman from day to day, and from month to month, to the twelfth month, that is, the month Adar."

Of these three verses the name of the first month is not given but it is given in the next two which is Nisan. This is the basis for the first denoted triangle. Of the three verses the name of the Persia King is given also, Artaxerxes and Ahasuerus respectively. This is the basis for the second denoted triangle. Of the three verses the name of Nisan is referred to as the first month in the last two verses. Another identified triangle,△. It is said that the name of the month Abib is a Canaanite name while the name of the month

Nisan/Nissan is a Jewish name which seems to be derived from the Babylonian name Nisanu.[16]

Job

▽/▽ **There are three supernatural / divine discussions relating to Job:**

1) Job 1:6-12.
2) Job 2:1-6.
3) Job chapters 38-42.

The first two instances relate to a discussion between God and Satan about Job and God allowing Satan to tempt and afflict Job to test his faith in God. These two conversations were held in heaven of the three. The third instance is with God and Job and Job's friends as it relates to what Job was put through via Satan. This conversation was held down here on earth via a whirlwind by God. The participants of the three conversations are God and Satan in the first two and God and Job with his friends in the third. This is the basis for the first denoted triangle. The second denoted triangle is based on the location of those conversations. The first two are in heaven while the third conversation is on earth. God's conversation with Job and his friends is the third time God used a whirlwind in reality. First two times were for Enoch and Elijah going into heaven. This is another identified triangle,▽.

▽/▽ **Three things were taken from Job by Satan.**

---

16   Source - Wikipedia, Nisan-year, 2014, http://en.wikipedia.org/wiki/Nisan-years, Retrieved 08.11.2014 (Month chart)

1) The first was all "His substance" or material posses-sions, the animals and the servants that were over them in 1:13-17.
2) The next were his 10 children, seven sons and three daughters in 1:18-19.
3) The third thing was his health in 2:7, "Satan. . . smote Job with sore boils from the sole of his foot unto his crown."

The first two things are linked to being external to Job. The third item is his personal health. This is the first denoted triangle. Of these three things the first two are mentioned as being taken in chapter 1 while the third item is taken in chapter 2. The second denoted triangle. This analysis is based on me watching a television show called "Hell: The Devil's Domain" on the History Channel 2 called "H2."

△ **Three friends come to comfort and counsel Job.**

1) Eliphaz the Temanite, from the town of Teman in Edom Territory (Nation of Jordan today),
2) Bildad the Shuhite, and
3) Zophar the Naamathite (Job 2:11)

The last two men seem to, based on some research, have a connection to Arabia. This is the basis for the denoted triangle.

△ **In Job 1:2 and 42:13-14 states he had fourteen sons and six girls.**
The last three girls born unto him are named:

1) Jemima translated as Dove
2) Kezia translated as Cinnamon/Cinnamon-like bark
3) Kerenhappuch as translated Antimony for eyeshadow.

The last two translated names of the three are linked to cosmetology in meaning. The basis for the denoted triangle. (Note: Read of two other verses pertaining to perfumes of the Bible in Psalms 45:8 which states, "All thy garments smell of myrrh, and aloes, and cassia," and Proverbs 7:17 states, "I have perfumed my bed with myrrh, aloes, and cinnamon." Of the three mentioned perfumes of the time in both verses the first two items are of resins/sap and the third of a tree bark/cinnamon. Two other identified triangles, ▽/▽)

Psalms, Proverbs, and Song of Solomon

▽/△ Three scriptures that mention the phrase ". . .people under me. . ."

There are those who may question the authorship of some of the Psalms as it relates David. Here is a clear example, confirmation and proof in my view, of David being the author of at least some of them with these three scriptures:

1) 2 Samuel 22:48 "It is God that avengeth me, and that bringeth down the people under me."
2) Psalms 18:47 "It is God that avengeth me, and sub-dueth the people under me."
3) Psalms 144:2 "My goodness, and my fortress; my high tower, and my deliverer; my shield, and he in whom I trust; who subdueth my people under me."

Notice that the first two scriptures are very similar of the three, the first denoted triangle, while the last two scriptures state the word "subdueth" along with the mentioned phrase and being in the same book, Psalms. The second denoted triangle. Also to confirm that he did, it is stated in Luke 20:42 "And David himself saith in the book of Psalms . . .".

△ **Read three verses in the book of Psalms that state "Make a joyful noise unto God/the LORD, all. . .":**

1) In Psalms 66:1 "Make a joyful noise unto God, all ye lands:"
2) In Psalms 98:4 "Make a joyful noise unto the LORD, all the earth: make a loud noise, and rejoice, and sing praise."
3) In Psalms 100:1 "Make a joyful noise unto the LORD, all ye lands."

Of the three verses the last two verse state "the LORD" while the first verse states "God". The basis of the denoted triangle. Note, the first and third verses state "all ye lands". All three verses should be viewed as giving praise to God. No of the verses pertain to King David.

△ **There are three recorded instances relating to the story of water being tuned into blood in Egypt.**

The first instance is the first plague as mentioned in Exodus 7:19. The next two times it is mentioned is in Psalm 78:44 and Psalm 105:29. The last two of the three are in the same book and pertain to instance in Exodus. This is the basis for the denoted triangle. It is noted that in Revelation 8:8 it states, "And the second angel sounded, and . . . the third part of the sea became blood," an act that is the same as the first plague of Egypt but this time on a much wider scale.

▽/▽ **Read three verses where "arrows" and "lightning" are stated by King David that was used or to be used by God against his enemies:**

1) In 2 Samuel 22:15 "And he sent out arrows, and scattered them; lightning, and discomfited them."

2) In Psalms 18:14 "Yea, he sent out his arrows, and scattered them; and he shot out lightnings, and discomfited them."

3) In Psalms 144:6 "Cast forth lightning, and scatter them: shoot out thine arrows, and destroy them."

In the first two verses of the three arrows are used to scatter the enemy and lightning to ". . .discomfited them". In the third verse lightning is to be used to ". . .scatter them. . ." and arrows to ". . .destroy them.". This is the basis for the first denoted triangle. Of the three verses the first two states "he sent" being past tense while the third verse is a request to do the action in the present tense. This is the basis for second denoted triangle. Note Zechariah 9:14 states "And the Lord shall be seen over them, and his arrow shall go forth as the lightning: and the Lord God shall blow the trumpet, and shall go with whirlwinds of the south."

△/△ **Read in three scriptures that state the "roaring of the/a lion".**

These scriptures are in Job 4:10, Proverbs 19:12, and 20:2. Of the three the last two verses relate to a King and his wrath as "a" lion. The first verse pertains to Job and his troubles. The first denoted triangle. The last two verses of the three are in same book. The second denoted triangle. Here are the mentioned verses:

1) Job 4:10 "The roaring of the lion, and the voice of the fierce lion, and the teeth of the young lions, are broken."

2) Proverbs 19:12 "The king's wrath is as the roaring of a lion; but his favour is as dew upon the grass."

3) Proverbs 20:2 "The fear of a king is as the roaring of a lion: whoso provoketh him to anger sinneth against his own soul."

Note the verse of Isaiah 5:29 that states "Their roaring shall be like a lion, they shall roar like young lions: yea, they shall roar, and lay hold of the prey, and shall carry it away safe, and none shall deliver it". This verse refers to the wicked.

△ **Read three scriptures that state "my dove" relating to the love of someone in Song of Songs/Solomon.**

The verses are 2:14, 5:2, and 6:9. Of the three verses the object of the love is also referred to as "my undefiled" in the last two verses. This is the basis for the denoted triangle. Here are the verses:

1) Song of Solomon 2:14 "O my dove, that art in the clefts of the rock, in the secret places of the stairs, let me see thy countenance, let me hear thy voice; for sweet is thy voice, and thy countenance is comely."

2) Song of Solomon 5:2 "I sleep, but my heart waketh: it is the voice of my beloved that knocketh, saying, Open to me, my sister, my love, my dove, my undefiled: for my head is filled with dew, and my locks with the drops of the night."

3) Song of Solomon 6:9 "My dove, my undefiled is but one; she is the only one of her mother, she is the choice one of her that bare her. The daughters saw her, and blessed her; yea, the queens and the concubines, and they praised her."

△/▽ **God's name, JEHOVAH, is mentioned in three books, four verses, alone in the Bible.**

1) God introducing Himself to Moses in Exodus 6:3, "And I appeared unto Abraham, unto Isaac, and unto Jacob, by the name of God Almighty, but by my name JEHOVAH was I not known to them."

2) In Psalm 83:18 is a definition of Him, "That men may know that thou, whose name alone is JEHOVAH, art the most high over all the earth."

3) In Isaiah 12:2 and 26:4 "strength" is mentioned with his name which is a definition of Him also. Isaiah 12:2 "Behold, God is my salvation; I will trust, and not be afraid: for the LORD JEHOVAH is my strength and my song; he also is become my salvation." Isaiah 26:4 "Trust ye in the LORD forever: for in the LORD JEHOVAH is everlasting strength:"

The basis for the first denoted triangle is in the using of the second, third, and fourth scriptures relating to the definition of God along with is name. The second verse relates to what he is "most high". The last two verses relate to the definition of "strength" for Him. Note the last two scriptures are in the same book of Isaiah and refer to him as "LORD JEHOVAH." Of the three books the third book has two verses for his name with other two books having one verse each. The second denoted triangle.

Babylonian Captivity of the Children of Israel

△ **The first three empires that the children of Israel had to deal with were the Egyptian, the Assyrian, and the Babylonian empires.**
The Egyptians were forced to release the Jewish people via the divine plagues which in part allow them to become a nation. Later in history when the children of Israel occupied the land the Assyrian and Babylonian empires conquered the people through war. The Assyrian empire dominated the Jewish people in the Northern Kingdom of Israel. Later the Kingdom of Judah to the south was dominated by Babylonian empire. The Babylonian empire was the first in the image of King Nebuchadnezzar after the interpretation, gold, as stated

in Daniel 2:37-38 and it was the third empire as it relates to the children of Israel they encountered.

The last two empires of the three are mentioned after the children of Israel had occupied the Promised Land, Assyrian and Babylonian. This is the basis for the denoted triangle. The kingdom of Judah had to deal with all three empires as stated in scriptures such as 1 Kings 14:25-26 and 2 Chronicles 12:2-9 relating to Egypt, in 2 Kings 18:13-16 and 2 Chronicles 32:9-10 relating to Assyria, and in 2 Kings chapters 24 and 25 relating to Babylon. This was due to the fact that there were power struggles between the three over time pertaining to the kingdom of Judah.

Here are some biblical specific examples of how the kingdom of Judah had to deal with the three empires while the people were in their own land:

1) In 1 Kings 14:26 "Shishak king of Egypt" came up against King Rehoboam of Judah "And he took away the treasures of the house of the LORD, and the treasures of the king's house; he even took away all." This story is also recorded in 2 Chronicles 12:2-9.

2) In 2 Kings 18:15 "Sennacherib king of Assyria" came up against King Hezekiah of Judah and also acquired treasures where ". . .Hezekiah gave him all the silver that was found in the house of the LORD, and in the treasures of the king's house." This story is also mentioned of how King of Assyria came up against Jerusalem in 2 Chronicles 32:1-23.

3) In Daniel 1:2 "Nebuchadnezzar king of Babylon" came up against "Jehoiakim king of Judah" and king Nebuchadnezzar took "part of the vessels of the house of God." This story is also recorded in 2 Chronicles 36:5-8.

△/▽/△ **There were three waves of captives deported from the Kingdom of Judah to Babylon under king Nebuchadnezzar of Babylon:**

1) In Daniel 1:1-2, "In the third year of the reign of Jehoiakim king of Judah came Nebuchadnezzar king of Babylon unto Jerusalem, and besieged it. And the Lord gave Jehoiakim king of Judah into his hand, with part of the vessels of the house of God:" Along with the treasures from the Temple of God he took "certain of the children of Israel, and of the king's seed, and of the princes" as stated in verse 3. Also taken were those ". . .skilful in all wisdom, and cunning in knowledge, and understanding science" as stated in verse 1: 4. Among them were Daniel, Hananiah, Mishael, and Azariah or of the last three listed also known as Shadrach, Meshach, and Abednego. This was the **first wave** of those captive and deported to Babylon. This event is also mentioned in 2 Chronicles 36:5-8, "Jehoiakim was twenty and five years old when he began to reign, . . . Against him came up Nebuchadnezzar king of Babylon, and bound him in fetters, to carry him to Babylon. Nebuchadnezzar also carried of the vessels of the house of the LORD to Babylon."

2) The **second wave** of captives deported to Babylon is recorded in 2 Kings 24:10-17 where Nebuchadnezzar, King of Babylon, "came up against Jerusalem, and the city was besieged" in verse 10. Afterwards King Jehoiachin, King Jehoiakim's son, surrendered the city to Nebuchadnezzar king of Babylon, "he, and his mother, and his servants, and his princes, and his officers: and the king of Babylon took him in the eighth year of his reign" (verse 12). The king of Babylon also "carried out thence all the treasures of

the house of the LORD, and the treasures of the king's house, and cut in pieces all the vessels of gold which Solomon king of Israel had made in the temple of the LORD, as the LORD had said" (verse 13). "And he carried away all Jerusalem, and all the princes, and all the mighty men of valour, even ten thousand captives, and all the craftsmen and smiths" (verse 14). "And he carried away Jehoiachin to Babylon, and the king's mother, and the king's wives, and his officers, and the mighty of the land, those carried he into captivity from Jerusalem to Babylon" (verse 15). King Nebuchadnezzar established Jehoiachin's uncle, and brother to King Jehoiakim, Mattaniah on to the throne of Judah as King and changing his name to Zedekiah. The prophet Ezekiel is noted as being taken in this second wave as recorded in Ezekiel 1:2-3, in ". . .the fifth year of king Jehoiachin's captivity. . .The word of the LORD came expressly unto Ezekiel the priest, . . .in the land of the Chaldeans[Babylonians]. . . ." This event is also mentioned in 2 Chronicles 36: 9-10, ". . .king Nebuchadnezzar sent, and brought him to Babylon, with the goodly vessels of the house of the LORD, and made Zedekiah his brother king over Judah and Jerusalem" (verse 10).

3) The **third wave** of captives that were taken to Babylon is recorded in 2 Kings 24:20, 25:1-21 where Zedekiah, 21st King of Judah, rebelled against the king of Babylon" (verse 24:20) and ". . .in the ninth year of his reign, . . .Nebuchadnezzar king of Babylon came, he, and all his host, against Jerusalem, and pitched against it; and they built forts against it round about." (verse 25:1) "And the city was besieged unto the eleventh year of king Zedekiah" (verse 25:2). Afterwards the city fell and Zedekiah was later captured and taken to king Nebuchadnezzar where

". . .they slew the sons of Zedekiah before his eyes, and put out the eyes of Zedekiah, and bound him with fetters of brass, and carried him to Babylon" (verse 25:7). I noticed that Zedekiah/Mattaniah is the third son of King Josiah of Judah. In the ". . . nineteenth year of king Nebuchadnezzar king of Babylon, came Nebuzaradan, captain of the guard, a servant of the king of Babylon, unto Jerusalem" (verse 25:8) and ". . .he burnt the house of the LORD, and the king's house, and all the houses of Jerusalem, and every great man's house burnt he with fire" (verse 25:9). Note: This is also recorded in Jeremiah 39:8 and 52:13-14. They also took all the treasures of the Temple/house of God as stated in verses 25:13-17. "Now the rest of the people that were left in the city, and the fugitives that fell away to the king of Babylon, with the remnant of the multitude, did Nebuzaradan the captain of the guard carry away" (verse 25:11). Also "the captain of the guard took Seraiah the chief priest, and Zephaniah the second priest, and the three keepers of the door" (verse 25:18). These and others as stated in verses 18-21 were shortly slain. "So Judah was carried away out of their land" (verse 25:21). This event is also mentioned in 2 Chronicles 36:13-21, "And all the vessels of the house of God, great and small, and the treasures of the house of the LORD, and the treasures of the king, and of his princes; all these he brought to Babylon" (2 Chronicles 36:18).

In summary, the second and third wave of the deportations as stated in 2 Kings of the Jews to Babylon are recorded in more detail than the first deportation wave as stated in the book of Daniel. The first denoted triangle.

In the first and second deportations a Judean King and a major prophet are among the captives, Jehoiakim and Daniel in the first wave and Jehoiachin and Ezekiel, who was a priest also, in the second wave. In the third deportation wave a Judean king and two priests of God were among those that were taken captive, Zedekiah and "Seraiah the chief priest, and Zephaniah the second priest." This is the second denoted triangle.

In the second and third waves priests are taken, but not the first wave or it is not recorded for the first wave. The third denoted triangle. The most significant event of the three waves is the destruction of the Temple/"house" of God. This was not done in the first two waves but in the third wave. Another identified triangle, ∇. Also of the three priests taken, of the last two deportations, one was left alive, Ezekiel, while the other two mentioned were slain," Seraiah the chief priest, and Zephaniah the second priest". Another identified triangle,$\triangle$.

All three times Jerusalem was stated to be "besieged," but in the third instance some length of time is stated in the book of 2 Kings 25:1-2, 18 months it seems. Another identified triangle, ∇. Also note what was stated in the scriptures in 2 Kings 25:21 that some of the upper echelon of the kingdom were slain in the third wave unlike the other two waves. Another identified triangle, ∇.There were three Major Prophets pertaining to these three Babylonian deportations, Jeremiah, Daniel, and Ezekiel. The first, the prophet Jeremiah foretold of its coming and mentions how long it would be, seventy years which is mentioned in 2 Chronicles 36:21, Jeremiah 25:11-12, 29:10, and Daniel 9:2. Note: Of the four scriptures the last three of these scriptures relate to prophets, "For thus saith the LORD, That after seventy years be accomplished at Babylon I will visit you, and perform my good word toward you, in causing you to return to this place" (Jeremiah 29:10). When the first wave happens, the prophet Jeremiah is not taken but the prophet Daniel is. Later in the second wave the prophet Ezekiel is taken. Base on who was taken of the three prophets another triangle is identified,△.

Just before the third wave the prophet Jeremiah has a conversation with King Zedekiah in Jerusalem and is later thrown into prison for his prediction against the King relating to the King's forthcoming encounter with the Babylonians as stated in Jeremiah 37:17-21. Jeremiah is later released from prison by the Babylonians and is not taken as part of the third wave in Jeremiah 40:1-6.

Note: "Your country is desolate, your cities are burned with fire: your land, strangers devour it in your presence, and it is desolate, as overthrown by strangers" (Isaiah 1:7) This verse could be viewed as a prophecy of what was going to happen.

▽ **Three verses concerning the reign of King Zedekiah of Judah:**

1) In 2 Kings 24:18-20, He began to reign at the age of twenty-one and "reigned eleven years in Jerusalem."
2) In 2 Chronicles 36:11-13, He also did "evil in the sight of the Lord."
3) In Jeremiah 52:1-3, He ". . .rebelled against the king of Babylon (Nebuchadnezzar)."

Of these three verses the first two are from a historical perspective while the third instance is from the prophet Jeremiah's perspective. This is the basis for the denoted triangle.

▽ **It is stated three times "he is the God" in 1 Kings 18:39 and Ezra 1:3.**

The first verse states the clause twice in 1 Kings 18:39 which states, "And when all the people saw it, they fell on their faces: and they said, The LORD, he is the God; the LORD, he is the God.". In Ezra 1:3 it states, "Who is there among you of all his people? his God be with him, and let him go up to Jerusalem, which is in Judah, and build the house of the LORD God of Israel, (he is the God,) which is in Jerusalem." This is the basis for the denoted triangle. Also note that in Jeremiah 10:10 and Daniel 6:26 it is stated, "he is the living God."

△/△/△/△ There were three waves when the Jews returned from the exile of the Babylonian captivity as recorded in the books of Ezra and Nehemiah to Jerusalem and Judah. These returns happened because of the Persian Kings of Persia who conquered Babylon:

1) The **first wave** is stated in Ezra 2:1-70 under the leadership of Zerubbabel who led the first group of returnees numbering 42,360 based on a decree from Cyrus, King of Persia. Note: Zerubbabel is referred to as governor of Judah in the book of Haggai in 1:1 and 2:1 under the Persian King Darius.

2) The **second wave** is stated in Ezra 7:6-26 led by the scribe, priest, and prophet Ezra under Artaxerxes, king of Persia who allowed Ezra to return to Jerusalem. "I make a decree, that all they of the people of Israel, and of his priests and Levites, in my realm, which are minded of their own freewill to go up to Jerusalem" (Ezra 7:13). Some of those that returned with Ezra were ". . .some of the children of Israel, and of the priests, and the Levites, and the singers, and the porters, and the Nethinims, unto Jerusalem, in the seventh year of Artaxerxes the king" (Ezra 7:7). A list of those "males" that came with Ezra is stated in Ezra 8:1-14 but no total is given

3) The **third wave** is stated in Nehemiah 2:1-9 headed by Artaxerxes king of Persia's cupbearer Nehemiah, a prophet. He is allowed, decreed, to return as stated

"And I said unto the king, If it please the king, and if thy servant have found favour in thy sight, that thou wouldest send me unto Judah, unto the city of my fathers' sepulchers, that I may build it." (verse 5) "And the king said unto me, (the queen also sitting by him,) For how long shall thy journey be? and when wilt thou return? So it pleased the king to send me; and I set him a time." (verse 6) Along with Nehemiah "Now the king had sent captains of the army and horsemen with me" (verse 9).

In summary, of the three returning waves the last two are released by the same king of Persia, Artaxerxes. The first denoted triangle. Of the three leaders of the returnees job descriptions are recorded for the last two before their return to Jerusalem. The second denoted triangle. Of these three waves it is decreed of Cyrus, recorded in Ezra 1:2 and Isaiah 44:28, that the temple in Jerusalem be rebuilt which is part of the first wave. The third denoted triangle. Of these three waves only the first wave provides the total number of people returning. The fourth and last denoted triangle.

Note that there are those who state that the true first wave was led by Sheshbazzar based on the scripture of Ezra 1:7-8 and 1:11 where the "vessels" of silver and gold that were taken out of the "house of the LORD" in Jerusalem were being returned. Also there are some who claim that Sheshbazzar and Zerubbabel are in fact one and the same person. With this in mind noticed that there is no biblical information to support that there was a wave of returnees who were led by one Sheshbazzar. The three waves of returnees to Jerusalem and Judah from Babylon that are mentioned are based on the biblical evidence. Of the three returning waves the first two are recorded in the book of Ezra while the third is recorded in the book of Nehemiah. Another identified triangle, ▽.

▽ **Based on Ezra 6:14 there are three Kings of Persia mentioned Cyrus, Darius, and Artaxerxes who made decrees or a "commandment" relating to those returning Jewish exiles to Jerusalem:**

1) The decree of Cyrus, recorded in Ezra 1:1-4, who specifically gave instructions to ". . .build the house of the LORD God of Israel" and released those who wanted to leave. This action of "Thou shalt be built; and to the temple,. . ." is stated in Isaiah 44:28 relating to Cyrus also.

2) The decree of Darius recorded in Ezra 6:12 was a decree that endorsed the decree of Cyrus as stated in Ezra 1:1-4 and stated again in Ezra 6:1-12 relating to ". . . the building of this house of God" (Ezra 6:8).

3) In the decree of Artaxerxes as recorded in Ezra 7:15, 17, 21, 25-26 he was providing resources for the affairs such as religious and civic of the Jewish state. Here are the verses:

Ezra 7:15 "And to carry the silver and gold, which the king and his counsellors have freely offered unto the God of Israel, whose habitation is in Jerusalem. . . ."

Ezra 7:17 "That thou mayest buy speedily with this money bullocks, rams, lambs, with their meat offerings and their drink offerings, and offer them upon the altar of the house of your God which is in Jerusalem."

Ezra 7:21 ". . .I Artaxerxes the king, do make a decree to all the treasurers which are beyond the river, that whatsoever Ezra the priest, the scribe of the law of the God of heaven, shall require of you, it be done speedily."

Ezra 7:25 "And thou, Ezra, after the wisdom of thy God, that is in thine hand, set magistrates and judges, which may judge all the people that are beyond the river, all such as know the laws of thy God; and teach ye them that know them not."

Ezra 7:26 "And whosoever will not do the law of thy God, and the law of the king, let judgment be executed speedily upon him, whether it be unto death, or to banishment, or to confiscation of goods, or to imprisonment."

Of these three decrees the first two are related to the "house of the LORD." This is the basis for the denoted triangle.

△/△ **Read three instances where Cyrus, King of Persia, is mentioned in building for the God of Israel.**

Of the three instances the building of the temple is mentioned in the first two verses. The third instance just mentions ". . .he shall build my city. . ." there is no mentioning of the Temple. Of the three verses the last two verses the Lord makes the statements about King Cyrus while the first verse Cyrus makes the statements of himself. The first denoted triangle. Of the three instances the last two are in the same book. The second denoted triangle. Here are the verses:

1) Ezra 1:2 "Thus saith Cyrus king of Persia, The LORD God of heaven hath given me all the kingdoms of the earth; and he hath charged me to build him an house at Jerusalem, which is in Judah."

2) Isaiah 44:28 "That saith of Cyrus, He is my shepherd, and shall perform all my pleasure: even saying to Jerusalem, Thou shalt be built; and to the temple, Thy foundation shall be laid."

3) Isaiah 45:1 "Thus saith the LORD to his anointed, to Cyrus, whose right hand I have holden, to subdue nations before him; and I will loose the loins of kings, to open before him the two leaved gates; and the gates shall not be shut. . . . I have raised him up in righteousness, and I will direct all his ways: he shall build my city, and he shall let go my captives, not for price nor reward, saith the LORD of hosts."

△/▽ The Three built Houses of God:

1) The Tabernacle of the congregation under Moses in Exodus 25-31.
2) The First Temple under King Solomon (1 Kings 6:1-38, 1 Kings Chapter 7, and Chapter 8).
3) The Second Temple in the book of Ezra, a prophet, and under foreign rule in 2 Chronicles 36:22-23, Ezra 1:1-4, Ezra 5.

The second temple was started by either Zerubbabel in Zechariah 4:9, "The hands of Zerubbabel have laid the foundation of this house" or Sheshbazzar in Ezra 5:16, "Then came the same Sheshbazzar, and laid the foundation of the house of God which is in Jerusalem." In Ezra 2:2 Zerubbabel is stated to be some of the first to return to Jerusalem from Babylon. The first house was mobile and the other two houses were stationary. This is the basis for the first triangle. The Ark of the Covenant only occupied the first two of the three houses of God. The basis for the second denoted triangle. Also the configuration of the three had a place called the Holy of Holies in the midst of them. Triangle diagram is shown below:

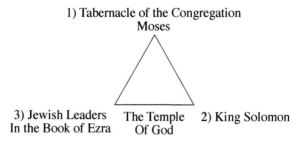

Based on this Three triangle pattern, the Jewish Temple has been built twice in history with both of those times being before Christ in 1 Kings 6, Ezra 3, and 2 Chronicles 36:22-23. They are linked by time, ancient times, and their location. The third one is different in the time and location. The current site for the previous Jewish temples, Temple Mount, is in part occupied by the Islamic shine the Doom of the Rock. The third future Jewish temple is called by some the visionary temple of Ezekiel because it is describe in the Book of Ezekiel starting in chapter 40. The three temples, the two of the past and the one of the future is the basis for another identified triangle, ▽. The second Jewish temple was recorded to have been destroyed in 70 A.D. by the Romans. A major remnant of this Temple was left standing which is called today the "Western Wall" since 70 A.D. I would think that whenever the third Jewish temple is built there it will incorporate this remnant linking the Second Jewish Temple to the Third one of the three. Another identified triangle, △. Scholars have also stated that animal sacrifices in the Temple will be reinstated. According to the Hebrew Bible, the Book of Ezekiel is the third of the Latter Prophets. Note the three major inner Courts of the Second/Herod's Temple based on diagrams:

1) Court of the Women.
2) Court of the Israel/Israelites, also known as the court of men.

3) Court of the Priests.

Of these three the Court of the Priests is the most sacred. Another identified triangle, $\triangledown$. Note that the last two of these inner Courts are for the men of the three. Another identified triangle, $\triangle$.

Isaiah

$\triangle$ **Biblical scholar(s) critiqued the book of Isaiah, the prophet Isaiah son of Amoz, which is the only book in the Christian Bible that has 66 chapters akin to the number of books in the entire Bible.**

Based on some scholar(s) critique of the book is divided it into three parts:

1) "Chapters 1 to 39 (First Isaiah, Proto-Isaiah or Original Isaiah): the work of the original prophet Isaiah, who worked in Jerusalem. . ."

2) "Chapters 40 to 55 (Second Isaiah or Deutero-Isaiah): by an anonymous author who lived in Babylon near the end of the Babylonian captivity."

3) "Chapters 56 to 66 (Third Isaiah or Trito-Isaiah): the work of anonymous disciples committed to continuing Isaiah's work in the years immediately after the return from Babylon. . . . This section includes visions of new heavens and new earth. . . . (Other scholars suggest that chapters 55–66 were written by Deutero-Isaiah after the fall of Babylon.)"[17]

Based on this work I noticed that the first thirty-nine chapters of the book are actually attributed to the prophet while

---

[17] Source - Wikipedia, Book of Isaiah, 2013, http://en.wikipedia.org/wiki/Book_of_Isaiah, Retrieved 01.22.2013

the other twenty-seven chapters, divided into two parts, are attributed to "anonymous" writers and relate to the Babylonian captivity. This is the basis for the denoted triangle. The entire Bible is composed of thirty-nine books of the Old Testament and twenty-seven books of the New Testament.

"The first 39 chapters prophesy doom for a sinful Judah and for all the nations of the world that oppose God, while the last 27 prophesy the restoration of the nation of Israel and a new creation in God's glorious future kingdom."[13] This statement critiquing this entire book of Isaiah makes me think that it could be applicable to the entire Bible as a summation for the entire Bible. It is stated that the prophet Isaiah is quoted in the New Testament of the Bible sixty-six times.

▽ **Read of Isaiah's vision: "Above it stood the seraphim: each one had six wings; with twain he covered his face, and with twain he covered his feet, and with twain he did fly" (Isaiah 6:2).**

Of the three pairs of wings the seraphim have two pair are stated to cover parts of their body while the third pair is used as the functional use of wings i.e. flying. This is the basis for the denoted triangle.

▽/▽ **Three verses where the king of Assyria, Sennacherib, came against king Hezekiah of Judah and the cites that were "fenced."**

The first two verses are based on the author of the books, and are viewed as providing a historical perspective of ancient Israel. The verse from Isaiah is providing a view from a prophet's perspective which is similar to the other verses. The firs denoted triangle. Notice that the first two verses stated "fenced" while the third states "defenced" relating to the cities. The second denoted triangle. The verses are as follows:

1) 2 Kings 18:13 "Now in the fourteenth year of king Hezekiah did Sennacherib king of Assyria come up against all the **fenced cities** of Judah, and took them."

2) 2 Chronicles 32:1 "After these things, and the establishment thereof, Sennacherib king of Assyria came, and entered into Judah, and encamped against the **fenced cities**, and thought to win them for himself."

3) Isaiah 36:1 "Now it came to pass in the fourteenth year of king Hezekiah, that Sennacherib king of Assyria came up against all the **defenced cities** of Judah, and took them."

▽ **Three verses where it is stated that king Hezekiah of Judah is sick that he is about to die.**

The two verses of 2 Kings and 2 Chronicles, one each respectively, are viewed as providing a historical perspective of the monarchy, while the verse from Isaiah provides a view from a prophet's perspective and his activities to the king which is similar to the other verses. The basis for the denoted triangle. Here are the verses:

1) 2 Kings 20:1 "**In those days was Hezekiah sick unto death.** And the prophet Isaiah the son of Amoz came to him, and said unto him, Thus saith the LORD, Set thine house in order; for thou shalt die, and not live."

2) 2 Chronicles 32:24 "**In those days Hezekiah was sick to the death**, and prayed unto the LORD: and he spake unto him, and he gave him a sign."

3) Isaiah 38:1 "**In those days was Hezekiah sick unto death.** And Isaiah the prophet the son of Amoz came unto him, and said unto him, Thus saith the LORD, Set thine house in order: for thou shalt die, and not live."

After hearing the news from Isaiah that he was going to die in the first and third verses he prayed to God he was given fifteen more years to live which was later told to him by Isaiah.

△/△ Three times the word "Creator" is stated in the Old Testament.

1) In Ecclesiastes 12:1 "Remember now **thy Creator** in the days of thy youth, while the evil days come not, nor the years draw nigh, when thou shalt say, I have no pleasure in them;"
2) In Isaiah 40:28 "Hast thou not known? hast thou not heard, that the everlasting God, the LORD, **the Creator** of the ends of the earth, fainteth not, neither is weary? there is no searching of his understanding."
3) In Isaiah 43:15 "I am the LORD, your Holy One, **the creator** of Israel, your King."

Of the three verse "thy" is used in the first verse while "the" is used in the next two verses. The basis for the first denoted triangle. Of the three verses the last two are in the same book. The second denoted triangle. Of the three verses the last two states what he has created. Another identified triangle,△. Note the word is also stated in Romans 1:25 as "the Creator" and in 1 Peter 4:19 as ". . .a faithful Creator" in the New Testament. Five times in all.

△/▽/△ A metaphor of garments being moth eaten is recorded three times in the Old Testament:

1) In Job 13:28 "And he, as a rotten thing, consumeth, as a garment that is moth eaten."
2) In Isaiah 50:9 "Behold, the Lord GOD will help me; who is he that shall condemn me? Lo, they all shall wax old as a garment; the moth shall eat them up."

3) In Isaiah 51:8 "For the moth shall eat them up like a garment, and the worm shall eat them like wool: but my righteousness shall be forever, and my salvation from generation to generation."

First, notice that the second and third usages of the metaphor are linked to the same book. The first denoted triangle. Notice also that the phrase in the first two scriptures of the three ". . .as a garment. . ." is stated. The second denoted triangle. Lastly looked at what was being consumed in all three scriptures based on the metaphor. The first relates to Job and his perceived sins and transgressions and he himself being consumed. The last two scriptures relate to one's enemies being consumed. The third denoted triangle. Note: The metaphor is also mentioned once in the New Testament in James 5:2 ". . .and your garments are moth eaten" relating to the riches of men.

Jeremiah and Lamentations

▽/▽ **There are three verses in the book of Jeremiah where he is told ". . .pray not . . . for this people".**

1) In Jeremiah 7:16 "Therefore pray not thou for this people, neither lift up cry nor prayer for them, neither make intercession to me: for I will not hear thee."
2) In Jeremiah 11:14 "Therefore pray not thou for this people, neither lift up a cry or prayer for them: for I will not hear them in the time that they cry unto me for their trouble."
3) In Jeremiah 14:11 "Then said the Lord unto me, Pray not for this people for their good."

Of the three verses the first two states "pray not thou for this people" while the third verse states ". . .Pray not for this people for their good." The first denoted triangle.

Of the three verses the first two also state ". . .neither lift up cry nor prayer for them. . .". The second denoted triangle. For a prophet to be told not to do this is a strong example of God's anger towards his people. Based on these verses the Babylonian exile was on God's mind "for this people". I think of the statement, "According to Jewish law, once something is done three times it is considered a permanent thing."[18] "The Latin phrase, **'omne trium perfectum'** (everything that comes in threes is perfect, or, every set of three is complete). . ."[19]

▽ **Three scriptures state "I am black."**

The first two scriptures can be viewed as Solomon noting his complexion. The third scripture relates to the prophet Jeremiah's emotional state. This is the basis for the denoted triangle. Here are the verses:

1) Song of Solomon 1:5 "**I am black**, but comely, O ye daughters of Jerusalem, as the tents of Kedar, as the curtains of Solomon."

2) Song of Solomon 1:6 "Look not upon me, because **I am black**, because the sun hath looked upon me: my mother's children were angry with me; they made me the keeper of the vineyards; but mine own vineyard have I not kept."

3) Jeremiah 8:21 "For the hurt of the daughter of my people am I hurt; **I am black**; astonishment hath taken hold on me."

---

[18] The Significance of The Number Three,2014, http://www. betemunah.org/three.html, Retrieved 08.13.2014

[19] Rule of three (writing), 2014, http://en.wikipedia.org/wiki/Rule_of_ three_(writing), Retrieved 09.06.14

Note the complexion issue is stated in Job 30:30, "My skin is black upon me. . ." and in Lamentations 4:8, "Their visage is blacker than a coal."

▽ **Three other verses relating to black or blackness.**
Of these three the first two verses state that the "skin" is/ was black and the third verse relating to the emotional state of the people. This is the basis for the denoted triangle. The verses are as follows:

1) Job 30:30 "My skin is **black** upon me, and my bones are burned with heat."
2) Lamentations 5:10 "Our skin was **black** like an oven because of the terrible famine."
3) Joel 2:6 "Before their face the people shall be much pained: all faces shall gather **blackness**."

▽/△ **In Jeremiah 52:28-30 King Nebuchadrezzar of Babylon in three instances carried away or had carried away, 4600 people captive from the kingdom of Judah.**

1) In his seventh year he took 3023 captives in the first wave.
2) In his eighteenth year he took 832 people captive in the second wave.
3) In his twenty-third year Nebuchadrezzar's "captain of the guard," Nebuzaradan carried away 745 captive in the third wave.

All the captives were sent to Babylon. In the first two instances of the three it is stated that the King was involved in taking the captives to Babylon. The first denoted triangle. Also, in the first instance thousands were taken and in the second and third hundreds were taken. The second denoted triangle. Gleaning as much detail as I could, focused on how each of these three scripture begins with the time of the activities relating to the king. The first verse states ". . .whom Nebuchadrezzar . . . in the seventh year . . .". The second verse states "In the eighteenth year of Nebuchadrezzar . . . ". The third verse states "In the three and twentieth year of Nebuchadrezzar . . .". Notice that the time is being stated afterwards in the first verse and the time being mentioned first in the next two verses. Another identified triangle, △.

△ **Read of the three times where it is recorded that King Zedekiah of Judah sons are slain in front of him and his eyes are put out and he is carried to Babylon in the third wave of the Babylonian captivity.**

The last two recorded times of the three are in the same book and stated over two scriptures. The first verse is from a historical perspective and the last times are from the prophet Jeremiah's perspective. The basis for the denoted triangle. Here are the scriptures:

1) 2 Kings 25:7 "And they slew the sons of Zedekiah before his eyes, and put out the eyes of Zedekiah, and bound him with fetters of brass, and carried him to Babylon."

2) Jeremiah 39:6-7 "⁶Then the king of Babylon slew the sons of Zedekiah in Riblah before his eyes: also the king of Babylon slew all the nobles of Judah. ⁷Moreover he put out Zedekiah's eyes, and bound him with chains, to carry him to Babylon."

3) Jeremiah 52:10-11 "¹⁰And the king of Babylon slew the sons of Zedekiah before his eyes: he slew also all the princes of Judah in Riblah. ¹¹Then he put out the eyes of Zedekiah; and the king of Babylon bound him in chains, and carried him to Babylon, and put him in prison till the day of his death."

Ezekiel

△ **Ezekiel 1 speaks of the vision of the prophet.**
It has four winged living creatures who have four faces, and four wings: man, lion, ox, and an eagle. Each of the four winged living creatures had a wheel within a wheel beside them. Over and above the four winged living creatures and the wheels was God sitting on his throne in all his glory. Based on the description given we have God in his glory over the groups the creatures and the wheels in which the last two are together or linked. This is the basis for the denoted triangle.

▽ **Ezekiel 5:12 states, "A third part of thee shall die with the pestilence, and with famine shall they be consumed in the midst of thee: and a third part shall fall by the sword round about thee; and I will scatter a third part into all the winds, and I will draw out a sword after them."**
Based on the scripture two thirds will succumb to destruction and one third will escape. This is the basis for the denoted triangle. This is similar to Zechariah 13:8 which states, "And it shall come to pass, that in all the land, saith the LORD, two parts therein shall be cut off and die; but the third shall be left therein". Another identified triangle,▽.

▽ **The Lord spoke to the Prophet Ezekiel about three men: Noah, Daniel, and Job who were righteous in God's sight in Ezekiel 14:12-20.**
To summarize these scriptures, if God sends his ". . . four sore judgments . . ." of famine, the noisome beast, the sword, or the pestilence "through/upon/into. . . the/that land. . ." these three men, if they were in the land, would be spared the desolation because of their righteousness.
In reviewing the Biblical history of the three men mentioned:

1) Noah was spared after the destruction of all men because of their sin during the flood.
2) Daniel was spared during the captivity of Judah and had visions of the destruction of sinful men.
3) Job's faith was put to the test by Satan.

Of the three men the first two are linked in that they both had to view the destruction of men. The basis for the denoted triangle. Note that the prophets Daniel and Ezekiel were taken in the Babylonian exile from Judah. The first and second Babylonian deportation waves respectively.

▽ **An analysis done on the book of Ezekiel states that the book is ". . .structured around three themes:**

1) Judgment on Israel (chapters 1-24)
2) Judgment on the nations (chapters 25-32)
3) Future blessings for Israel (chapters 33-48)."[20]

Based on this information we can view the first two of these themes as being linked to "judgment." The basis for the denoted triangle.

Daniel

▽ **The three Hebrew men spoken of in the book of Daniel: Shadrach, Meshach, and Abednego.**
These men were assigned Babylonian names but their given Hebrew names were Hananiah, Mishael, and Azariah respectively. Based on further research the two names Shadrach and Meshach are associated with the Babylonian moon-god called Aku while the name Abednego relates to

---

[20]   Source - Wikipedia, Book of Ezekiel, 2013, http://en.wikipedia.org/wiki/Book_of_Ezekiel, Retrieved 03.07.2013

the Babylonian god Nebo, the Babylonian god of wisdom or Nergal another Babylonian god. This is the basis for the denoted triangle. Note the god Nebo is mentioned in Isaiah 46:1 and Jeremiah 48:1.

▽/▽ In Daniel 5:25-28 Divine judgment was decreed at that time against King Belshazzar and his kingdom.

"MENE, MENE, TEKEL, UPHARSIN", these four words follow the pattern where the first two words are the same, linked, and the third and fourth are different. The first two words relate to the judgment of the kingdom and third to the king himself and the fourth back to judgment of the kingdom. Noticed that God could have just written the three words only.

Daniel 5:25 "And this is the writing that was written, MENE, MENE, TEKEL, UPHARSIN."

Daniel 5:26 "This is the interpretation of the thing: MENE; God hath numbered thy kingdom, and finished it."

Daniel 5:27 "TEKEL; Thou art weighed in the balances, and art found wanting."

Daniel 5:28 "PERES [UPHARSIN]; Thy kingdom is divided, and given to the Medes and Persians."

In essence God used three words for his message against the king. Daniel gave the king the interpretation of God's message using the last three written words. Again, three of the words written are related to the judgment of the Kingdom of King Belshazzar, the first, second and the fourth. This is the basis for the first denoted triangle. The first two words the same and the last word different. Notice of the last three words written, the third word used by God, UPHARSIN, is also replaced by PERES when it is interpreted by Daniel. This is the basis for the second denoted triangle. The third word used strips the king of his kingdom. From another perspective the first three words are the basis for the another identified triangle, ∇, where the first two words are the same, judgment for the kingdom, and the third written word used as judgment for the king himself.

∇ The finger of God wrote on stone three times.

The first two times relates to the Ten Commandments on stone tablets in Exodus 20:3-16 and Deuteronomy 5:6-21 that were given to Moses twice. The third time is in Daniel 5:25-28 on the wall. This is the basis for the denoted triangle. The third time God writes it is out of anger with the written four words against King Belshazzar. The first two times of the three when God writes he is calm. Another identified triangle, ∇.

∇ There are three interpretations the prophet Daniel gave or provided to kings while he is in Babylon.

1) The first interpretation is of the multi-metal image dream of King Nebuchadnezzar in chapter 2.
2) The second interpretation is also for King Nebuchadnezzar and his tree dream in chapter 4.
3) The third interpretation Daniel provided was for King Belshazzar, who was king some time after king Nebuchadnezzar based on the reading of the scriptures, of the words that were written on the wall in chapter 5 by God.

Of these three interpretations the first two are of the dreams of King Nebuchadnezzar and the third to King

Belshazzar. This is the basis for the denoted triangle. Here are the relevant verses:

1) Daniel 2:36 "This is the dream; and we will tell the interpretation thereof before the king."
2) Daniel 4:24 "This is the interpretation, O king, and this is the decree of the most High, which is come upon my lord the king."
3) Daniel 5:26 "This is the interpretation of the thing: MENE; God hath numbered thy kingdom, and finished it."

Note of the three verses presented the last two starts with, "This is the interpretation. . . .". Another identified triangle,△.

△ **In Daniel 6:2 it states, ". . .three presidents; of whom Daniel was first". He was under the rule of King Darius.**
Daniel was "over "a hundred and twenty princes" of the kingdom and ". . .was preferred above the presidents . . .and the king thought to set him over the whole realm." Daniel was the head President and the other two were lesser presidents. The basis for the denoted triangle.

△ **There are three instances of extraordinary and extreme tests of faith in God where something is done to an individual or individuals.**

1) Job had to endure Satan's taking of all his possessions and afflicting his body to prove his or lack of commitment to God.
2) The three Hebrews boys, Shadrach, Meshach, and Abednego, were thrown into the fiery furnace in Daniel 3:1-30 for continuing to worship God and not a golden idol and surviving the ordeal.

147

3) Daniel is thrown into a den of lions in Daniel 6:4-28 for continuing to worship God praying "three times a day", verse 10, and he survives his ordeal.

Of the three instances the first instance is from and of heaven in the "land of Uz." The last two instances are ordeals that relate to orders or decrees by a King demanding obedience or face severe consequences in the land of Babylon. This is the basis for the denoted triangle. These last two instances are done under King Neberchanazzer and King Darius respectively.

▽ **Read in the book of Daniel the four verses where it is stated "O King, liver for ever".**

1) In Daniel 2:4 "Then spake the Chaldeans to the king in Syriack, O king, live for ever: tell thy servants the dream, and we will shew the interpretation."
2) In Daniel 3:9 "They spake and said to the king Nebuchadnezzar, O king, live for ever."
3) In Daniel 5:10 "Now the queen by reason of the words of the king and his lords came into the banquet house: and the queen spake and said, O king, live for ever: let not thy thoughts trouble thee, nor let thy countenance be changed:"
4) In Daniel 6:21 "Then said Daniel unto the king, O king, live for ever."

Of the four verses the first three verses pertain to the Babylonians saying it. The first two verses of the three pertain to a group of people with the third verse attributed to the queen. The first two verses are of groups and the third verse by and individual. The basis for the denoted triangle. The fourth verse is stated by Daniel to King Darius. Note the verse of Daniel 6:6 "Then these presidents and princes assembled together to the king, and said thus unto him, King Darius, live for ever."

▽ **In Daniel chapter 7, "1 In the first year of Belshazzar king of Babylon Daniel ..." had a vision of four great beasts that "...came up from the sea...". These beasts are described in Daniel 7:3-7.**

1) "...like a lion, and had eagle's wings" in verse 4.
2) "...like to a bear, and it had three ribs in the mouth of it between the teeth of it" in verse 5.
3) "...like a leopard, which had upon the back of it four wings of a fowl; the beast had also four heads;" in verse 6.
4) Unknown "...dreadful and terrible, and strong exceedingly; and it had great iron teeth: ...and it had ten horns" in verse 7.

Of the four beasts described the first three are "like" known beasts. Of the three known type of beasts, or liked, the first two beasts have one head each while the third beast has four heads. The basis for the denoted triangle. The fourth beast is an unknown type of beast.

▽ **In Daniel chapter 8, "¹ In the third year of the reign of king Belshazzar a vision appeared unto me, even unto me Daniel...".**

The prophet Daniel has a vision of "...a ram which had two horns: and the two horns were high; but one was higher than the other, and the higher came up last" in verse 8:3, and a "...he goat came from the west on the face of the whole earth, and touched not the ground: and the goat had a notable horn between his eyes" (verse 8:5). The interpretation is given in Daniel 8:20-21, "The ram which thou sawest having two horns are the kings of Media and Persia. And the rough goat is the king of Grecia: and the great horn that is between his eyes is the first king."

The three horns where two kings together are on the ram and a third king separate on the goat. This is the basis for the denoted triangle.

▽ **Three verses that state the salutation phrase, ". . .Peace be unto thee. . . ."**

The first two people who this phrase is addressed to are leaders of the children Israel: Gideon a judge and David a king. The third person who it is addressed to is Daniel a prophet of God. This is the basis for the denoted triangle. The first and third instances are stated by angels. Here are the verses:

1) Judges 6:23 "And the LORD said unto him, Peace be unto thee; fear not: thou shalt not die."

2) 1 Chronicles 12:18 "Then the spirit came upon Amasai, who was chief of the captains, and he said, Thine are we, David, and on thy side, thou son of Jesse: peace, peace be unto thee, and peace be to thine helpers; for thy God helpeth thee. Then David received them, and made them captains of the band."

3) Daniel 10:19 "And said, O man greatly beloved, fear not: peace be unto thee, be strong, yea, be strong. And when he had spoken unto me, I was strengthened, and said, Let my lord speak; for thou hast strengthened me."

▽/△ **In Daniel 9:23 he was told "for thou art greatly beloved" and in 10:11 and 10:19 he was told twice that he was a ". . .man greatly beloved. . .". Based on what he was called, reviewed a confluence of threes associated with him:**

1) There are the three interpretations he gave or provided to kings while he is in Babylon. Two that relate to the dreams of King Nebuchadnezzar and the third to King Belshazzar relating to the three words written on the wall.

2) In Daniel 6:2 it states, ". . .three presidents; of whom Daniel was first". He was under the rule of King Darius.

3) In Daniel chapter 8, "¹ In the third year of the reign of king Belshazzar a vision appeared unto me, even unto me Daniel. . .". The prophet Daniel has a vision of ". . .a ram which had two horns" and a ". . .he goat. . ." that ". . . had a notable horn between his eyes". Three horns amongst the two animals.

Of these three in the first and the third there is some association with King Belshazzar. This is the basis for first denoted triangle. Note, of the three times Daniel is told he is "greatly beloved" it is by the angel Gabriel face to face once and twice, in the same chapter, in a vision he had "In the third year of Cyrus king of Persia" (verse 10:1) by an angel. The second denoted triangle.

Hosea through Haggai

△/△ **Hosea the prophet has three children where God had given the children their names.**

1) The first is a son named Jezreel which means "God will sow" based on the review of the Hebrew translation of the "baby" name, or some would say "God scatters/The Lord sowing", relating to how God would ". . .avenge the blood of Jezreel on the house of Jehu, and will cause to cease the kingdom of the house of Israel" in Hosea 1:4.

2) The second child is Hosea's daughter Loruhamah. Her name means "no more mercy upon the house of Israel" as stated in Hosea 1:6. Some would say "not pitted" or not accepted.

3) The third child is Hosea's son named Loammi with his name meaning "not my people" as stated in Hosea 1:9.

These names were chosen for his children as a sign of God's displeasure with the people of Israel for not following his ways i.e. serving other gods. The first name being attributed to vengeance and last two names to disobedience. The first denoted triangle. Note that last two children's names start with same letter "L" in English and the same letter in Hebrew. The second denoted triangle.

$\nabla/\triangle/\triangle$ There "are three products of ancient Israel that were important to its economy and a sign of God's blessing: grain[corn i.e. wheat/barley], [new] wine, and [olive] oil."[21]

All three are mentioned in the following scriptures with corn being the most predominant (which is also referenced as wheat and/or barley): Numbers18:12, Deuteronomy 11:14, 12:17, 14:23, 18:4, 28:51; 2 Kings 18:32; 2 Chronicles 2:10, 15, 31:5, 32:28; Ezra 6:9, 7:22; Nehemiah 10:39, 13:5, 13:12; Jeremiah 31:12; Hosea 2:8, 22; Joel 1:10, 2:19, 2:24; Haggai 1:11.

The predominate order of the three is corn, wine, and oil based on these scriptures. All three products are used as part of a sacred religious ritual. The oil and corn were mixed in as part of the meat/meal offering and the wine used as the drink offering measure by "hin" or about five liters as indicated in

---

[21] Source - Use of Three in the Bible, 2011, http://Bible.org/seriespage/use-three-Bible, Retrieved 08.21.2011

Exodus, Leviticus, and Numbers. The first denoted triangle. Only oil was use in the consecration of someone of the three. The other two items are not. The second denoted triangle. The wine and oil are liquids based on the arrangement of the stated items. The third denoted triangle.

▽ **The three animals mentioned in Amos 5:19, "As if a man did flee from a lion, and a bear met him; or went into the house, and leaned his hand on the wall, and a serpent bit him."**

Of the three animals mentioned a lion, bear, and snake, the snake is the animal that is stated causing harm. The basis for the denoted triangle. Of the three animals the first two beasts are larger. Another identified triangle, ▽. The context of the scripture is stated in Amos 5:18, "Woe unto you that desire the day of the LORD! to what end is it for you? the day of the LORD is darkness, and not light."

▽ **In Jonah 4:6-8 God prepared three things for Jonah after he preached or "he cried" to the people of Nineveh:**

1) a gourd for shade in verse 6
2) a worm that ". . .smote the gourd that it withered" in verse 7
3) ". . .God prepared a vehement east wind" to cool him off in verse 8.

The first two items mentioned are linked relating to the "gourd". The basis for the denoted triangle.

▽/▽/△/△ **Three men made a request to God to kill them or take their life:**

1) Moses in Numbers 11:15 because of the burden of the people, "And if thou deal thus with me, kill me, I pray thee, out of hand. . ."
2) Elijah in 1 Kings 19:4 because of King Ahab and Queen Jezebel, ". . .and he requested for himself that he might die; and said, It is enough; now, O LORD, take away my life."
3) Jonah in Jonah 4:3 because God did not destroy Nineveh, "Therefore now, O LORD, take, I beseech thee, my life from me. . . ."

The first two men of the three are linked by being "forty days and forty nights" in or around Mount Horeb/Sinai in Exodus 24:18, 34:28-29; Deuteronomy 9:11, 10:10; and 1 Kings 19:8. The first denoted triangle. The first two men of the three were also under the pressure of men. The second denoted triangle. The last two men of the three can be viewed as prophets of God. The first person is a leader of the people. The third denoted triangle. Notice that the last two of the three reference God as "O LORD." The fourth denoted triangle. Note also that the first two men were mentioned at the Transfiguration in the New Testament of the three. Note also that Job did not asked God directly to take his life, or it is not recorded, but he gets close based on his situation in Job 6:9, "Even that it would please God to destroy me; that he would let loose his hand, and cut me off!"

Zechariah

▽ **Read of three instances, seven verses, where it is stated "And the LORD said unto Satan,. . .".**

1) Job 1:7 "And the LORD said unto Satan, Whence comest thou? Then Satan answered the LORD, and

said, From going to and fro in the earth, and from walking up and down in it."

2) Job 1:8 "And the LORD said unto Satan, Hast thou considered my servant Job, that there is none like him in the earth, a perfect and an upright man, one that feareth God, and escheweth evil?"

3) Job 1:12 "And the LORD said unto Satan, Behold, all that he hath is in thy power; only upon himself put not forth thine hand. So Satan went forth from the presence of the LORD."

4) Job 2:2 "And the LORD said unto Satan, From whence comest thou? And Satan answered the LORD, and said, From going to and fro in the earth, and from walking up and down in it."

5) Job 2:3 "And the LORD said unto Satan, Hast thou considered my servant Job, that there is none like him in the earth, a perfect and an upright man, one that feareth God, and escheweth evil? and still he holdeth fast his integrity, although thou movedst me against him, to destroy him without cause."

6) Job 2:6 "And the LORD said unto Satan, Behold, he is in thine hand; but save his life."

7) Zechariah 3:2 "And the Lord said unto Satan, The Lord rebuke thee, O Satan; even the Lord that hath chosen Jerusalem rebuke thee: is not this a brand plucked out of the fire?"

The first two instances, three verses in Job chapter 1 and three verses in chapter 2, pertain to Job and Satan's test of him. The third instance, one verse, pertains to a vision that the prophet has relating to "Jerusalem". This is the basis for the denoted triangle.

△ **Zechariah 4:2-3 has a vision of a golden candlestick and two olive trees.**

"And said unto me, What seest thou? And I said, I have looked, and behold a candlestick all of gold, with a bowl upon the top of it, and his seven lamps thereon, and seven pipes to the seven lamps, which are upon the top thereof: And two olive trees by it, one upon the right side of the bowl, and the other upon the left side thereof". The candlestick and the two olive trees are the basis for the denoted triangle.

△ Zechariah 5:7-9 speaks of three women.

One is of wickedness sitting in the ephah and the other two are winged flying carrying the ephah, "⁷. . .and this is a woman that sitteth in the midst of the ephah". "⁸And he said, This is wickedness. . .". "⁹Then lifted I up mine eyes, and looked, and, behold, there came out two women, and the wind was in their wings; for they had wings like the wings of a stork". Note: An ephah is around five gallon container. Of the three women one is wicked and the other two are not. This is the basis for the denoted triangle.

▽ Zechariah 13:8 states, "And it shall come to pass, that in all the land, saith the LORD, two parts therein shall be cut off and die; but the third shall be left therein."

Two-thirds part shall die and a third shall be spared. The basis for the denoted triangle. This is another scriptural example that is akin to Ezekiel 5:12 that is the epitome of the divine triangle pattern. In Zechariah 13:9 it states what happens to the third part," I will bring the third part through the fire, and will refine them as silver is refined, and will try them as gold is tried." There is not mention of what happens to the other two-thirds part. Another identified triangle,△.

▽ The three stated Babylonian Captivity post-exilic "Minor" prophets of Haggai, Zechariah, and Malachi for the people of Israel.

These three continue to state God's message to Israel. Of these three the first two are linked in which Zechariah was a co-worker with Haggai in Ezra 5:1, "Then the prophets, Haggai the prophet, and Zechariah the son of Iddo, prophesied unto the Jews that were in Judah and Jerusalem in the name of the God of Israel, even unto them." In Ezra 6:14, "And the elders of the Jews builded, and they prospered through the prophesying of Haggai the prophet and Zechariah the son of Iddo. And they builded, and finished it, according to the commandment of the God of Israel, and according to the commandment of Cyrus, and Darius, and Artaxerxes king of Persia." The denoted triangle is based on the relationship of the three with the first two men working together. Working alone of the three, Malachi's message to the people is recorded in the book of Malachi.

△ **There are three verses where the phrase ". . .valley of Jezreel. . ." is stated.**

The last two verses of the three relate to a battle and the first relates to the inheritance of the "Children of Joseph." This is the basis for the denoted triangle. Here are the verses:

1) Joshua 17:16 "And the children of Joseph said, The hill is not enough for us: and all the Canaanites that dwell in the land of the valley have chariots of iron, both they who are of Bethshean and her towns, and they who are of the valley of Jezreel."

2) Judges 6:33 "Then all the Midianites and the Amalekites and the children of the east were gathered together, and went over, and pitched in the valley of Jezreel."

3) Hosea 1:5 "And it shall come to pass at that day, that I will break the bow of Israel in the valley of Jezreel."

The place also is known for Megiddo the place where the battle of Armageddon will take place. It is said that Armageddon or "The Mount of Megiddo" was the earliest known battle in human history that was documented by the military scribe called Tjaneni for the Egyptian Pharaoh Thutmose III, sixth Pharaoh of the 18th Dynasty, against the Canaanite forces.

Note that the place called Megiddo is mentioned eleven times in the Bible in Joshua 12:21, 17:11; Judges 1:27, 5:19; 1 Kings 4:12, 9:15, 9:27; 2 Kings 23:29, 23:30; 1 Chronicles 7:29; and 2 Chronicles 35:22. An Ancient Map of the major trade route called Via Maris (Latin term for "Way of the Sea") shows that from Megiddo (Armageddon), which it is said to be a control point and way station of the times, the route went in three directions: North towards Anatolia (Asia Minor/Modern day Turkey along the coast line of Israel), Northeast towards Syria and Mesopotamia (Iraq, Iran, etc.) and South towards Egypt[22]. Two routes going north and one going south. Another identified triangle,▼.

▽/△ **There are three verses where the phrase ". . .the day of the LORD is near . . ." is stated.**

All three verses relate to the judgment of "the heathen" or the enemies of Israel based on further reading of other verses that are either before or after the mentioned verses.

1) The heathen of Egypt and its confederates in Ezekiel 30:3, "For the day is near, even **the day of the LORD is near**, a cloudy day; it shall be the time of the heathen."

2) Those of Egypt, Edom and others in Joel 3:14, "Multitudes, multitudes in the valley of decision: for **the day of the LORD is near** in the valley of decision."

---

[22]   Map Source: Via Maris, 2010, http://www.jewishvirtuallibrary.org/jsource/History/ViaMaris.html, Retrieved 05.11.2010

3) The heathen of Edom in Obadiah 1:15, "For **the day of the LORD is near** upon all the heathen: as thou hast done, it shall be done unto thee: thy reward shall return upon thine own head."

Of the three verses Egypt is mentioned in the first two but not the third. The first denoted triangle. Edom is mentioned for the last two verses of the three. The second denoted triangle. Note in Zephaniah 1:14 it states, "The great day of the LORD is near, it is near, and hasteth greatly, even the voice of the day of the LORD."

▽ **There are three verses that state the phrase "for the day of the LORD is at hand. . ."**
Of the three verses the first two verses state what it is going to be, ". . .as a destruction from the Almighty." Also a sense of emotion is expressed with the first two verses but with the third there is a sense of calm. This is the basis of the denoted triangle. Here are the verses:

1) Isaiah 13:6 "Howl ye; **for the day of the LORD is at hand**; it shall come as a destruction from the Almighty."
2) Joel 1:15 "Alas for the day! **for the day of the LORD is at hand**, and as a destruction from the Almighty shall it come."
3) Zephaniah 1:7 "Hold thy peace at the presence of the Lord GOD: **for the day of the LORD is at hand**: for the LORD hath prepared a sacrifice, he hath bid his guests."

△/▽ **There are three verses that state the phrase "The burden of the word of the Lord. . ."**
Of the three verses the first verse also states "in the land of Hadrach and Damascus. . ." while the last two verses are

159

"for" or "to" Israel respectively. The first denoted triangle. Of the three verses the first two are in the same book Zechariah and the third in the book Malachi. The second denoted triangle. Here are the verses:

1) Zechariah 9:1 "The burden of the word of the Lord in the land of Hadrach, and Damascus shall be the rest thereof: when the eyes of man, as of all the tribes of Israel, shall be toward the Lord."

2) Zechariah 12:1"The burden of the word of the Lord for Israel, saith the Lord, which stretcheth forth the heavens, and layeth the foundation of the earth, and formeth the spirit of man within him."

3) Malachi 1:1 "The burden of the word of the Lord to Israel by Malachi."

▽ **The details of the Book of Leviticus, third book of Bible and the divine number.**

"Leviticus contains laws and priestly rituals, but in a wider sense is about the working out of God's covenant with Israel set out in the book of Genesis and the Book of Exodus—what is seen in the Torah as the consequences of entering into a special relationship with God. The first 16 chapters and the last chapter make up the Priestly Code with rules for ritual cleanliness, sin-offerings, and the Day of Atonement, including Chapter 12, which mandates male circumcision. Chapters 17–26 contain the Holiness Code, including the injunction in chapter 19 to 'love one's neighbor as oneself' (the Great Commandment). The book is largely concerned with 'abominations,' largely dietary and sexual restrictions. The rules are generally addressed to the

Israelites, except for several prohibitions applied equally to 'the strangers that sojourn in Israel.' "[23]

Based on this information and the test performed as part Bible Code/Torah code and the finding of the word "Torah" (TORH) in the first two books and last two books which points to the center book Leviticus, it can be seen as to how it is the book of Leviticus where God in the Old Testament, with the stated activities for children of Israel his special possession, is providing the path in creating "a kingdom of priests, and an holy nation" (Exodus 19:6) unto himself. The basis for the denoted triangle is a focus on the third book starting from Genesis based on the mentioned test. The word was not found in the third book. The name of God was, YaHWeh (YHWH).

---

[23]   Sources - Book of Leviticus, 2011, Wikipedia, http://en.wikipedia. org/wiki/Book_of_Leviticus / Book of Leviticus, http://saintscriptures.com/leviticus.asp, Retrieved 11.30.2012)

✝ Examples of the Divine Pattern in the New Testament

Th ere was no sort of test or experiment done that could be compared to what was done with the Torah or first five books of the Bible, but I knew that this divine triangle pattern had to extend into the New Testament also as it did in the Old Testament.

The Gospels

△/△ **The three appearances of an angel in the dreams of Joseph in Matthew**.

1) In 1:20 relating to take Mary to be his wife even though she is pregnant
2) In 2:13 telling them to go to Egypt for safety
3) In 2:19 telling him to come out of Egypt the danger is over

The last two appearances of the angel in the dreams of Joseph are linked to Egypt. The basis for the denoted triangle. Also the last two dreams are in the second chapter. The second denoted triangle.

△ **Matthew 2:11 states the three gifts that were given to Jesus at his birth: Gold, Frankincense and Myrrh.**

The latter two gifts of the three are both resins from tree sap that is dried and was brought to him by the Magi. The basis for the denoted triangle. There are those who mention the three Magi/scholars came from Arabia, Persia, and India. If true I view the geographical link of Arabia and Persia being close and India further away. Another identified triangle,▽. There are those who think that the three Magi were of different origins. One from Europe, another from Africa (Ethiopian), and one from the Arabian Peninsula. The European is often portrayed with the Gold as the other two gifts were native to Africa (Ethiopia and/or Somalia) and Asia (Arabia, Yemen and Oman). The Myrrh and Frankincense vary between the latter two. There are those who say that the three Magi came from Persia, Mesopotamia, and Ethiopia. Of these three the first two lands are linked to each other. Another identified triangle,▽.

▽ **The three instances where Jesus is recognized as a "special" child while in the temple in Luke chapter 2.**

1) "Simeon; and the same man was just and devout, waiting for the consolation of Israel: and the Holy Ghost was upon him. And it was revealed unto him by the Holy Ghost, that he should not see death, before he had seen the Lord's Christ" (Luke 2:25-26).

2) Anna "a prophetess, the daughter of Phanuel, . . . which departed not from the temple, but served God with fastings and prayers night and day. . . . And she coming in that instant gave thanks likewise unto the Lord, and spake of him to all them that looked for redemption in Jerusalem" (Luke 2:36-38).

3) When his parents went looking for him in Jerusalem, ". . .after three days they found him in the temple,

sitting in the midst of the doctors, both hearing them, and asking them questions" (Luke 2:41-50).

Twice as a baby and the third time is when Jesus is twelve years old. This is the basis for the denoted triangle. Jesus as a baby is viewed by five people as special. The three Magi, Simeon, and Anna.

▽ **In Luke 3:1 there are the three tetrarchs: ". . .Herod [Antipas] being tetrarch of Galilee, and his brother Philip tetrarch of Ituraea and of the region of Trachonitis, and Lysanias the tetrarch of Abilene."**

Of these three the first two are related as brothers while the third person is not based on the scripture. This is the basis for the denoted triangle. There was no other researched information indicating that the third man was related to the first two men. Also notice that the two brothers are stated to control three areas. Herod Antipas of Galilee and his brother Philip of Ituraea and Trachonitis. Another identified triangle, △.

△ **Jesus was tempted three times by the devil as stated in the Gospels of Matthew 4:1-11, Mark 1:12-13, and Luke 4:1-13.**

1) The first time the devil wants Jesus to address his hunger while on the ground by turning stone into bread in Matthew 4:3, "If thou be the Son of God, command that these stones be made bread", and Luke 4:3," If thou be the Son of God, command this stone that it be made bread."

2) The second time he takes Jesus to the pinnacle of the Jewish temple in Matthew 4:5, "Then the devil taketh him up into the holy city, and setteth him on a pinnacle of the temple," and Luke 4:9, "And he brought him to Jerusalem, and set him on a pinnacle of the temple.

3) The third time the devil takes Jesus to a high or big/ tall mountain to show him "the kingdoms of the world" based on Matthew 4:8, "Again, the devil taketh him up into an exceeding high mountain, and sheweth him all the kingdoms of the world, and the glory of them", and Luke 4:5, "And the devil, taking him up into an high mountain, shewed unto him all the kingdoms of the world in a moment of time."

The denoted triangle is based on the three temptations of the devil with the last two being in high places. Read in Matthew 4:2, Mark 1:13, and Luke 4:2 of how each refer to the forty days Jesus spent in wilderness, with the last two verses stating, being "tempted of Satan/ the devil". Another identified triangle,△.

△ **As Jesus was being tempted by Satan three times according to Luke chapter 4, verses 4, 8, 12, Jesus responds each time to Satan from a quote, in part, in the book of Deuteronomy.**

1) After Satan's first temptation Jesus quotes Deuteronomy. 8:3 which states ". . .man doth not live by bread only, but by every word that proceedeth out of the mouth of the LORD doth man live."

2) After the second temptation Jesus quotes Deuteronomy 6:13 which states ". . . fear the LORD thy God, and serve him, and shalt swear by his name."

3) After Satan's third temptation Jesus quotes Deuteronomy 6:16 which states "Ye shall not tempt the LORD your God, as ye tempted him in Massah."

Of the three quotes the last two are from the sixth chapter of Deuteronomy while the first is from the eighth chapter. This is the basis for the denoted triangle. .

▽ **According to the Gospels of Matthew, Mark, and John, which detail the order of the choosing of the disciples Peter and Andrew who were brothers were among the first three with someone else being third. The basis for the denoted triangle.**

The Gospel of Matthew and Mark states Simon called Peter and Andrew and his brother were the first two disciples Jesus chose with James the son of Zebedee the third as mentioned in Matthew 4:18, 21 and 10:2; Mark 1:16-19. In Luke 5:8-10, as part of the miraculous fish catching narrative, it indicates that the first three named disciples are Simon, James, and John, the two sons of Zebedee. "And so was also James, and John, the sons of Zebedee, which were partners with Simon." (Luke 5:10). Another identified triangle,△. Perhaps this is the reason that these three were singled out by Jesus on occasions. These three are also the first disciples listed in **Mark 3:16-17, "And Simon he surnamed Peter; [17]And James the son of Zebedee, and John the brother of James; and he surnamed them Boanerges, which is, The sons of thunder".** No others are "surnamed" after these three by Jesus. Another identified triangle,△. The listing of the disciples is also given in Luke 6:14 where Simon Peter, Andrew his brother, and James the son of Zebedee are the first three named disciples. Another identified triangle,▽. The Gospel of John, in 1:37-42, has two of John the Baptist's disciples, one of which is Andrew, leaving him and following Jesus. Then Andrew goes and finds his brother Simon who becomes the third disciple. The other disciple of John's who also followed Jesus is not named but is of the 12. Another identified triangle,△. Perhaps the other was John the son of Zebedee who was a disciple of John the Baptist it is said.

▽/▽/▽ **According to the Gospels, Jesus had as disciples three sets of brothers, seven men.**

Of these three sets of brothers the last set has three men while the first two has two men each. The basis for the first denoted triangle. According to Matthew 4:18, 21 and Mark 1:16, 19 the occupation of the first two sets of brothers of the three is that they are all fishermen. The second denoted triangle. Of these three sets of brothers the first two sets, according to Matthew 10:2 and Luke 6:14, are mentioned among the first of his disciples. The basis for the third denoted triangle. The brothers are as follows:;

1) Simon Peter and his brother Andrew
2) James, "the greater" and his brother John, the sons of Zebedee
3) James the son of Alphaeus "James the less(er)", (Matthew 10:3; Mark 3:18; Luke 6:15; Acts 1:13), and his brother Judas (a.k.a Lebbaeus, whose surname was Thaddaeus), (Luke 6:16; Acts 1:13), and their other brother Matthew/Levi the son of Alphaeus (Mark 2:14).

▽ **Jesus has three pairs of disciples with the same first name.**

The three pairs of disciples with the same name of Jesus' are mentioned in Matthew 10:2-4, Mark 3:14-19, and Luke 6:13-16. Of the three pairs two of them have a significant individual, Simon Peter who Jesus called him "the rock" where "I will build my church" and Judas Iscariot who betrayed Jesus. Here are the pairs:

1) Simon, whom he also named Peter in Mark 3:16 and John 1:42, and Simon called Zelotes (a.k.a "the Canaanite")
2) James (the son of Zebedee) "James the greater" and James the son of Alphaeus "James the less(er)"
3) Judas (a.k.a Lebbaeus, whose surname was Thaddaeus) and Judas Iscariot

The denoted triangle is based on those two significant men of the three pairs, Simon Peter and Judas in two of the pairs. Note in Mathew 13:55 and Mark 6:3 Jesus has brothers whose names are James, Judas, and Simon.

△ **The name of Matthew/Levi is used three times in the Gospels.**

1) In Matthew he is called Matthew in 9:9
2) In Mark he is called Levi in 2:13
3) In Luke he is also called Levi in 5:27.

The last two Gospels are linked to the recorded name for him. This is the basis for the denoted triangle.

▽/ ▽ **Jesus raised three people from the dead based on the harmonizing of the Gospels**:

1) The only son of a widow from Nain in Luke 7:14 "And he said, Young man, I say unto thee, Arise."
2) The twelve-year-old daughter of "one of the rulers of the synagogue" Jairus in Mark 5:41 ". . .said unto her, Talitha cumi; which is, being interpreted, Damsel, I say unto thee, arise." This story is also recorded in Matthew 9:18-19, 23-26 and Luke 8:40-42, 49-56, but the words are not mentioned.
3) Lazarus, the third person and friend in John 11:43 "when he thus had spoken, he cried with a loud voice, Lazarus, come forth."

Of the three people the words "I say unto thee, Arise" is said to the first two people for their resurrection. For the third person he says "come forth." The first denoted triangle. Two are young people and the other one is an adult or older person. I think of what Jesus did with the three in the pattern as being akin to Numbers 6:14 with the sacrifice of two young lambs, male and female, and a ram. The second denoted triangle. "And he shall offer his offering unto the LORD, one he lamb of the first year without blemish for a burnt offering, and one ewe lamb of the first year without blemish for a sin offering, and one ram without blemish for peace offerings,. . ." This was done in relating to a ". . . vow a vow of a Nazarite, to separate themselves unto the LORD" (Numbers 6.2). In Numbers 6:13-14 it is stated what was to be done when the vow was complete: "And this is the law of the Nazarite, when the days of his separation are fulfilled: he shall be brought unto the door of the tabernacle of the congregation" offering the three animals.

Note also in John 11:43 three words were used in the resurrection of the third person, "Lazarus, come forth" of which the first word is the name of his friend. Another identified triangle, △.

▽ **Jesus used three words, some say utterances, that were interpreted in the performance of a miracle in Mark 5:41 and 7:32-34.**

The first two words "Talitha cumi" were used on the daughter of the Jewish leader Jairus in her resurrection ". . .which is, being interpreted, Damsel, I say unto thee, arise." The third word was used on "one that was deaf, and had an impediment in his speech" in 7:32. Jesus ". . .put his fingers into his ears, and he spit, and touched his tongue; . . . and saith unto him, Ephphatha, that is, Be opened." The use of the three words is the basis for the denoted triangle.

▽ **Three times the clause ". . .Get thee behind me, Satan" is recorded.**

The first two times mentions Peter, Jesus' disciple, who has the saying directed at him once. The third recorded scripture is directed at Satan himself after Jesus is tempted by him. This is the basis for the denoted triangle. Here are the verses:

1) Matthew 16:23 "But he turned, and said unto Peter, Get thee behind me, Satan: thou art an offence unto me: for thou savourest not the things that be of God, but those that be of men."

2) Mark 8:33 "But when he had turned about and looked on his disciples, he rebuked Peter, saying, Get thee behind me, Satan: for thou savourest not the things that be of God, but the things that be of men."

3) Luke 4:8 "And Jesus answered and said unto him, Get thee behind me, Satan: for it is written, Thou shalt worship the Lord thy God, and him only shalt thou serve."

Note that in Matthew 4:10 Jesus says to Satan, "Get thee hence, Satan: for it is written. . ." Note also that Satan is rebuked by the Lord in Zechariah 3:2, "And the LORD said unto Satan, The LORD rebuke thee, O Satan; even the LORD that hath chosen Jerusalem rebuke thee."

△/▽/△ **There are three women who were healed by Jesus in Luke 8:2-3.**

They were Mary Magdalene, Joanna wife of Herod's steward Chuza, and Suzanna. The first person is healed from "evil spirits" which is Mary Magdalene. The other two women, Joanna and Susanna, are assumed to have been healed from their "infirmities" since it is not stated in the verses. The first denoted triangle. The first two women are identified more in detail than the third, Mary Magdalene and Joanna wife of Herod's steward Chuza. The second denoted triangle. The last two women of the three are mentioned together in verse 3 while the first in the second verse. The third denoted triangle. Luke 8:2-3 "And certain women, which had been healed of evil spirits and infirmities, Mary called Magdalene, out of whom went seven devils, [3]And Joanna the wife of Chuza Herod's steward, and Susanna, and many others. . . ."

△/△ In Matthew 17:1-9, Mark 9:2-8, and Luke 9:28-36, Peter, James, son of Zebedee, and his brother John were with Jesus upon the "high" mountain during the transfiguration of Jesus where ". . .his face did shine as the sun, and his raiment was white as the light" (Matthew 17:2).

The first denoted triangle is based on the three disciples. Appearing along with Jesus were Moses and Elijah the two preeminent figures of Judaism and who spent some time around Mount Sinai/Horeb, "40 days and 40 Nights", in Exodus 24:18, 34:28-29; Deuteronomy 9:18, 25, 10:10; and 1 Kings 19:8. These three together is the second denoted triangle. Note, this is also mentioned in 2 Peter 1:16-18.

▽ In Mark 9:44, 46, and 48 states, "Where their worm dieth not, and the fire is not quenched."

Prior to each of the three mentioned verses the following is stated before each respectively:

1) In 9:43 "And if thy hand offend thee, cut it off."
2) In 9:45 "And if thy foot offend thee, cut it off."
3) In 9:47 "And if thine eye offend thee, pluck it out."

Of the three prior verses the first two state "cut it off" while the third prior verse states "pluck it out." The first two of the three relate to a person's limbs. This is the basis for the denoted triangle. In Isaiah 66:24 it states, "And they shall go forth, and look upon the carcasses of the men that have transgressed against me: for their worm shall not die, neither shall their fire be quenched; and they shall be an abhorring unto all flesh." I also noted that in Matthew 5:30 it states, "And if thy right hand offend thee, cut it off." The place that is referred to is Hell.

▽ **In Luke 10:30-37 Jesus told the parable of a man who had been robbed.**

Three men saw him in his condition. The third person, the Samaritan helped him while the other two, a Priest and a Levite both who are linked to the Temple, "passed by on the other side" (verses 31 and 32) as they looked at him and did nothing to help. This is the basis for the denoted triangle.

▽ **Read the Parable of the Great Banquet, "A certain man made a great supper, and bade many" and the three excuses given as to why they could not come in Luke 14:16-20.**

1) In verse 18 "And they all with one consent began to make excuse. The first said unto him, I have bought a piece of ground, and I must needs go and see it: I pray thee have me excused."

2) In verse 19 "And another said, I have bought five yoke of oxen, and I go to prove them: I pray thee have me excused.

3) In verse 20 "And another said, I have married a wife, and therefore I cannot come."

Of these three excuses the first two are linked to having "bought" something and needing to go and inspect the purchase. This is the basis for the denoted triangle.

▽ **There are three instances where Jesus speaks regarding rich men.**

1) The first, the parable of the "certain rich man" laying up goods for himself only to be called a fool by God and God requiring his soul in Luke 12:16-20.

2) The second is again a parable of the "certain rich man" who lived an opulent lifestyle and the poor man Lazarus in Luke 16:19-31.

3) The third time in Matthew 19:16, Mark 10:17-25, and Luke 18:18-25 where a rich young man ask Jesus. "What good thing shall I do, that I may have eternal life?" Jesus tells him what he what he must do and he is "sorrowful" at Jesus' answer. Jesus later states, "It is easier for a camel to go through the eye of a needle, than for a rich man to enter into the kingdom of God."

The first two instances of the three relate to parables and the third to an actual event. This is the basis for the denoted triangle.

▽/△ Jesus was confronted by three adulterous women separately. He responses to the three of them.

1) The first is the woman of Samaria at "Jacob's well" as recorded in John 4:4-42. It is stated in verses 17-18, "The woman answered and said, I have no husband. Jesus said unto her, Thou hast well said, I have no husband: [18] For thou hast had five husbands; and he whom thou now hast is not thy husband: in that saidst thou truly."

2) The second is the woman who was caught in the act of adultery in John 8:2-11. John 8:4 states, "They say unto him, Master, this woman was taken in adultery, in the very act." In John 8:11, after Jesus has persuaded those who brought her to him to leave her alone, "She said, No man, Lord. And Jesus said unto her, Neither do I condemn thee: go, and sin no more."

3) The third woman is stated in Luke 7:36-50. The woman ". . . was a sinner. . ." and anointed Jesus with "an alabaster box of ointment" in verse 37. " And stood at

his feet behind him weeping, and began to wash his feet with tears, and did wipe them with the hairs of her head, and kissed his feet, and anointed them with the ointment" in verse 38. In Luke 7:47-48 it is stated by Jesus to the woman, "Wherefore I say unto thee, her sins, which are many, are forgiven; for she loved much: but to whom little is forgiven, the same loveth little. And he said unto her, Thy sins are forgiven."

Based on the latter two stated verses along with other scholars, there is a strong implication that she was an adulterous woman. The first two women of the three stories are told in the book of John. The first denoted triangle. The last two women of the three are told by Jesus not to sin anymore or their sins were forgiven. Nothing is mentioned by Jesus about the first woman's sins afterwards. The second denoted triangle. This third event is also recorded in Matthew 26:6-13, Mark 14:3-9, and John 12:2-8. These three references to the same story make no mention or indicate that the woman is a sinner. Just a woman who performed an act of kindness towards Jesus in the house of "Simon the leper" as stated in the books of Matthew and Mark. In the book of John the act is stated to be done by Mary in the house, it seems, of Jesus' friends, Mary, Martha, and Lazarus. There is no mention of one "Simon the leper" in the last book of the three. Another identified triangle, $\triangledown$.

$\triangledown/\triangledown$ Jesus did something relating to the ground three times.

1) In John 8:6 "But Jesus stooped down, and with his finger wrote on the ground, as though he heard them not."
2) In John 8:8 "And again he stooped down, and wrote on the ground."

3) In John 9:6 "When he had thus spoken, he spat on the ground, and made clay of the spittle, and he anointed the eyes of the blind man with the clay."

The first two activities are recorded in chapter 8 and the third in chapter 9. This is the basis for the first denoted triangle. The first two times Jesus does something on the ground it relates to the "adulterous woman." The third time to the blind man. The second denoted triangle.

△ **In John 10:10 it lists three things, "The thief cometh not, but for to steal, and to kill, and to destroy."**
Of the three items listed the last two are linked in that to kill is the destroying of life. The basis for the denoted triangle.

△ **The three pairs of people listed in Luke 17:34-36 as it relates to the Judgment day of God or what some may say "The rapture" or "taken away" to be with Christ.**

1) In verse 34 "I tell you, in that night there shall be two men in one bed; the one shall be taken, and the other shall be left."
2) In verse 35 "Two women shall be grinding together; the one shall be taken, and the other left."
3) In verse 36 "Two men shall be in the field; the one shall be taken, and the other left."

Of the three pairs the first pair are at rest and the last two pairs are at work. The basis for the denoted triangle.

△/△ **Three times it is recorded that the question relating to what is needed to ". . .inherit eternal life" is asked.**
Once in the book of Mark and twice in the book of Luke. The first denoted triangle. The last two verses of the three relate to the question being asked by two different men and

they both state also, "what shall I do to . . .". The second denoted triangle. The first and third verses indicate that the same person asked the question. The last two verses of the three refer to the "certain" men. Another identified triangle, △. Here are the verses:

1) Mark 10:17 "And when he was gone forth into the way, there came one running, and kneeled to him, and asked him, Good Master, what shall I do that I may inherit eternal life?"

2) Luke 10:25 "And, behold, a certain lawyer stood up, and tempted him, saying, Master, what shall I do to inherit eternal life?"

3) Luke 18:18 "And a certain ruler asked him, saying, Good Master, what shall I do to inherit eternal life?"

▽/ ▽ **There are two similar parables that was told by Jesus in Matthew 25:14-28 and Luke 19:15-25 where three servants had been given talents/pounds.**

The first two servants explain they had put what they were given to work and increased the value of what they were entrusted with and they were each rewarded. But the third servant merely hidden his one talent/pound and is punished. The two denoted triangles are formed based on the two parables which are similar. Two good servants and one evil one in each book.

▽ **Three times Jesus predicts his death and resurrection, some may call it the Passion, within the first three Gospel books:**

1) The first time is in Matthew 16:21, Mark 8:31, and Luke 9:22 where he states he must suffer/be rejected ". . .of the elders and chief priests and scribes. . ." and be killed/slain and rise on the "third day."

Of these three books he states ". . .and be killed" in the first two books. The basis for the denoted triangle. Note that the last two verses in the last two Gospels of the three are similar where he calls himself "Son of man" and state that he will "be rejected". Another identified triangle, △. Also note that the place Jerusalem is mentioned in the first book and not in the last two of these three books. Another identified triangle,△. Of these three books the first scripture in the first book states that Jesus ". . .shew unto his disciples" his prediction. Another identified triangle, △.

2) The second time he mentions his prediction it is in the Gospels of Matthew 17:22-23, Mark 9:31, and Luke 9:44 where he states "The Son of man shall be betrayed/delivered into the hands of men. . ." and be killed.

Of these three books the first two are similar and state that he will be killed but not in Luke where nothing is mentioned about his death. Another identified triangle,▽. The last two of these three books also state "delivered" while the first states "betrayed". Another identified triangle,△.

3) The third time he mentions the prediction it is in the Gospels of Matthew 20:17-19, Mark 10:32-34, and Luke 18:31-33 where he is more graphic and detailed as to what is going to happen to him. The ". . .chief priests, and . . . the scribes" shall ". . .deliver him to the Gentiles. . . where they shall mock him, spit on him, . . .shall scourge him" and "crucify him" / "kill him"/ "put him to death".

All three of these scriptures state "he shall rise again" on the "third day".

177

The first of these three books states how he will die, via crucifixion while the other two state he will be killed/put to death. Another identified triangle, $\triangle$. In Matthew 20:17, Mark 10:32 and Luke 18:31 it states that Jesus "took. . .the twelve" and told them the prediction .

Overall the three predictions that Jesus stated were said to his disciples in private. Of the three predictions, the third one is detailed and graphic as opposed to the other two predictions which are not. This is an overall triangle of the subject matter within all three Gospels, $\triangledown$.

$\triangledown / \triangle$ **Over the course of Jesus' life, in three stages, he is mentioned as going to the Temple.**

1) The first time was when he was a baby and was taken there by his parents as indicated in Luke 2:25-26, 36-38.
2) The second time he was there it was as a boy in Luke 2:39-52 most likely taken there again by his parents.
3) The third time is when he is a man and he is driving out the money changers and teaching and talking with others in Matthew 21:12–17, 21:23–27; Mark 11:15–19, 11:27–33; Luke 19:45–48, 20:1–8; and John 2:14–16.

Of the three stages he is taken there by his parents the first two times. This is the basis for first denoted triangle. Also the last two time records him conversing with others in the Temple of the three. This is the basis for the second denoted triangle. I would think that Jesus has come full circle in his life where he visited the Temple at the start of his life and being in it as one of the last places he visits before his demise.

$\triangle / \triangle$ **When Jesus went to go pray in ". . .a place called Gethsemane . . ." he took with him Peter and the two sons**

of Zebedee [James and John],. . ." in Matthew 26:36-37 and Mark 14:32-33. He prayed three times.

The first denoted triangle is based on who he took with him Peter, James and John. The first time he "prayed, saying, O my Father, if it be possible, let this cup pass from me: nevertheless not as I will, but as thou wilt" in Matthew 26:39 and Mark 14:36, 39. The second time he "prayed, saying, O my Father, if this cup may not pass away from me, except I drink it, thy will be done" in Matthew 26:42. Then in Matthew 26:44 it states, "and prayed the third time, saying the same words." Based on the scriptures he prayed three times with the last two prayers of the three being the same based on the account in Matthew. This is the basis for the second denoted triangle.

△/△/▽ **The activities in the Garden of Gethsemane.**

Jesus checked on the three disciples, "And he taketh with him Peter and James and John. . ." in Mark 14:33. The mentioning of the three men is the first denoted triangle noting that the last two men are brothers.

Three times he checked in on them as stated in Mark 14:37, 40, 41, "And he cometh, and findeth them sleeping, and saith unto Peter, Simon, sleepest thou? couldest not thou watch one hour? [40] And when he returned, he found them asleep again, (for their eyes were heavy,) neither wist they what to answer him. [41] And he cometh the third time, and saith unto them, Sleep on now, and take your rest: it is enough, the hour is come; behold, the Son of man is betrayed into the hands of sinners."

Note the first time Jesus finds the three sleeping he tries to wake them by asking Peter two questions in verse 37. He does not mention all three of them. The next two times Jesus finds them asleep in verses 40 and 41 he is not as heavy-handed as the first time. This is the basis for the second denoted triangle.

The third time he checks on them he tells them to "Sleep on now, and take your rest. . . ." after wanting them awake after the first two times. This is the basis for the third denoted triangle.

▽ **The three denials of Jesus by Peter his disciple as stated in Matthew 26:69-74, Mark 14:66-72, Luke 22:54-62, and John 18:16-18, 25-27.**

Based on an analysis of the first three of the four Gospels, his first two denials were at the insistence of a female servant. In Matthew it states two maids, in Mark it could be two of them or perhaps one, and in Luke a maid and someone else perhaps another maid. There are not enough details to make the determination for Mark and Luke in my view. In these two instances of Peter's denial it could have been made to the same person or if it were two of them they would be linked by occupation.

He later makes his third denial at the insistence to someone with others around in a group directly based on Peter's accent that was heard as he spoke. The denoted triangle is based on the same individual or two female servants and to a group of people.

Jesus did tell Peter that "thou shalt deny me thrice" or some variation of it within a statement in Matthew 26:34, Mark 14:30, Luke 22:34, and John 13:38. For the book of John, Peter's first denial is to a "damsel that kept the door" (John 18:17). His second denial is to a group of people in John 18:25. The third denial is to "One of the servants of the high priest, being his kinsman whose ear Peter cut off" (John 18:26). Then "immediately the cock crew" (John 18:27).

▽ **Three separate individuals tried Jesus in the Gospel of John chapter 18.**

1) The first was Ananias in John 18:12-13, 19-24. Ananias was the Jewish official High Priest at the time, but was deposed and replaced by his son-in-law Caiaphas who was appointed by the Romans.

2) Jesus was then sent to the appointed High Priest Caiaphas in John 18:24, 28 to be tried.

3) Then Jesus was lead to Pilate in 18:28-38 to be tried.

Based on this information Jesus was tried by two High Priests first and then by the Roman governor. The basis for the denoted triangle.

▽/▽ **There are four verses that pertain to the release of a prisoner "at that/the feast" or for Passover .**
The release of the prisoner was a choice between Jesus and Barabbas. Here are the verses:

1) Matthew 27:15 "Now at that feast the governor was wont to release unto the people a prisoner, whom they would."
2) Mark 15:6 "Now at that feast he released unto them one prisoner, whomsoever they desired."
3) Luke 23:17 "(For of necessity he must release one unto them at the feast.)"
4) John 18:39 "But ye have a custom, that I should release unto you one at the passover: will ye therefore that I release unto you the King of the Jews?"

The first three verses of the four state "at that feast" or "at the feast". Of these three verses the first two states "at that feast" while the third verse states "at the feast". The first denoted triangle. Also of these first three verses the first two verses state "one" or "a" and "prisoner". The second denoted triangle. Of these first three the last two mentions "one". Another identified triangle,△.

▽/△ **Jesus was crucified between two thieves as stated in Matthew 27:38, Mark 15:27, and John 19:18.**
Of the three verses cited, the first two states "two thieves" while the third does not . The third verse states ". . .two other with him, on either side one, and Jesus in the midst." The basis for the first denoted triangle. Of the three men, two of them were guilty of their crimes while one was not, Jesus

181

". . .because he had done no violence, neither was any deceit in his mouth." (Isaiah 53:9) This is the basis for the second denoted triangle. Read in Isaiah 53:12 which states, ". . .and he was numbered with the transgressors".

△ **The sign on the cross of Jesus stated, "JESUS OF NAZARETH, THE KING OF THE JEWS" was written in Hebrew, Greek, and Latin (John 19:20).**

The last two languages are both linked or are based out of Europe and the Hebrew language, perhaps Aramaic, being of the Middle East. This is the basis for the denoted triangle. There is no mention of the other two men having signs on their crosses. Another identified triangle, △.

△ **There are four verses that state the title "The King Of The Jews" as it relates to Jesus' crucifixion.**

1) In Matthew 27:37 "And set up over his head his accusation written, This Is Jesus The King Of The Jews."
2) In Mark 15:26 "And the superscription of his accusation was written over, THE KING OF THE JEWS."
3) In Luke 23:38" And a superscription also was written over him in letters of Greek, and Latin, and Hebrew, This Is The King Of The Jews."
4) In John 19:19 "And Pilate wrote a title, and put it on the cross. And the writing was Jesus Of Nazareth The King Of The Jews."

Of the four verses the first three verses states that the words were "over his head", "over" or "over him" and "written". Of these three verses the second and third verse also states "superscription". This is the basis for the denoted triangle. The fourth verse states that the words were "put . . . on the cross". No exact location is given.

▽/△/▽ **Two of three men dying on their crosses were going to heaven or "paradise" while one was not in Luke 23:43-44.**

"And Jesus said unto him, Verily I say unto thee, To day shalt thou be with me in paradise. And it was about the sixth hour, and there was a darkness over all the earth until the ninth hour." The first denoted triangle. The two thieves are linked by occupation of the three. The basis of the second denoted triangle. According to the book of Mark 15:34-37 Jesus died at the "ninth hour" which corresponds to 3 pm. Of the three men on the crosses one would be raised from the dead. The third denoted triangle.

△ **There were three Marys who were very close to Jesus when he lived.**

His mother, and devoted two friends Mary Magdalene who was cleansed of seven "devils" by Jesus according to Luke 8:2 and Mark 16:9, and Mary the sister of Martha and Lazarus. This is basis for the denoted triangle. Note Lazarus is the one he raised from the dead in John 11:31-32 and 12:1-3.

△/▽ **In John 19:25 it states, "Now there stood by the cross of Jesus his mother, and his mother's sister, Mary the wife of Cleophas, and Mary Magdalene."**

Notice that his mother Mary is there with two other friends named Mary based on my view of the scripture. The first denoted triangle. John 19:32-33 states that the legs of the two thieves were broken first but not Jesus because he was dead. The second denoted triangle.

▽ **John 20:11-14 states there were three astral beings in and around Jesus' sepulcher when Mary Magdalene came and looked: two angels on the inside and he, Jesus, on the outside.** The basis for the denoted triangle.

▽/△ **Three questions were asked of Mary Magdalene in John 20:13 and 15.**

The first by the two angels in white, "they say unto her, Woman, why weepest thou?" Later Jesus appears and asked her the same question and a follow-up question, "Woman, why weepest thou? Whom seekest thou?" Notice that the three of them together asked her the same first question, why is she weeping? The two angels first then Jesus. This is the basis for the first denoted triangle. There were three individuals who asked of her questions. One question was asked by the two angels and two questions are asked by Jesus. This is the basis for the second denoted triangle.

▽ **Three men named "Simon" had some interaction with Jesus in the Gospels.**

1) The first man is the apostle Simon Peter who is mentioned at length in the four Gospels.

2) The second man is Simon the apostle the "Canaanite" or "called Zelotes" in Matthew 10:4, Mark 3:18, and Luke 6:15. Note he is also mentioned in Acts 1:13.

3) The third man is "Simon a Cyrenian" who was compelled to bear the cross for Jesus in Matthew 27:32, Mark 15:21, and Luke 23:26.

Of the three men named Simon, the first two are disciples/apostles of Jesus while the third man is a bystander. This is the basis for the denoted triangle. There are three other men named Simon in the New Testament, Simon the leper in Matthew 26:6 and Mark 14:3, Simon the sorcerer in Acts 8:9, 13, 18, 24 and "Simon a tanner" in Acts 10:6, 32 who had Simon Peter lodge with him. Of these three the first man could be consider a friend of Jesus. Another identified triangle,△.

▽ **The resurrection of Jesus refers to the return to bodily life three days after his death by crucifixion.**

He rose on the third day indicating that two of the three days he was not alive. The basis for the denoted triangle. It is akin to the Jonah story with him being in a whale's belly.

△ **The Walk to Emmaus, Jesus with two other men, as stated in Mark 16:12-13 and Luke 24:13-35.**

After Jesus' resurrection he walked with two other men, the three altogether, who were called disciples. Believers who later came and told the eleven they had seen him. Jesus and the two unnamed men is the basis for the denoted triangle.

△ **Jesus is seen resurrected based on the harmonizing of the Gospels**.

He is seen twice before seeing the disciples/Apostles. The four noted appearances, pertaining to groups mostly, including seeing the disciples/Apostles are as follows:

1) Jesus appears first to the women who came to check on him in Matthew 28:9-10, Mark 16:9-11, and John 20:14-18.
2) Jesus appears to two men who are believers on the way to Emmaus in Mark 16:12-13 and Luke 24:13-35.
3) Jesus appears to the disciples with Thomas not being present in Mark 16:14-15, Luke 24:36-43, and John 20:19-25.
4) Jesus appears to his disciples again with Thomas being present in John 20:24-29.

Note the last three instances are with men. The last two of these three are with his disciples and according to the book of John are in a room. The basis for the triangle is the appearances to the men.

△/▽ **There are three instances where Jesus is accompanied by individuals from heaven.**

1) In Matthew 4:11 and Mark 1:13 after Jesus is tempted of the Devil angels came and ". . .ministered unto him" afterwards;
2) In Matthew 17:1-9, Mark 9:2-8, and Luke 9:28-36 when Jesus is seen with both Moses and Elijah during his transfiguration.
3) In Luke 24:4 and John 20:12-14 Jesus is with two angels after his resurrection.

The last two of the three are linked in that two heavenly individuals are mentioned. The first denoted triangle. The first does not indicate a particular number of heavenly individuals. Also the first two instances occurred while he was alive and the third one after he died and was resurrected. The second denoted triangle.

▽/△ **Peter was restored by Jesus in John 21:15-17 while Jesus was with his disciples the third time after being resurrected.**

Jesus asked Peter a question three times, the first question is different then the other question which is asked twice. His response to Peter's answer was different the first time and the same the next two times. Peter's response to the question was the same twice and differently the third time. Here are the verses pertaining to Peter and Jesus' conversation:

1) "Jesus saith to Simon Peter, Simon, son of Jonas, lovest thou me more than these? He saith unto him, Yea, Lord; thou knowest that I love thee. He saith unto him, Feed my lambs" (verse 15).

2) "Simon, son of Jonas, lovest thou me? He saith unto him, Yea, Lord; thou knowest that I love thee. He saith unto him, Feed my sheep" (verse 16).

3) "Simon, son of Jonas, lovest thou me? . . . And he said unto him, Lord, thou knowest all things; thou knowest that I love thee. Jesus saith unto him, Feed my sheep" (verse 17).

Based on this conversation I know that this was done for a reason and to demonstrate the three pattern of the divine. It confirmed Peter's first two denials were by the same type of person(s) and that Jesus mimicked Peter's previous actions. The two denoted triangles shown at the beginning are illustrated below relating to the conversation between the two men:

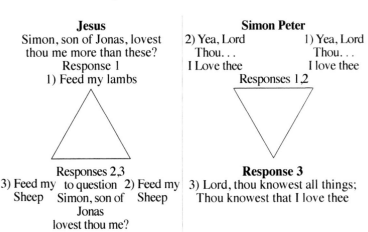

Jesus
Simon, son of Jonas, lovest thou me more than these?
Response 1
1) Feed my lambs

Responses 2,3
3) Feed my to question 2) Feed my
Sheep   Simon, son of   Sheep
         Jonas
         lovest thou me?

Simon Peter
2) Yea, Lord   1) Yea, Lord
   Thou. . .   Thou. . .
   I Love thee   I love thee
        Responses 1,2

Response 3
3) Lord, thou knowest all things;
   Thou knowest that I love thee

▽ **In John 20:19, 21, and 26 Jesus says "Peace be unto you" three times.**

The first two times Jesus is with the disciples without Thomas and says it twice, then eight days later with the disciples again with Thomas, he says it once. The basis for the denoted triangle. Here are the verses:

1) John 20:19 "Then the same day at evening, being the first day of the week, when the doors were shut where the disciples were assembled for fear of the Jews, came Jesus and stood in the midst, and saith unto them, Peace be unto you."

2) John 20:21 "Then said Jesus to them again, Peace be unto you: as my Father hath sent me, even so send I you."

3) John 20:26 "And after eight days again his disciples were within, and Thomas with them: then came Jesus, the doors being shut, and stood in the midst, and said, Peace be unto you."

This salutation that Jesus states to his disciples is first recorded in Luke 24:36, "And as they thus spake, Jesus himself stood in the midst of them, and saith unto them, Peace be unto you."

▽ In John 21:1, and 14 Jesus showed himself to the disciples a third time at the sea of Tiberius.

In verse 1, "After these things Jesus shewed himself again to the disciples at the sea of Tiberias; and on this wise shewed he himself. . . . [14] This is now the third time that Jesus shewed himself to his disciples, after that he was risen from the dead." The first two times he was seen by the disciples is recorded in John 20:19 and 26 which were inside a room where he stated, "Peace by unto you" three times. This is the basis for the denoted triangle.

▽/△ The Holy Trinity, "three in one."

In Matthew 28:19 Jesus states to his disciples, "Go ye therefore, and teach all nations, baptizing them in the name of the Father, and of the Son, and of the Holy Ghost." Some call it the Great Commission and used in the Trinitarian formula. Two of the three names of the "commission" have been given in the Bible. God the Father's name which is given is JEHOVAH mentioned in three books, four verses, in Exodus 6:3, Psalm 83:18, Isaiah 12:2, and Isaiah 26:4. A previously identified triangle, $\triangledown$, within the three books. God the Son's name, Jesus is stated in Matthew 1:25, ". . . and he called his name JESUS" and other various instances in the New Testament. The name of the Holy Spirit we don't know as of yet of the three. This is the first denoted triangle.

I also notice how beginning in Matthew we are introduced to the existence of Jesus and Holy Ghost or Holy Spirit, the second and third members of the Holy Trinity. These two members are not mentioned at all in the Old Testament, at least not as we know them in the New Testament. The Bible is divided as relating to the trinity, God the Father is of and in the Old Testament predominantly, and Jesus and the Holy Ghost are introduced in and of the New Testament predominantly. This is the basis for the second denoted triangle.

In Isaiah 9:6 it states, "For unto us a child is born, unto us a son is given: and the government shall be upon his shoulder: and his name shall be called Wonderful, Counsellor, The mighty God, The everlasting Father, The Prince of Peace." Scholars and theologians view this as the prophecy of Jesus to come in the Old Testament as well as Micah 5:2 which states, "But thou, Bethlehem Ephratah, though thou be little among the thousands of Judah, yet out of thee shall he come forth unto me that is to be ruler in Israel; whose goings forth have been from of old, from everlasting." It is in the New Testament that we learn the nature of who he is in detail.

Based on the pattern, the name of God and his son both begin with the letter "J" in English, in Latin "I" and in Hebrew ` (*Yod*) or "Y" in English. I would think that the name of the Holy Spirit would begin with the letter J as well. Of the three Jesus is the only one to have been born into this world. Another identified triangle, $\triangle$.

There are other scriptures that refer to and support the concept of the trinity which are stated as follows:

Matthew 3:16-17 "And Jesus, when he was baptized, went up straightway out of the water: and, lo, the heavens were opened unto him, and he saw the Spirit of God descending like a dove, and lighting upon him: [17]And lo a voice from heaven, saying, This is my beloved Son, in whom I am well pleased."

John 14:16-17 "And I will pray the Father, and he shall give you another Comforter, that he may abide with you forever; [17] Even the Spirit of truth; whom the world cannot receive, because it seeth him not, neither knoweth him: but ye know him; for he dwelleth with you, and shall be in you."

Acts 2:32-33 "This Jesus hath God raised up, whereof we all are witnesses. [33] Therefore being by the right hand of God exalted, and having received of the Father the promise of the Holy Ghost, he hath shed forth this, which ye now see and hear."

2 Corinthians 13:14 "The grace of the Lord Jesus Christ, and the love of God, and the communion of the Holy Ghost, be with you all. Amen."

1 Peter 1:2 "Elect according to the foreknowledge of God the Father, through sanctification of the Spirit, unto obedience and sprinkling of the blood of Jesus Christ: Grace unto you, and peace, be multiplied."

The "Shield of the Trinity" shows the interrelationship of the three. This diagram and the second denoted triangle that shows the structure of the three within the bible are shown below:

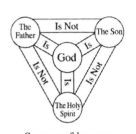

Source of image:
http://en.wikipedia.org/wiki/
Shield_of_the_Trinity

God, The Father, Jehovah
of the
Old Testament

Introduced in & of
the New Testament
(Predominantly)

God, The Holy Spirit   God, The Son
Name unknown   Jesus

△ It is not in the Bible but what some call "The **Eye of Providence** (or the **all-seeing eye of God**) is a symbol showing an eye often surrounded by rays of light or a glory and usually enclosed by a triangle. In the modern era, the most notable depiction of the eye is the reverse of the Great Seal of the United States, which appears on the United States one-dollar bill." "A Christian version of the Eye of Providence, emphasizing the triangle representing the Trinity"[24] is shown below: The denoted triangle is the referenced symbol:

Source of image: http://en.wikipedia.org/wiki/Eye_of_Providence

---

[24] Source - Wikipedia, Eye of Providence, 2013, http://en.wikipedia. org/wiki/Eye_of_Providence, Retrieved 05.11.2013

▽ Taking a closer look at the image above noticed that the three lines on each side of the triangle image shown is a triangle itself. The basis for the denoted triangle. There are other symbols that are said to be associated with the Christian trinity which are the Trefoil, a graphic that is an outline of three overlapping rings, another identified triangle▽, and the Borromean Rings that is the interlocking of three circles. Another identified triangle,△.

▲**Commentary**: There are those who do not believe in the notion of the Holy Trinity and are dubbed "Nontrinitarians." Some focus only on Jesus Christ. They seem to omit that most of the information for the "Great Commission" is provided with the two names of Jehovah and Jesus. There are those that cite the scripture of Acts 2:38 as Nontrinitarians for their position which states, "Then Peter said unto them, Repent, and be baptized every one of you in the name of Jesus Christ for the remission of sins, and ye shall receive the gift of the Holy Ghost."

I noticed that two members of the Holy trinity are mentioned "Jesus Christ" and receiving ". . .the gift of the Holy Ghost." In one respect I can say that their position has some validity. For me the question is how does one reconcile such scriptures as Luke 23:34, John 3:16, 10:30, and 14:6 based on the position they have taken? Here is what they state:

Luke 23:34 "Then said Jesus, Father, forgive them; for they know not what they do."

John 3:16 "For God so loved the world, that he gave his only begotten Son, that whosoever believeth in him should not perish, but have everlasting life."

John 10:30 "**I and my Father are one**"

John 14:6 "Jesus saith unto him, I am the way, the truth, and the life: no man cometh unto the Father, but by me."

Their position, as a Nontrinitarian, could be a challenge based on the analysis I am providing. In Genesis 1:26 it is stated, "And God said, Let us make man in our image, after our likeness." The question has to be asked, who is God referring to as "us"? As a Nontrinitarian where the focus is on Jesus, that would be appropriate in my view but there should also be some thought of there being a next step based on the scriptures such as Matthew 10:32-33 and Revelation 3:5 that state:

Matthew 10:32 "Whosoever therefore shall confess me before men, him will I confess also before my Father which is in heaven."

Matthew 10:33 "But whosoever shall deny me before men, him will I also deny before my Father which is in heaven."

Revelation 3:5 "He that overcometh, the same shall be clothed in white raiment; and I will not blot out his name out of the book of life, but I will confess his name before my Father, and before his angels."

Genesis 1:26 "And God said, Let us make man in our image, after our likeness."

There was a voice that came from heaven twice that stated ". . .my beloved son in whom I am well pleased" after Jesus was baptized by John the Baptist, in Matthew 3:17, Mark 1:11, and Luke 3:22, and during Jesus' transfiguration in Matthew 17:5, Mark 9:7, and Luke 9:35. The question begs to be asked, who is making those statements from heaven while Jesus is on the earth? Lastly, there are eight verses that state or suggests that Jesus either sat on or is standing by or is on "the right hand of God" in Mark 16:19, Acts 2:33, 7:55, 7:56, Romans 8:34, Colossians 3:1, Hebrews 10:12, and 1 Peter 3:22.

▽ **The history of Roman emperors when Jesus is alive and the three who are mentioned in the Bible with the title "Caesar":**

1) Gaius Julius Caesar Augustus (63 BC – 14 AD) was the First ever Roman Emperor of the Roman Empire and 2nd Caesar (". . .Caesar Augustus. . .", Luke 2:1).
2) Tiberius Julius Caesar Augustus/Tiberius I (42 BC – 37 AD) was the second Roman Emperor and stepson of Augustus and Third Caesar (". . .Tiberius Caesar. . .", Luke 3:1). Tiberius was the Emperor when Jesus was crucified before the third emperor came to power in 37A.D.
3) Tiberius Claudius Caesar Augustus Germanicus (10 BC – 54 AD) (". . .Claudius Caesar. . .", Acts 11:28 & 18:2) Claudius was the fourth Roman Emperor and fifth Caesar

The three emperors were alive, in or out of power, during the life of Jesus and they are all part of what is called the Julio-Claudian dynasty. The first five Roman emperors. Jesus lived during the lives of the second and third Caesars, Augustus and Tiberius, who were the first two Roman emperors of the three mentioned men. This is the basis for the denoted triangle. The first two Caesars were related by blood, Julius was great-uncle to Augustus. Note: After the death of Gaius Julius Caesar, considered by some one of the last rulers of the Roman republic, that name Caesar continued on as a title for future rulers of the Roman empire. It is said that

Augustus was adopted by Julius. Note that these first two emperors are also mentioned in the in the same book of Luke while the third is not. Another identified triangle, ∇. The title of Caesar is after the names of Tiberius and Claudius but not Augustus. Another identified triangle, $\triangle$.

The third Roman emperor, and fourth Caesar, Caligula is not mentioned at all in the text. It is said that Caligula, as the third Roman emperor, viewed himself as deity and had "ordered the erection of a statue of himself in the Jewish Temple of Jerusalem. . . ."[25]. An act that should exclude an individual from being mentioned in the text in my view. It is said that Caligula is the first emperor to bribe the Praetorian guard to become emperor. "Caligula had both Julian and Claudian ancestry, making him the first actual 'Julio-Claudian' emperor."[26] There are those who believe that Nero is alluded to as the character called "The Beast" in the book of Revelation being the fifth and last Roman emperor of the Julio-Claudian dynasty. Note, there is a stated name called "Augustus" in Acts 25:21, 25, and 27:1 which is said to refer to the emperor Nero. Note that part of Nero's full name is Augustus based on the listing of the members of the Julio-Claudian dynasty. These verses pertain to the apostle Paul who makes an appeal to Caesar.

The Synoptic Gospels, the first three books/gospels of the New Testament which are Matthew, Mark, and Luke. With Matthew being the first book/gospel of the New Testament you would assume that it was the first book/gospel written. It is said, and many believe, that the gospel/book of Mark was the first gospel written and that is was the source for

---

[25]   Source - Wikipedia, Caligula, 2013, http://en.wikipedia.org/wiki/ Caligula, Retrieved 01.02.2013)

[26]   Source-Wikipedia,Julio-Claudiandynasty,2013,http://en.wikipedia.org/ wiki/Julio-Claudian_dynasty, Retrieved 07.20.2013

the gospels/books of Matthew and Luke. I focused on what is called the "Triple tradition" where many of the stories and events are present in all three books/gospels. As I looked at certain verses from these three books/gospels, I saw the divine pattern. Either the first two or the last two of the verses are closely the same with the first or the third one having a "minor" variation from the other two verses. Here is a diagram of the subject matter:

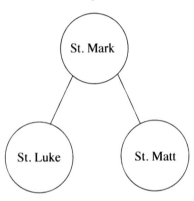

Below are fifteen scriptural examples from those three gospels, that are proceeded with a triangle or two, that exhibit the pattern where either the first two of the three are closely aligned or the last two are or in some cases it could be either or of the three based on how the three scriptures, or more in the first example, are viewed. Again, a triangle or more is denoted prior to each of three verses to show the triangle direction of the three verses:

△

Matthew 3:3 "For this is he that was spoken of by the prophet Esaias, saying, The voice of one crying in the wilderness, Prepare ye the way of the Lord, make his paths straight.
Mark 1:2-3 "**As it is written in the prophets**, Behold, I send my messenger before thy face, which shall prepare thy way before thee. ³The voice of one crying in the wilderness, Prepare ye the way of the Lord, make his paths straight."

Luke 3:4 "**As it is written in the book of the words of Esaias the prophet**, saying, The voice of one crying in the wilderness, Prepare ye the way of the Lord, make his paths straight."

△

Matthew 3:17 "And lo a **voice from heaven, saying, This is my beloved Son, in whom I am well pleased.**"
Mark 1:11 "And there came **a voice from heaven, saying, Thou art my beloved Son, in whom I am well pleased.**"
Luke 3:22 "And the Holy Ghost descended in a bodily shape like a dove upon him, and **a voice came from heaven, which said, Thou art my beloved Son; in thee I am well pleased.**"

△ / ▽

Matthew 5:15 "Neither do men light a candle, and put it under a bushel, but on a candlestick; and it giveth light unto all that are in the house."
Mark 4:21 "And he said unto them, Is a candle brought to be put under a bushel, or under a bed? and not to be set on a candlestick?"
Luke 8:16 "No man, when he hath lighted a candle, covereth it with a vessel, or putteth it under a bed; but setteth it on a candlestick, that they which enter in may see the light."

△

Matthew 14:19 "And he commanded the multitude to sit down on the grass, and took the five loaves, and the two fishes, and looking up to heaven, he blessed, and brake, and gave the loaves to his disciples, and the disciples to the multitude."
Mark 6:41 "And when he had taken the five loaves and the two fishes, he looked up to heaven, and blessed, and brake the loaves, and gave them to his disciples to set before them; and the two fishes divided he among them all."

Luke 9:16 "Then he took the five loaves and the two fishes, and looking up to heaven, he blessed them, and brake, and gave to the disciples to set before the multitude."

▽

Matthew 20:18 "Behold, we go up to Jerusalem; and the Son of man shall be betrayed unto the chief priests and unto the scribes, and they shall condemn him to death,"

Mark 10:33 "Saying, Behold, we go up to Jerusalem; and the Son of man shall be delivered unto the chief priests, and unto the scribes; and they shall condemn him to death, and shall deliver him to the Gentiles:"

Luke 18:31 "Then he took unto him the twelve, and said unto them, Behold, we go up to Jerusalem, and all things that are written by the prophets concerning the Son of man shall be accomplished."

▽

Matthew 21:9 "And the multitudes that went before, and that followed, cried, saying, Hosanna to the Son of David: Blessed is he that cometh in the name of the Lord; Hosanna in the highest."

Mark 11:10 "Blessed be the kingdom of our father David, that cometh in the name of the Lord: Hosanna in the highest."

Luke 19:38 "Saying, Blessed be the King that cometh in the name of the Lord: peace in heaven, and glory in the highest."

△ / ▽

Matthew 24:2 "And Jesus said unto them, See ye not all these things? verily I say unto you, There shall not be left here one stone upon another, that shall not be thrown down."

Mark 13:2 "And Jesus answering said unto him, Seest thou these great buildings? there shall not be left one stone upon another, that shall not be thrown down."

Luke 21:6 "As for these things which ye behold, the days will come, in the which there shall not be left one stone upon another, that shall not be thrown down."

Matthew 24:6 "And ye shall hear of wars and rumours of wars: see that ye be not troubled: for all these things must come to pass, but the end is not yet."

Mark 13:7 "And when ye shall hear of wars and rumours of wars, be ye not troubled: for such things must needs be; but the end shall not be yet."

Luke 21:9 "But when ye shall hear of wars and commotions, be not terrified: for these things must first come to pass; but the end is not by and by."

Matthew 24:15 "When ye therefore shall see the abomination of desolation, spoken of by Daniel the prophet, stand in the holy place, (whoso readeth, let him understand:)"

Mark 13:14 "But when ye shall see the abomination of desolation, spoken of by Daniel the prophet, standing where it ought not, (let him that readeth understand,) then let them that be in Judaea flee to the mountains:"

Luke 21:20 "And when ye shall see Jerusalem compassed with armies, then know that the desolation thereof is nigh."

Matthew 24:19 "And woe unto them that are with child, and to them that give suck in those days!"

Mark 13:17 "But woe to them that are with child, and to them that give suck in those days!"

Luke 21:23 "But woe unto them that are with child, and to them that give suck, in those days! for there shall be great distress in the land, and wrath upon this people.

△ / ▽

Matthew 24:30 "And then shall appear the sign of the Son of man in heaven: and then shall all the tribes of the earth mourn, and they shall see the Son of man coming in the clouds of heaven with power and great glory."
Mark 13:26 "And then shall they see the Son of man coming in the clouds with great power and glory."
Luke 21:27 "And then shall they see the Son of man coming in a cloud with power and great glory."

△

Matthew 26:18 "And he said, Go into the city to such a man, and say unto him, The Master saith, My time is at hand; I will keep the passover at thy house with my disciples."
Mark 14:14 "And wheresoever he shall go in, say ye to the goodman of the house, The Master saith, Where is the guestchamber, where I shall eat the passover with my disciples?"
Luke 22:11 "And ye shall say unto the goodman of the house, The Master saith unto thee, Where is the guest-chamber, where I shall eat the passover with my disciples?"

▽

Matthew 26:21 "And as they did eat, he said, Verily I say unto you, that one of you shall betray me."
Mark 14:18 "And as they sat and did eat, Jesus said, Verily I say unto you, One of you which eateth with me shall betray me."
Luke 22:21 "But, behold, the hand of him that betrayeth me is with me on the table."

∇

Matthew 26:24 "The Son of man goeth as it is written of him: but woe unto that man by whom the Son of man is betrayed! it had been good for that man if he had not been born."

Mark 14:21 "The Son of man indeed goeth, as it is written of him: but woe to that man by whom the Son of man is betrayed! good were it for that man if he had never been born."

Luke 22:22 "And truly the Son of man goeth, as it was determined: but woe unto that man by whom he is betrayed!"

$\triangle$ / ∇

Matthew 27:45 "Now from the sixth hour there was darkness over all the land unto the ninth hour."

Mark 15:33 "And when the sixth hour was come, there was darkness over the whole land until the ninth hour."

Luke 23:44 "And it was about the sixth hour, and there was a darkness over all the earth until the ninth hour."

∇ **The three year ministry of Jesus, he being the Messiah, it can be summed up or categorized into three major activities.**

1) One of those activities was teaching his followers that were close to him, his disciples and others,
2) Another activity was preaching to the masses.

In both of these two activities he was using his voice to get the message of God the father over to the people either directly or via parables in many instances. That message that he was voicing was in essence he was/is the only way to God the Father in heaven.

3) The third major activity that Jesus was involved with was the working of miracles amongst the people. This was done to demonstrate the power of God.

The denoted triangle is based on Jesus using his voice, in the first two instances, and the display of miracles.

△ **There is a body of water that is prominent relating to story of Jesus. It is called by three names in the New Testament.**

Based on the harmonizing of the Gospels the body of water is called:

1) The "sea of Galilee" in Matthew 4:18 and 15:29; Mark 1:16, 7:31; and John 6:1.
2) The "Lake of Gennesaret" in Luke 5:1.
3) The "sea of Tiberias" in John 6:1 and 21:1.

Based on maps of the area, Galilee is a northern Israeli region in which the sea was located.[27] The last two names mentioned for the body of water relate to cities on north western and western shore of the lake/sea respectively. This is the basis for the denoted triangle. Note that two of the names began with "Sea" of the three. Another identified triangle,▽. Note that the body of water is also referred to in the Old Testament as the sea of Chinnereth in Numbers 34:11 and Joshua 13:27, and Chinneroth in Joshua 12:3.

---

[27] Map source: Map of Ancient Israel, 2013, www.Bible-history. com/geography/ancient-israel/israel-first-century.html, Retrieved 04.03.2013

Acts through Jude

△ The first four recorded visions of those in the book of Acts:

1) Stephen and seeing Jesus "on the right hand of God. . ." just before he is about to die by stoning after giving a sermon in Acts 7:55-56.
2) Saul has an encounter on the way to ". . .Damascus: and suddenly there shined round about him a light from heaven" with the voice of Jesus saying to him "Saul, Saul, why persecutest thou me?" in Acts 9:3-7. Note that Saul/Paul states that this is a vision in "Acts 26:19 ". . .I was not disobedient unto the heavenly vision,"
3) Ananias, a disciple of Jesus who was told in a vision to go and meet Saul of Tarsus in Acts 9:10-11. ". . .Arise, and go into the street which is called Straight, and enquire in the house of Judas for one called Saul, of Tarsus" (verse 11).
4) In Acts 9:12 Saul of Tarsus ". . . hath seen in a vision a man named Ananias coming in, and putting his hand on him, that he might receive his sight."

The last three recorded visions relate Saul and of these three visions the last two are linked in that there was a meeting of the two men and both of their visions could have been happening simultaneously based on the reading of the scriptures, Ananias and Saul. The first vision for Saul is from Jesus. The denoted triangle is based on this information. I noticed that Saul with his name changed to Paul has two other recorded visions also in Acts 16:9-10 and 18:9. There are two others who had visions in the book of Acts worth noting. Cornelius, a centurion, and how his ". . .prayers and thine alms are come up for a memorial before God. . .about the ninth hour of the day . . ." in Acts 10:1-4, and Peter and his vision of the unclean beasts on "a great sheet let down from heaven three times" in Acts 10:9-16 at ". . .about the sixth hour. . .". These two visions are linked also in that there was a meeting of the two men and that their visions were in and of an unconscious/sleep state.

△ **In Acts 7:55-56, 9:3-7, 9:10-11, 9:12, 10:1-4, and 10:9-16 six visions have been mentioned in order. One is by Stephen, one by Saul, one by Ananias, one by Saul again, one by Cornelius, and one by Peter respectively**.

The last four of these six can be viewed as being paired. Each pair of two visions are linked in that there was a meeting of the two men relating to their visions. There is no connection between the first two visions where there is meeting of the men, but it is mentioned that Stephen saw Jesus while Saul heard Jesus. The denoted triangle is form with the last two pair being linked to the men meeting each other. Ananias meeting Saul and Peter meeting Cornelius.

△/△ **In Acts 10:11, 13-16 Peter has a vision where "a great sheet knit" is let down from heaven three times.**

He is commanded in the first instance from heaven to "Rise, Peter; kill, and eat." He is told next, second, from heaven, "What God hath cleansed, that call not thou common" in verse 15. Based on the pattern, the third command would have to have been the same as the second, as in verse 16 states it was done "thice" and then "the vessel was received up again into heaven" The first denoted triangle. The only response Peter gave is indicated in verse 14, "Not so, Lord; for I have never eaten anything that is common or unclean," and no other response is recorded for the next two times that "a certain vessel descending unto him" in verse 11. The second denoted triangle. One notes that there were only two statements made from heaven that is recorded and not a third. Another identified triangle,▽.

△ As Peter thought on his vision, three men came to see him.

"A great sheet knit" being let down three times from heaven, Peter is later summoned within Acts 10:7-16, 19 where the pattern of three is exhibited:

> Verse 7 "And when the angel which spake unto Cornelius was departed, he called two of his household servants, and a devout soldier of them that waited on him continually; "

> Verse 8 "And when he had declared all these things unto them, he sent them to Joppa."

> Verse 19 "While Peter thought on the vision, the Spirit said unto him, "Behold, three 'men' seek thee.""

Three came to see Peter, a centurion and two servants. The basis for the denoted triangle. Based on verse seven Cornelius ". . .called two of his household servants, and a devout soldier". Another identified triangle,▽. This story is also repeated in Acts 11:5-10 by Peter, "And this was done three times: and all were drawn up again into heaven." (Acts 11:10)

△/▽ The three deaths in and of the New Testament:

1) Jesus, the Crucifixion, Matthew 27:33-44; Mark 15:22-32; Luke 23:33-43; John 19:17-30
2) Stephen, in Acts 6:8-7:60
3) James, Acts 12:1-2 son of Zebedee and brother of John

The first death was the greatest of the three which aided in establishing the Christian faith and the last two are martyrs of that faith. The first denoted triangle. There is no record of James giving a sermon or any other stated detailed activities relating to his faith as did the first two men. The second denoted triangle. Note that the death of John the Baptist in Matthew 14:1-12 and Mark 6:14-29 cannot be, technically, attributed to the spreading of the Gospel of Jesus.

▽ **There are three miraculous acts relating to the apostles being in prisons:**

1) Peter and others sent to prison and released with help of an angel in Acts 5:15-20, "But the angel of the Lord by night opened the prison doors, and brought them forth. . ." (verse 19).

2) Peter alone is sent to prison by Herod and an angel helped in his release again in Acts 12:5-11, "And, behold, the angel of the Lord came upon him, and a light shined in the prison: and he smote Peter on the side, and raised him up, saying, Arise up quickly. And his chains fell off from his hands. . ." (verse 7).

3) Paul and Silas locked in prison, prayed and God sent an earthquake to open prison doors in Acts 16:23-27, "And suddenly there was a great earthquake, so that the foundations of the prison were shaken: and immediately all the doors were opened, and every one's bands were loosed" (verse 26).

The first two acts are linked to an angel assisting in release of Peter twice. The third prison release was of God with him sending an earthquake. The basis for the denoted triangle.

▽ **In the book of Acts the Apostle Paul stayed in three stated places for a time of three months:**

206

1) In Ephesus for three months where he boldly "spake" in the synagogue there as stated in Acts 19:8.

2) In Acts 20:2-3 then subsequently later he stayed three months in Greece.

3) Later the ship that was carrying him to Rome to stand trial for preaching the gospel, was wrecked in a storm, Acts 27:41-44, and he and the other prisoners with him stayed on the island of Melita for three months in Acts 28:1,11.

I see the pattern where he had relatively two good three month journeys relating to preaching the gospel, and one not. The basis for denoted the triangle.

▽ A voice spoke from Heaven three times for the benefit of an individual.

The first two times are when after Jesus was baptized by John the Baptist and during the transfiguration the words that were spoken "This is my beloved Son, in whom I am well pleased." Both times the words were spoken by God the Father in Matthew 3:17, Mark 1:11, Luke 3:22, and in Matthew 17:5 and 2 Peter 1:17 with Mark 9:7 and Luke 9:35 being very similar. The third time is by Jesus to Saul/Paul "Saul, Saul, why persecutest thou me?" in Acts 9:4. This is the basis for the denoted triangle. Note in John 12:28-30 states a voice coming out of heaven which is for the benefit of a group of people. "Jesus answered and said, This voice came not because of me, but for your sakes." (John 12:30)

△/▽/▽ There are three gods of Roman mythology that are mentioned in the New Testament in seven verses.

The three Roman gods that are mentioned are Jupiter, king of the gods, Mercuris or Mercury, god of messages among other activities, and Diana goddess of the hunt among other activities. Here are the verses that mention the gods:

1) Acts 14:12 "And they called Barnabas, Jupiter; and Paul, Mercurius, because he was the chief speaker."
2) Acts 14:13 "Then the priest of Jupiter, which was before their city, brought oxen and garlands unto the gates, and would have done sacrifice with the people."
3) Acts 19:24 "For a certain man named Demetrius, a silversmith, which made silver shrines for Diana, brought no small gain unto the craftsmen;"
4) Acts 19:27 "So that not only this our craft is in danger to be set at nought; but also that the temple of the great goddess Diana should be despised, and her magnificence should be destroyed, whom all Asia and the world worshippeth."
5) Acts 19:28 "And when they heard these sayings, they were full of wrath, and cried out, saying, Great is Diana of the Ephesians."
6) Acts 19:34 "But when they knew that he was a Jew, all with one voice about the space of two hours cried out, Great is Diana of the Ephesians."
7) Acts 19:35 "And when the townclerk had appeased the people, he said, Ye men of Ephesus, what man is there that knoweth not how that the city of the Ephesians is a worshipper of the great goddess Diana, and of the image which fell down from Jupiter?"

Of the three gods the first is the king of them while the last two are lesser ones. The first denoted triangle. Of the three gods two of them were assigned to men, the apostles of Jesus, Banabas and Paul. The second denoted triangle. Of the three gods the first two are male and the third is female. The third denoted triangle. Note that Jupiter is mentioned in three verses in the first, second, and fourth verses of which the first and second verses are in the same chapter of the three. Another identified triangle, $\triangledown$.

$\triangledown$ Three men are raised from the dead by men of God:

1) The only son of the widow of Nain by Jesus in Luke 7:14 "And he said, Young man, I say unto thee, Arise."

2) Lazarus, the friend of Jesus by Jesus in Luke 11:43 "when he thus had spoken, he cried with a loud voice, Lazarus, come forth."

3) "A certain young man named Eutychus. . .[who]fell down from the third loft and was taken up dead" by the Apostle Paul in Acts 20:9-10.

First two men were raised by Jesus and third by Paul. This is the basis for the denoted triangle.

$\triangle$/$\triangle$/$\triangledown$ There are three men who were involved in raising people from the dead.

1) Jesus who raised three people, the only son of the widow of Nain (Luke 7:11-14), Jairus' daughter (Matthew 9:18-19, 23-26; Mark 5:41-43; Luke 8:40-42, 49-56), and Lazarus (Luke 11:1-44).

2) Apostle Peter who raised a woman, "Tabitha, which by interpretation is called Dorcas" (Acts 9:40-41).

3) Apostle Paul who raised "a certain young man named Eutychus" (Acts 20:9-10).

The last two are disciples of the first man. The first denoted triangle. The first man did three people while the last two men did one each. The second denoted triangle. The first two men were together in life, the third man, Paul, was not with them. The third denoted triangle.

▽/△/△/▽ **There are three recorded instances of baptisms with water of someone of authority by named individuals in the New Testament.**

1) Jesus was baptized by John the Baptist in Matthew 3:13-17, Mark 1:9-10, and also along with others, in Luke 3:21 and John 1:28.
2) The apostle Philip baptized "a man of Ethiopia, an eunuch of great authority" in Acts 8:35-39.
3) The apostle Simon Peter baptized with water the Roman Centurion Cornelius and his followers in Acts 10:47-48.

Of these three baptisms the first two are baptisms of a single individual, while the third is of a number of people. This is the basis for the first denoted triangle. Of the three baptisms the first instance is done be a prophet while the next two are done by Apostles of Jesus. This is the basis for the second denoted triangle. Of the three baptisms in and by water only the first instance mentions the name of the body of water, the Jordan river. This is the third denoted triangle. The second instance mentions "they came unto a certain water:. . .and they went down both into the water, both Philip and the eunuch. . ." (Acts 8: 36,38). Of these three baptisms the first two ended with a miraculous event happening. For the first "the Holy Ghost descended in a bodily shape like a dove upon him, and a voice came from heaven" (Luke 3:22). In the second instance "the Spirit of the Lord caught away Philip" in Acts 8:39. There was no such miraculous event for the third baptism but there was the falling of the "Holy Ghost" on them prior to the baptism in Acts 10:44. This is the basis for the fourth denoted triangle. Read in the book of Acts of other baptisms in 2:41, 8:12-13, 16:14-15, 33, 18:8 and 19:5 but none of them are as such as the three mentioned.

▽ **The three deaths where divinity was involved in the New Testament.**

The first two are stated in Acts 5:1-11 when Ananias and his wife Sapphira lied to Peter about the price they got for selling "a possession." The third person is Herod Antipas being "smoted" by the angel of the Lord in Acts 12:21-23. This is the basis for the denoted triangle. These three people also either ". . .gave up" or "yielded up" "the ghost". Here are verses of the deaths:

1) The first person is Ananias who ". . .fell down, and gave up the ghost." in verse 5:5

2) The second person is Sapphira who ". . .fell she down straightway at his feet, and yielded up the ghost" in verse 5:10

3) The third person is King Herod who ". . .he gave not God the glory: and he was eaten of worms, and gave up the ghost" in verse 12:23.

The two men of the three "gave up the ghost". Another identified triangle, ▽. Note the first two people of the three are stated to have "fell . . .down" dead. Another identified triangle, ▽.

△/▽ **There are three Roman governors who ruled the province of "Judaea", i.e. Judea, that are mentioned in the New Testament.**

1) Pontius Pilate the governor who tried Jesus and is mentioned in the scriptures such as Matthew 27:2 and Luke 3:1.

2) Felix the governor (Antonius) who is mentioned in Acts 23:24, 26, and 24:22.

3) Poricus Festus mentioned in Acts 24:26 also in chapters 25 and 26.

Paul appeared before the Roman governors Felix and Festus to tell his story or as some would say to be tried before them. It is stated for both Felix and Festus that they were "willing to shew the Jews a pleasure" in Acts 24:27, "willing to do the Jews a pleasure" in Acts 25:9 as it related to Paul respectively. Pilate was also "willing to do the Jews a pleasure" when he allowed the people to choose between Jesus and Barabbas as mentioned in the Gospels. The first mentioned governor dealt with Jesus while the last two dealt with Paul. The three governors tried an individual. The first denoted triangle. The first two mentioned governors have the title mentioned with their names while the third one does not. His title is mentioned later on in Acts 26:30. The second denoted triangle. Festus was also the successor to Felix. I can conclude that the acts of each of the three governors mentioned were done because of politics. Also note that King Agrippa, who is mentioned in the book of Acts, is a ruler of the Jews when Felix and Festus are Roman governors. Based on other information, the three stated governors were either a Roman Prefect, as was Pontius Pilate, or a Roman Procurator as was Felix and Festus. Another identified triangle, △.

▽/△ Three times the word "Christian(s)" is found in the New Testament:

In the first instance it is plural and in the last two verses it is singular. The first denoted triangle. It is mentioned in the book of Acts twice and in 1 Peter the third time. The second denoted triangle. Here are the verses:

1) Acts 11:26 "And when he had found him, he brought him unto Antioch. And it came to pass, that a whole year they assembled themselves with the church, and taught much people. And the disciples were called Christians first in Antioch."

2) Acts 26:28 "Then Agrippa said unto Paul, Almost thou persuadest me to be a Christian."

3) 1 Peter 4:16 "Yet if any man suffer as a Christian, let him not be ashamed; but let him glorify God on this behalf."

▽ **The three, what some call, "theological virtues" that are stated in 1 Corinthians 13:13.**

"And now abideth faith, hope, charity, these three; but the greatest of these is charity." The first two words of faith and hope are linked by the word trust. The word charity, LOVE, can stand alone of the three and is stated to be the "greatest" of the three. This is the basis for the denoted triangle.

▽ **Read of the glory of the sun, moon, and stars in 1 Corinthians 15:41.**

"There is one glory of the sun, and another glory of the moon, and another glory of the stars." The three are mentioned in Day 4 of Creation in Genesis 1:14-19 where the sun is the greater light and the moon the lesser light and then the stars. The first two of these three are mentioned as lights. The basis for the denoted triangle.

▽ **Read of two of the three Jewish feasts in the New Testament:**

"The feast of unleavened bread drew nigh, which is called the Passover" in Luke 22:1, Matthew 26:17, and Mark 14:1. The "feast of tabernacles" in John 7:2. Both of these are the seven day festivals. The second stated feast, feast of weeks/harvest, is not mentioned in the New Testament but it is called Pentecost which is, in a way, analogous to the same day of the Old Testament. The basis for the denoted triangle.

▽/△ **There are three verses where the word "Pentecost" is stated.**

It is a day in which for Christians, the Holy Spirit descended from heaven onto the apostles in Acts 2:1-4. The three verses are Acts 2:1, 20:16, and 1 Corinthians 16:8. The first two verses of the three state ". . .day of Pentecost. . .". The first denoted triangle. The last two verses of the three relate to the Apostle Paul and his location for the day, in Ephesus. The basis for the second denoted triangle. Apostle Paul was not present or an apostle the first stated day of the three mentioned. Here are the verses:

1) Acts 2:1,3 "And when the day of Pentecost was fully come, they were all with one accord in one place. ³And there appeared unto them cloven tongues like as of fire, and it sat upon each of them."
2) Acts 20:16 "For Paul had determined to sail by Ephesus, because he would not spend the time in Asia: for he hasted, if it were possible for him, to be at Jerusalem the day of Pentecost."
3) 1 Corinthians 16:8 "But I will tarry at Ephesus until Pentecost."

▽ **There are three times the Apostle Paul mentions the word "thrice."**
The first two are in the same verse as it relates to what has happened to him being involved in his vocation, "beaten with rods" and shipwrecked. The third time relates to "a thorn in the flesh" that he has asked the Lord to remove. This is the basis for the denoted triangle. Here are those verses:

2 Corinthians 11:25 "Thrice was I beaten with rods, . . .thrice I suffered shipwreck, . . ."

2 Corinthians 12:8 "For this thing I besought the Lord thrice, that it might depart from me."

△ **There are three verses where ". . .Abba, Father. . ." is stated.**

The first instance Jesus utters it as he makes his appeal to God the Father. The next two verses are connected to the epistles of Paul and are prefaced by "cry" or "crying" respectively. This is the basis for the denoted triangle. Here are the verses:

1) Mark 14:36 "And he said, **Abba, Father**, all things are possible unto thee; take away this cup from me: nevertheless not what I will, but what thou wilt."
2) Romans 8:15 "For ye have not received the spirit of bondage again to fear; but ye have received the Spirit of adoption, whereby we cry, **Abba, Father**."
3) Galatians 4:6 "And because ye are sons, God hath sent forth the Spirit of his Son into your hearts, crying, **Abba, Father**."

▽ **The articles that are listed as a metaphor for battle garments, a spiritual battle in this case, in Ephesians 6:11-17.**

Focused on the mentioning of actual articles of battle i.e. belt, breastplate, shield, helmet, and sword. It is stated twice to put on the "whole armour of God" in verses 11 and 13. The first item to put on is a belt or sash/girdle of truth in verse 14. Next is the item is the breastplate of righteousness in verse 14. Next is the shield of faith in verse 16. The next two articles are the helmet of salvation, and the sword of the Spirit in verse 17. Of the first three articles the belt and breastplate are stated in the same verse with the shield stated alone in verse 16. The basis for the denoted triangle. Also the first two articles mentioned are put on the abdominal and chest areas of the body of the three. The shield can be used by the hand or arm. Another identified triangle, ▽. The sword is the only offensive weapon with the others being defensive or protective gear. The list of battle garments are as follows:

Ephesians 6:11 "Put on the whole armour of God."

Ephesians 6:13 "Wherefore take unto you the whole armour of God."

Ephesians 6:14 "having your loins girt about with truth and having on the breastplate of righteousness."

Ephesians 6:16 "taking the shield of faith."

Ephesians 6:17 "And take the helmet of salvation, and the sword of the Spirit, which is the word of God."

△ **Philippians 2:10 states, "That at the name of Jesus every knee should bow, of things in heaven, and things in earth, and things under the earth."**
The first part of the verse mentions Heaven and the second and third parts mentions "earth." The basis for the denoted triangle.

△ **It is noted three times that in the Bible one should "Walk worthily."**

1) In Ephesians 4:1 ". . .walk worthy of the vocation."
2) In Colossians 1:10 " . . .walk worthy of the Lord."
3) In 1 Thessalonians 2:12 " . . .walk worthy of God."

The last two state of the three "the Lord" and "God" which can be viewed as linked or the same. The basis for the denoted triangle.

▽ **There are three verses where it is stated and/or implied of something "made without hands."**

1) In Mark 14:58 "I will destroy this temple that is made with hands, and within three days I will build another made without hands."

2) In 2 Corinthians 5:1 ". . .we have a building of God, an house not made with hands."

3) In Colossians 2:11 "In whom also ye are circumcised with the circumcision made without hands, in putting off the body of the sins of the flesh by the circumcision of Christ."

The first two relate to the "building of God" as Jesus and God the father respectively. The third focuses on the faith in "Christ." This is the basis for the denoted triangle.

△ **Read three instances where the "saints" rise in the New Testament.**

1) In Matthew 27:52-53 "And the graves were opened; and many bodies of the saints which slept arose, . . . [53]And came out of the graves after his resurrection, and went into the holy city, and appeared unto many."

2) In 1 Corinthians 15:51-53 "Behold, I shew you a mystery; We shall not all sleep, but we shall all be changed, [52] In a moment, in the twinkling of an eye, at the last trump: for the trumpet shall sound, and the dead shall be raised incorruptible, and we shall be changed. [53] For this corruptible must put on incorruption, and this mortal must put on immortality."

3) In 1 Thessalonians 4:16-17 ". . . and the dead in Christ shall rise first: . . .[17]Then we which are alive and remain shall be caught up together with them in the clouds, to meet the Lord in the air: and so shall we ever be with the Lord."

The first instance was an actual event. The next two are stated future events. This is the basis for the denoted triangle.

△/▽ **Read in three books, three verses, where the Apostle Paul states the salutation to fellow believers, "Grace, mercy, and peace from God our/the Father and Jesus Christ/Christ Jesus/the Lord Jesus Christ".**

1) In 1 Timothy 1:2 "Unto Timothy, my own son in the faith: Grace, mercy, and peace, from God our Father and Jesus Christ our Lord."

2) In 2 Timothy 1:2 "To Timothy, my dearly beloved son: Grace, mercy, and peace, from God the Father and Christ Jesus our Lord."

3) In Titus 1:4 "To Titus, mine own son after the common faith: Grace, mercy, and peace, from God the Father and the Lord Jesus Christ our Saviour."

Of the three the first two verses are directed to Timothy while the third at Titus. This is the basis for the first denoted triangle. He calls both men "my own son" of the "faith". The Apostle Paul was the mentor to both Timothy and Titus. Of the three the first verses refer to Jesus as ". . .our Lord" while the third verse refers to him as ". . .our Saviour". The second denoted triangle. Of the three verses the first starts with "Unto" while the last two verses start with "To". Another identified triangle,△. Of the three verses "God our Father" is stated in the first verse while "God the Father" is stated in the last two verses. Another identified triangle,△.

Note the verse of 2 John 1:3 which also provides a similar salutation, "Grace be with you, mercy, and peace, from God the Father, and from the Lord Jesus Christ, the Son of the Father, in truth and love."

△ **There are three verses relating to the phase that states ". . .principalities and powers."**

1) In Ephesians 3:10 ". . .principalities and powers in heavenly places. . ."
2) In Colossians 2:15 "And having spoiled principalities and powers, he made a shew of them openly. . ."
3) In Titus 3:1 "Put them in mind to be subject to principalities and powers. . ."

The last two verses of the three relate to those being on earth in authority. This is the basis for the denoted triangle.

△ **Read in three books that reference the subject of the Rapture, the end-times event, where believers in Christ will be taken from the earth and a trumpet and/or trump is used.**

Note trump and trumpet have been both defined as instruments. Of the three books, for the first the subject matter is stated by Jesus about himself while the last two books the subject matter relates to letters of the apostle Paul to the Corinthians and the Thessalonians. This is the basis for the denoted triangle. Here are the verses

1) Matthew 24:30 "And then shall appear the sign of the Son of man in heaven: and then shall all the tribes of the earth mourn, and they shall see the Son of man coming in the clouds of heaven with power and great glory. [31] And he shall send his angels with a great sound of a trumpet, and they shall gather together his elect from the four winds, from one end of heaven to the other."
2) 1 Corinthians 15:51-52 "Behold, I shew you a mystery; We shall not all sleep, but we shall all be changed, [52]In a moment, in the twinkling of an eye,

at the last trump: for the trumpet shall sound, and the dead shall be raised incorruptible, and we shall be changed."

3) 1 Thessalonians 4:16-17 "For the Lord himself shall descend from heaven with a shout, with the voice of the archangel, and with the trump of God: and the dead in Christ shall rise first: [17] Then we which are alive and remain shall be caught up together with them in the clouds, to meet the Lord in the air: and so shall we ever be with the Lord."

Based on how Jesus ascended into heaven I would think that these "saints" who are "taken" will mimic his ascension.

▽ **1 Thessalonians 5:23 states that, and there are those who say, the created man has three parts.**
"Whole spirit and soul and body" or mind, soul and body. Soul and spirit are closely linked with the body separate. This is the basis for the denoted triangle. The entire verse is as follows, "And the very God of peace sanctify you wholly; and I pray God your whole spirit and soul and body be preserved blameless unto the coming of our Lord Jesus Christ." It could also be viewed that soul and body are linked closely and the spirit is separate. Another identified triangle,▽.

△ **Evangelist(s), a title in the Christian faith, is found three times in the New Testament.**
The first time it is assigned to the Apostle Philip with the next two times being used in general as a Christian title that is given. This is the basis for the denoted triangle. Note that the second time it is plural. Here are the verses:

1) Acts 21:8 "And the next day we that were of Paul's company departed, and came unto Caesarea: and we entered into the house of Philip the evangelist, which was one of the seven; and abode with him."

2) Ephesians 4:11 "And he gave some, apostles; and some, prophets; and some, evangelists; and some, pastors and teachers."

3) 2 Timothy 4:5 "But watch thou in all things, endure afflictions, do the work of an evangelist, make full proof of thy ministry."

▽ **There are three verses that relates to and states Jesus weeping/crying.**

The first two verses relate to Jesus weeping for *others*, Jerusalem and Lazarus, and in the third verse it implies he weeps for himself. This is the basis for the denoted triangle. Here are the verses.

1) Luke 19:41 "And when he was come near, he beheld the city, and wept over it."

2) John 11:35 "Jesus wept."

3) Hebrews 5:7 "Who in the days of his flesh, when he had offered up prayers and supplications with strong crying and tears unto him that was able to save him from death, and was heard in that he feared."

Of the three verses the word "wept" is stated in the first two. Another identified triangle,△.

▽ **There are three things listed in Hebrews 9:4 relating to the contents of the Ark of the Covenant.**

"The Ark of the Covenant overlaid roundabout with gold, wherein was . . ."

1) ". . .the golden pot that had manna, and. . ."

2) "Aaron's rod that budded,"

3) "the tables of the covenant."

221

Of these three things listed the most sacred of the three are "the tables of the covenant." This is the basis for the denoted triangle.

△/▽ The phase "Before the Foundation of the World" is stated three times.

The first time is when Jesus is stating it to God the Father and the last two times are stated by apostles about themselves in Christ and Christ only respectively. The first denoted triangle. The first two verses mentioned are linked to love of the three. The first is the love between Jesus and the Father and the second is between believers and Christ. The third verse pertains to Jesus only. This is basis for the second denoted triangle. The first two verses also imply those that are chosen of God. The third verse relating to Jesus being chosen. Another identified triangle, ▽. Here are the verses:

1) John 17:24 "Father, I will that they also, whom thou hast given me, be with me where I am; that they may behold my glory, which thou hast given me: for thou lovest me before the foundation of the world."
2) Ephesians 1:4 "According as he hath chosen us in him before the foundation of the world, that we should be holy and without blame before him in love."
3) 1 Peter 1:20 "Who verily was foreordained before the foundation of the world, but was manifest in these last times for you."

▽/▽/△ As the four gospels are read you are led to believe that Jesus was crucified on a cross. There are five verses in three books that state or imply that Jesus was hung on a tree.

The first three verses are in the book of Acts which are statements made by the apostles Peter and Paul to others about Jesus' death. Peter is involved in verbally stating the subject matter twice in the first two verses about Jesus. In the third verse Paul implies that it was done and "they took him down from the tree, and laid him in a sepulcher" in his verbal statement to others. This is the basis for the first denoted triangle. Of the four verses of the first two books, the first, second and fourth verses mention the words "hanged" or "hangeth" "on a tree." Of these three verses Peter states twice "hanged on a tree" while Paul in a letter to the Galatians writes "hangeth on a tree." The second denoted triangle. Of the three books the first book, having three verses, are verbal statements made to others by Peter and Paul while the last two books, one verse each, are of letters to others about the subject matter by Paul and Peter respectively. The third denoted triangle. Here are the verses:

1) Acts 5:30 "The God of our fathers raised up Jesus, whom ye slew and hanged on a tree."
2) Acts 10:39 "And we are witnesses of all things which he did both in the land of the Jews, and in Jerusalem; whom they slew and hanged on a tree:"
3) Acts 13:29 "And when they had fulfilled all that was written of him, they took him down from the tree, and laid him in a sepulcher."
4) Galatians 3:13 "Christ hath redeemed us from the curse of the law, being made a curse for us: for it is written, Cursed is every one that hangeth on a tree:"
5) 1 Peter 2:24 "Who his own self bare our sins in his own body on the tree, that we, being dead to sins, should live unto righteousness: by whose stripes ye were healed."

Note, even though the cross was made out of wood you could be led to believe after reading these verses that he was hung from a tree with the use of a rope hanging from a tree limb. This was not the case. He died on the cross.

▽ **1 John 2:16 states that "For all that is in the world, the lust of the flesh, and the lust of the eyes, and the pride of life, is not of the Father, but is of the world."**

The first two items of the three are linked by the word "lust" the third is not. This is the basis for the denoted triangle.

▽ **1 John 5:7 states, "For there are three that bear record in heaven, the Father, the Word, and the Holy Ghost: and these three are one."**

In this case the "Father" and the "Word" are linked in that it is based on God's word that things are done in the universe. This is the basis for the denoted triangle.

Revelation

▽/△ **Revelation Chapters 6-16 states the 21 judgments in three groups of sevens.**

The first two groups of 7s, the seven seals and the seven trumpets, are linked via the seventh seal being opened and releasing the seven trumpets. "And when he had opened the seventh seal, there was silence in heaven about the space of half an hour. [30 minutes] And I saw the seven angels which stood before God; and to them were given seven trumpets" (Revelation 8:1-2). The seven vials/bowls are mentioned separately starting in chapter 16. The first denoted triangle for the three groups of 7s. I also viewed how the first group of 7 is handled by the Lamb of God and the last two groups of 7s are handled by two groups of seven angels. The second denoted triangle. These 21 judgments are preceded by seven messages to seven churches in Revelation chapters 2 and 3. The two triangle diagrams of the two views of the 21 judgments are shown below:

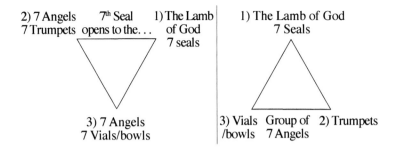

△ The "Lord GOD" will punish those by/to//from/with/ of the sword, by/from/to/with/of the famine, and by/from/ to/with/of the pestilence for their evil acts.[28]

The three mentioned punishments are mostly in that order given in the Bible. Famine and pestilence are linked as non-violent methods of destruction and the sword the opposite. The basis for the denoted triangle. Based on this data it leads me to make a correlation to the last three horsemen of the four of the apocalypse as mentioned in Revelation 6:3-8: the Red Horsemen being associated with war, the Black Horsemen being associated with famine, and the Pale Horsemen called Death being interpreted as pestilence by some accounts. I also noticed the third Black horseman, Famine, is not to hurt the oil and the wine, two of the three items important to ancient Israel. Another identified triangle,△.

Matthew 24:7 states, "For nation shall rise against nation, and kingdom against kingdom: and there shall be famines, and pestilences." I think in this verse of how the first two items in this list is analogous to being "The sword" (war) with famine and pestilence, the three which are mentioned by the prophets Jeremiah and Ezekiel also and the last three

---

[28] Jeremiah 14:12, 21:7, 21:9, 24:10, 27:8, 27:13, 29:17, 29:18, 32:24, 32:36, 34:17, 38:2, 42:17, 42:22, 43:13. Ezekiel 5:12, 6:11, 6:12, 7:15, 12:16. 2 Samuel 24:13. 1 Chronicles 21:12 and 2 Chronicles 20:9.

of the four horsemen in Revelation 6:2-8. "And power was given unto them over the fourth part of the earth, to kill with sword, and with hunger, and with death" (Revelation 6:8). I think of how the three wraths of God: the sword, famine, and pestilence are mentioned by the three men of God Jeremiah, Ezekiel, and Jesus. Of these three men the first two of them are prophets. Another identified triangle,▽.

▽ **Revelation 7:9 states, "After this I beheld, and, lo, a great multitude, which no man could number, of all nations, and kindreds, and people, and tongues."**
The last three have a closer association. Tongues, i.e. speech/language, would be the defining factor that clarifies the other two items of kindreds and people. This is the basis for the denoted triangle. This characteristic would have been more prevalent in biblical times than today. Also one could view the third item in the list of the four as a "singular" item as oppose to the other three which are stated as plural items, nation(s), kindred(s), and tongue(s). Of these three the last two are closely linked as stated previously. Another identified triangle,△. One notes that this verse is similar to Daniel 7:14 which states, "And there was given him dominion, and glory, and a kingdom, that all people, nations, and languages, should serve him." In this verse "people, nations, and languages" the first item could be viewed as a "singular" item as opposed to the other two which are stated as plural items. Another identified triangle,△.

In the context of the two verses mentioned, a congregation pays homage to the man of God, "the Lamb" in Revelation 7:9 and in Daniel 7:14 "the Son of Man" who are one and the same in my view. Daniel 3:4, 7, 4:1, 5:19, and 6:25 also mentions the three item list of people, nations, and languages. Of these they are mentioned as it relates to Nebuchadnezzar and Darius and the empires they ruled over. In Revelation 10:11, 11:9, and 17:15 these three verses mentions many "peoples, and nations, and tongues, and kings," and the "people and kindreds and tongues and nations," and "peoples, and multitudes, and nations, and tongues" respectively. The congregation of these that are listed are of what is done during the end times. Of the three verses mentioned in the book of Revelation the first two verses relate to those who must prophecy or had been speaking to all of the mentioned "groups" while the third verse pertains to a description of the "groups". The groups are called "waters". Another identified triangle, $\triangledown$.

$\triangle$ **Read in Revelation 8:7-12 and 9:15 and 18, as they relate to judgment, the "third part" of trees, grass, sea, sea creatures, ships, rivers, fountain of waters, sun, moon, stars, the day, and men are effected in some adverse manner.**

Mostly being "burnt up" for some of the items mentioned. "By these three . . . by the fire, and by the smoke, and by the brimstone. . ." (verse 9:18). This would indicate that two-thirds part will be spared from that adverse judgment mentioned. The basis for the denoted triangle. Notice in verse 9:18 the three that will be used as part of the judgment fire, smoke and brimstone. Of these three the fire and smoke are closely linked. Another identified triangle, $\triangledown$.

$\triangledown$ **The three woes which are the last three trumpets held by the angels as stated in Revelation 8:13.**

"And I beheld, and heard an angel flying through the midst of heaven, saying with a loud voice, Woe, woe, woe, to the inhabiters of the earth by reason of the other voices of the trumpet of the three angels, which are yet to sound!" The fifth to the seventh trumpets:

1) The Fifth Trumpet/First Woe in Revelation 9:1-12, is where ". . .the shapes of the locusts were like unto horses prepared unto battle." in verse 9:7.

2) The Sixth Trumpet/Second Woe in Revelation 9:13-14 is where horses that have men of battle on

them have ". . .the heads of the horses were as the heads of lions; and out of their mouths issued fire and smoke and brimstone" in verse 9:17.

3) The Seventh Trumpet/Third Woe in Revelation 11:15-19 is where ". . . the nations were angry,. . ." in verse 11:18 because of God's wrath and ". . .the temple of God was opened in heaven, and there was seen in his temple the ark of his testament: and there were lightnings, and voices, and thunderings, and an earthquake, and great hail." in verse 11:19.

The first two of these three woes are linked as having "horses" that are unique for battle. The basis for the denoted triangle. Also note that the first two woes are stated in the same chapter while the third is not. Another identified triangle,▽.

▽ **It is said that all demons were angels at one time and that one-third of all the angels fell according to an interpretation of Revelation 12:4.**
When the dragon, Satan, fell, "And his tail drew the third part of the stars of heaven." This would indicate that he took a third of the angels with him. This would also indicate that two-thirds of the angels are in heaven with God. Two-thirds with God and one-third with Satan. The basis for the denoted triangle.

△ **There are three levels of the Christian Angelic Hierarchy:**

1) The first Sphere/Triad/Choirs are Seraphim, Cherubim, Thrones/Ophanim.
2) The second Sphere/Triad/Choirs are Dominions, Virtues, Powers/Authorities.
3) The third Sphere/Triad/Choirs are Principalities/Rulers, Archangels, Angels.

It is said that the Second Sphere is linked or connected to the Third Sphere. The first subgroup Principalities/Rulers of the third Sphere "appear to collaborate, in power and authority, with the Powers/Authorities" the third subgroup of the Second Sphere and vice versa.[29] This is the basis for the denoted triangle. I can conclude that this is how God's heavenly Angelic Hierarchy is structured, in a triangular format. The Angelic Hierarchical triangle is shown below:

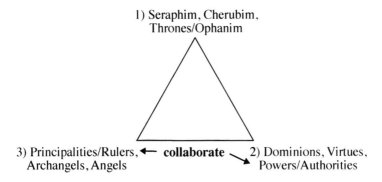

1) Seraphim, Cherubim, Thrones/Ophanim

3) Principalities/Rulers, ◄— **collaborate** ⟍ 2) Dominions, Virtues,
Archangels, Angels ➤ Powers/Authorities

▽ **Read of the three people in Revelation who are killed and are resurrected from the dead.**

In Revelation 11:3-12, the "two witnesses" of God who are killed by Satan, "the beast that ascendeth out of the bottomless pit" and are resurrected ". . .after three days and an half the Spirit of life from God entered into them." In Revelation 13:13-14, the Beast/the Antichrist is "wounded to death; and his deadly wound was healed" and "which had the wound by a sword, and did live." Satan resurrects him by indwelling in him as interpreted by some via the scriptures of Revelation 17:8-13. This is the basis for the denoted triangle. To me this would make sense in that Jesus was raised from the dead so

---

[29] Source - Wikipedia, Christian Angelic Hierarchy, 2012, http://en.wikipedia.org/wiki/Christian_angelic_hierarchy, Retrieved 05.25.2012

why would not the Beast/Antichrist via Satan. Based on all of the referenced scriptures here, Satan is involved in some way with all three. The death of God's two and the resurrection of his man the Antichrist. Another identified triangle, ∇.

△/△ The three descriptions of God's two in Revelation 11:3-4.

They are called "two witnesses" in verse 3, and "two olive trees", and "two candlesticks" in verse 4. Of the three descriptions the last two descriptions are in the fourth verse. The first denoted triangle. Of the three descriptions the first relates to being human while the last two descriptions relate to objects. This is the basis for the second denoted triangle. From another perspective the first two descriptions relate to life while the third description relate to an inanimate object. Another identified triangle, ∇.

△/△/▽/▽ The three beasts of the triumvirate, The unholy trinity, Satan a.k.a Beelzebub, The Anti-Christ (A.C.), and the False Prophet (F.P.)

1) The Beast of the Air, Ephesians 2:2 ". . .the prince of the power of the air. . .", - Great Red Dragon who ". . .having seven heads and ten horns, and seven crowns upon his heads" (Revelation 12:3) a.k.a The Dragon.

2) The Beast of the Sea, an evil fisher of men, ". . .having seven heads and ten horns, and upon his horns ten crowns, and upon his heads the name of blasphemy.", a.k.a The Beast /A.C. (Revelation 13:1).

3) The Beast of the Earth/Field, ". . .he had two horns like a lamb, and he spake as a dragon" a.k.a The F.P. (Revelation 13:11).

The first beast is not stated to be a beast but is described as one, a dragon. The last two "Beasts" of the three are recorded as "Beasts" being of the Sea and Earth. The first denoted triangle. Also the last two of the three, The Anti-Christ and False Prophet are linked as being human based on the interpretation of them and are described in the same chapter of the book. Satan is not in either case who is stated first. The second denoted triangle. The first two beasts of the three, of the air and sea, are connected based on the described characteristics, 7 heads, 10 Horns, and 7 or 10 crowns. The third denoted triangle. Since animals are consider beasts one thinks of Genesis 1:20-25 and the creation of beasts on Days 5 (sea and air) and 6 (earth/field) and makes the correlation that the beasts of Revelation are a mirror image and a dark opposite of the beasts of Creation. It is as if the Bible has come "full circle". The fourth denoted triangle is based on the two days for the beasts of creation. In the order and in the three areas where beasts were created man was given ". . .dominion over the fish of the sea, and over the fowl of the air, and over the cattle, and over all the earth, . . ." as stated in Genesis 1:26. The unholy trinity is the direct opposite of the Holy Trinity. The triangle diagrams of the Beasts are shown below based on my reading:

1) Great Red Dragon
Satan
(Beast of the Air)

3) Beast of the Earth (F.P.)   Human   2) Beast of the Sea (A.C.)

Rev. 12:3, 13:1, 11

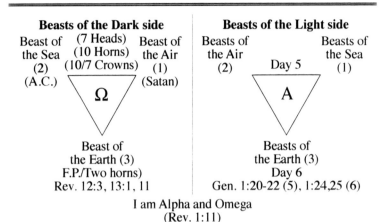

Beasts of the Dark side
Beast of (7 Heads) Beast of
the Sea (10 Horns) the Air
(2) (10/7 Crowns) (1)
(A.C.) (Satan)
Ω

Beast of
the Earth (3)
F.P./Two horns)
Rev. 12:3, 13:1, 11

Beasts of the Light side
Beasts of Beasts of
the Air Day 5 the Sea
(2) (1)
A

Beasts of
the Earth (3)
Day 6
Gen. 1:20-22 (5), 1:24,25 (6)

I am Alpha and Omega
(Rev. 1:11)

△/△ **According to Revelation 13:17 in order to be involved in commerce that is heavily influenced by the Anti-Christ a.k.a. "the Beast", i.e. to "buy or sell", one must have on themselves, the right hand or forehead, one of three items:**

1) the mark of the beast,
2) "or the name of the beast,"
3) "or the number of his name."

Of the three items mentioned the last two items pertain to his "name". This is the basis for the first denoted triangle. Of the three items only one item is required to participate in his trade environment. The second denoted triangle.

▽/△/▽ **Three scriptures in the book of Revelation mention "blood" as part of the judgment of the earth.**
    In the first verse where "hail and fire mingled blood. . .were cast upon the earth" it is stated as part of first angel sounding trumpet. In the second verse where "the third part of the sea became blood," it is stated as part of second angel sounding trumpet. In the third verse where a vial is poured out ". . .upon the sea; and it became as the blood

232

of a dead man" it is stated as part of the second angel who has one of the vials of the wrath of God. Of the three verses the first two verses are linked to trumpets sounding with the third verse associated with an angel and his vial. The first denoted triangle. The last two verses are linked to an angel who is "second" and judgment relating to the "sea." The second denoted triangle. Note the first two verses are in the same chapter of the three where trumpets are used. The third denoted triangle. Here are the verses:

1) Revelation 8:7 "The first angel sounded, and there followed hail and fire mingled with blood, and they were cast upon the earth: and the third part of trees was burnt up, and all green grass was burnt up."
2) Revelation 8:8 "And the second angel sounded, and as it were a great mountain burning with fire was cast into the sea: and the third part of the sea became blood."
3) Revelation 16:3 "And the second angel poured out his vial upon the sea; and it became as the blood of a dead man: and every living soul died in the sea."

▽/▽ **Revelation 17:3-7 describes a woman with a name written on her forehead.**

She is also called the "Whore of Babylon", who sits ". . .upon a scarlet coloured beast . . .having seven heads and ten horns." She has ". . .a golden cup in her hand full of abominations and filthiness of her fornication" and she was ". . .drunken with the blood of the saints, and with the blood of the martyrs of Jesus." In short, based on the description, the pattern is, there is a woman who has a golden cup in her hand, these two being linked, riding a seven headed ten horned beast. This is the basis for the denoted triangle. From another perspective two live corporeal beings, the woman and the beast, and an inanimate object, the golden cup. The second denoted triangle.

△ **Revelation 17:10 stated seven kings are broken into three, a group of five kings and two separate singular kings which is the basis for the denoted triangle.** "And there are seven kings: five are fallen, and one is, and the other is not yet come; and when he cometh, he must continue a short space."

△/▽ **The Beast (A.C.) and the False Prophet (F.P.) are mentioned three times together in the book of Revelation.**
The last two scriptures of the three relate to them going and being in the "lake of fire and brimstone." The first denoted triangle. View the first two verses of the three relating to miracles being done by The Beast and The False Prophet. The second denoted triangle. Note that Satan/Devil is mentioned with them both in the first and third verses. Here are the verses:

1) Revelation 16:13 "And I saw three unclean spirits like frogs come out of the mouth of the dragon, and out of the mouth of the beast, and out of the mouth of the false prophet."
2) Revelation 19:20 "And the beast was taken, and with him the false prophet that wrought miracles before him, with which he deceived them that had received the mark of the beast, and them that worshipped his image. These both were cast alive into a lake of fire burning with brimstone."
3) Revelation 20:10 "And the devil that deceived them was cast into the lake of fire and brimstone, where the beast and the false prophet are, and shall be tormented day and night for ever and ever."

△ **As part of the Judgment of God as recorded in the Book of Revelation the Devil/Satan is "cast out" and/ or down, in part for deceiving the nations of the world, three times after a battle.**

1) He is "cast out into the earth" with his angels after a fight with "Michael and his angels" (Revelation 12:7-9).
2) After a battle of "The Beast and The False Prophet" and their armies, in Revelation 19:19, Satan is chained and imprisoned in a place called the "bottomless pit" (Revelation 20:1-2). A place where there is smoke and heat for a millennium or "a thousand years" (Revelation 9:2).
3) The third time is " . . . when the thousand years are expired, Satan shall be loosed out of his prison,. . ." for ". . .a little season" to ". . .go out to deceive the nations. . ." and " . . .to gather them together to battle" (Revelation 20:3,7-8).

After this third and final battle Satan "the devil that deceived them was cast into the lake of fire and brimstone, where the beast and the false prophet are, and shall be tormented day and night for ever and ever" (Revelation 20:10) a place where there is smoke and heat also akin to the "bottomless pit." For years I wondered why would God let Satan out of the "bottomless pit" after putting him in. Now I see that it is part of His three, triangle, pattern. These three places for Satan are the basis for the denoted triangle with the last two of the three places being linked to smoke and heat, the bottomless pit and Hell respectively.

△/△ **Three particular men are mentioned and described who were or will be human individuals who ended or will end up in Hell/lake of fire.**

The First person, in the parable of the "certain rich man" in Luke 16:22-23 ". . .the rich man also died, and was buried; And in hell he lift up his eyes, being in torments, and seeth Abraham afar off, and Lazarus in his bosom." The second and third persons are The Beast and the False Prophet in Revelation 19:20,

"And the beast was taken, and with him the false prophet that wrought miracles before him, with which he deceived them that had received the mark of the beast, and them that worshipped his image. These both were cast alive into a lake of fire burning with brimstone." In Revelation 20:10 the two are also stated as being there. This is the basis for the first denoted triangle.

Of the three men, the first man is part of a parable and the last two men are of a vision. The second denoted triangle. Read of others who are in that place as stated in 2 Peter 2:4, "For if God spared not the angels that sinned, but cast them down to hell, and delivered them into chains of darkness, to be reserved unto judgment." Also in Revelation 20:13, "And the sea gave up the dead which were in it; and death and hell delivered up the dead which were in them: and they were judged every man according to their works."

Revelation 21:8 lists the types of people that join them, ". . .the fearful, and unbelieving, and the abominable, and murderers,. . .and all liars, shall have their part in the lake which burneth with fire and brimstone." Note: Matthew 5:22, Luke 10:15, Matthew 11:23, 23:15, and 33 lists those who are in danger or risk of going into Hell. Read in three books, four other notable scriptures, relating to the subject of Hell and its purpose in Psalms, Proverbs, and Isaiah:

Psalms 9:17 "The wicked shall be turned into hell, and all the nations that forget God."

Proverbs 27:20 "Hell and destruction are never full; so the eyes of man are never satisfied."

Isaiah 5:14 "Therefore hell hath enlarged herself, and opened her mouth without measure: and their glory, and their multitude, and their pomp, and he that rejoiceth, shall descend into it."

Isaiah 28:15 "Because ye have said, We have made a covenant with death, and with hell are we at agreement; when the overflowing scourge shall pass through, it shall not come unto us: for we have made lies our refuge, and under falsehood have we hid ourselves:"

Of the first three verses, the second and third are linked relating to the size of Hell. An identified triangle,△. Of the last three verses the fourth verse implies some level of comfort with it in my view. Of the three books the last book has two verses while the first two books have one verse each. Another identified triangle,▽.

△ Read three verses relating to God's name being written on his servants in Revelation:

1) In Revelation 3:12 "Him that overcometh will I make a pillar in the temple of my God, and he shall go no more out: and **I will write upon him the name of my God,. . .**".

2) In Revelation 14:1 ". . .a Lamb stood on the mount Sion, and with him an hundred forty and four thousand, **having his Father's name written in their foreheads**."

3) In Revelation 22:4 "And they shall see his face; and **his name shall be in their foreheads**."

The last two of the three are linked to God's name being in the bodily area, the foreheads of his servants. This is the basis for the denoted triangle.

△/▽ There are three verses that state the phrases "King of kings" and "Lord of lords" together relating to Jesus.

Of these three the last two scriptures are in the same book. The first denoted triangle. The first two verses state what he is while the last verse states that the phrases are written on him. The second denoted triangle. Here are the verses:

1) 1 Timothy 6:15 "Which in his times he shall shew, who is the blessed and only Potentate, the King of kings, and Lord of lords."
2) Revelation 17:14 "These shall make war with the Lamb, and the Lamb shall overcome them: for he is Lord of lords, and King of kings: and they that are with him are called, and chosen, and faithful."
3) Revelation 19:16 "And he hath on his vesture and on his thigh a name written, KING OF KINGS, AND LORD OF LORDS."

▽ Three verses are stated relating to the phrase "faithful and true."

Of the three verses the first two verses are about a person called the subject matter, the Lamb of God, while the third verse states "These sayings are. . ." relating to the subject matter. The basis for the denoted triangle. Here are the verses:

1) Revelation 3:14 "And unto the angel of the church of the Laodiceans write; These things saith the Amen, the faithful and true witness, the beginning of the creation of God."
2) Revelation 19:11 "And I saw heaven opened, and behold a white horse; and he that sat upon him was called Faithful and True, and in righteousness he doth judge and make war."
3) Revelation 22:6 "And he said unto me, These sayings are faithful and true: and the Lord God of the holy prophets sent his angel to shew unto his servants the things which must shortly be done."

○✡✝ Examples of the Divine Pattern Across the Old Testament and New Testament

There was no sort of test that was done that could be compared to what was done with the Torah or the first five books of the Bible, but I knew that this divine triangle pattern had to extend across the Old and New Testaments also as it did within the Old and New Testaments separately. Here are some examples of the Divine triangle pattern across the Old and New Testament where one or two of the items are found in either and linked to the same subject matter.

▽ **There are three times Adam and Eve are mentioned together in the Bible by name.**

Twice in the Old Testament, the same book, and once in the New Testament. The basis for the denoted triangle. Here are the verses:

1) Genesis 3:20 "And Adam called his wife's name Eve; because she was the mother of all living."
2) Genesis 4:1 "And Adam knew Eve his wife; and she conceived, and bare Cain, and said, I have gotten a man from the Lord."

3) 1 Timothy 2:13 "For Adam was first formed, then Eve."

▽/▽ Three times Abraham is referred to as a "Friend of God."

1) In 2 Chronicles 20:7 "who didst drive out the inhabitants of this land before thy people Israel, and gavest it to the seed of Abraham thy friend forever?"
2) In Isaiah 41:8 "Jacob whom I have chosen, the seed of Abraham my friend."
3) In James 2:23 "And the scripture was fulfilled which saith, Abraham believed God, and it was imputed unto him for righteousness: and he was called the Friend of God."

The first two verses are stated in the Old Testament, the third in the New Testament. This is the basis for the denoted triangle. Note of the three verses the phrase ". . .the seed of Abraham. . ." is stated in the first two verses. The second denoted triangle.

△/△ There are three instances where the story of Moses is told where he was hidden for three months as a child.

Once in the Old Testament and twice in the New Testament. This is the basis for the denoted triangle. In the first verse it is part of a narrative while the last two verses are statements made by Jesus' followers Stephen and, by many accounts, Paul. The second denoted triangle. Here are the verses:

1) Exodus 2:2 "And the woman conceived, and bare a son: and when she saw him that he was a goodly child, she hid him three months."

2) Acts 7:20 "In which time Moses was born, and was exceeding fair, and nourished up in his father's house three months"

3) Hebrews 11:23 "By faith Moses, when he was born, was hid three months of his parents, because they saw he was a proper child; and they were not afraid of the king's commandment."

△/▽ The angel Gabriel visited three people physically.

The first denoted triangle is formed based on the fact that the last two visits of the three are linked to the proclamations of the birth of sons who are cousins. The second triangle is based on the fact that the first two people of the three Gabriel sees are men of God, a prophet and a priest. Here are the relevant verses:

1) Daniel in Daniel 9:21 "Yea, whiles I was speaking in prayer, even the man Gabriel, whom I had seen in the vision at the beginning, being caused to fly swiftly, touched me about the time of the evening oblation."

2) Zacharias the Priest in Luke 1:19 "And the angel answering said unto him, I am Gabriel, that stand in the presence of God; and am sent to speak unto thee, and to shew thee these glad tidings."

3) Mary in Luke 1:26-27 "And in the sixth month the angel Gabriel was sent from God unto a city of Galilee, named Nazareth, [27] To a virgin espoused to a man whose name was Joseph, of the house of David; and the virgin's name was Mary."

Also note that of the three, two are praised by the angel Gabriel. Daniel in Daniel 9:23 "for thou art greatly beloved," and Mary in Luke 1:28 "Hail, thou that art highly favoured. . . blessed art thou among women."

△/▽ There were three single angelic birth announcements:

1) In Judges 13:3 by unnamed angel as stated in Judges 13:18 "And the angel of the LORD said unto him, Why askest thou thus after my name, seeing it is secret?" This is relating to the birth of Samson.
2) In Luke 1:5-25 by Gabriel and the birth of John, the Baptist
3) In Luke 1:26-38 by Gabriel and the birth of Jesus to Mary.

The first denoted triangle is based on the fact that Gabriel makes the last two announcements of the three and the two are linked where the parents/sons are cousins as well as being in the New Testament. The first two sons were to be Nazarites unto God, Samson and John, in that the angel mentions "drink no wine nor strong drink" in Judges 13:7 and "shall drink neither wine nor strong drink" in Luke 1:15 before they are born. This is an attribute of a Nazarite. The last son Jesus was not a Nazarite. This is the basis for the second denoted triangle. The first son was strong physically and the last two sons were strong spiritually. Another identified triangle,△. The Holy Ghost was involved with the last two births of the three as stated in Luke 1:15 "and he shall be filled with the Holy Ghost, even from his mother's womb" for John the Baptist and in Luke 1:35 "The Holy Ghost shall come upon thee, and the power of the Highest shall overshadow thee" for Jesus. Another identified triangle,△. These last two sons of the three being linked in this manner. Of the three sons the last two names are given by the angel Gabriel John and Jesus in Luke 1:13 and Luke 1:31, also in Matthew 1:21, respectively. Another identified triangle,△. (Note: In Genesis 18:10 "The Lord" with two others, provided the first birth announcement with the foretelling of the birth of Isaac.) A triangle diagram is shown below for the three mentioned sons:

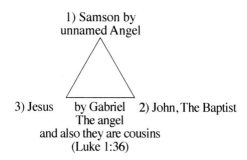

1) Samson by
unnamed Angel

3) Jesus   by Gabriel   2) John, The Baptist
The angel
and also they are cousins
(Luke 1:36)

△/▽ **There are only three men who are considered life-time Nazarites from birth in the Bible.**

1)   Samson in Judges 13:4-5
2)   Samuel in 1 Samuel 1:11
3)   John the Baptist in Luke 1:15.

The definition of a Nazarite, in part, is someone who is to "drink not wine nor strong drink, and eat not any unclean thing" in Judges 13:4, and in Luke 1:15 "no razor shall come on his head." For the first man of the three in Judges 13:5 the title of Nazarite is stated, "the child shall be a Nazarite unto God." This is not stated for the other two men but it is implied based on the scriptures. This is the basis for the first denoted triangle. The first two men are in the Old Testament, Samson and Samuel and it is stated that "no razor shall come upon his head" for both of them. No such statement is recorded for John the Baptist who is in the New Testament. The basis for the second denoted triangle.

△/△ **Three scriptures that state "a sign" as it relates to baby Jesus.**

The first verse is a prophecy while the last two scriptures mention "a sign" that is stated by an angel and a man of God, Simeon, respectively after Jesus' birth. This is the basis for the first denoted triangle. Also the last two verses of the three are the fulfillment of the prophecy in the first verse. Of the three verses, the last two are in the same book and chapter. The second denoted triangle. Here are the verses:

1) Isaiah 7:14 "Therefore the Lord himself shall give you a sign; Behold, a virgin shall conceive, and bear a son, and shall call his name Immanuel."

2) Luke 2:12 "And this shall be a sign unto you; Ye shall find the babe wrapped in swaddling clothes, lying in a manger."

3) Luke 2:34 "And Simeon blessed them, and said unto Mary his mother, Behold, this child is set for the fall and rising again of many in Israel; and for a sign which shall be spoken against."

$\nabla/\triangle$ **Read three verses where a lot of children are stated to have died all at one time.**

1) In Exodus 1:22 "And Pharaoh charged all his people, saying, Every son that is born ye shall cast into the river, and every daughter ye shall save alive."

2) In 2 Kings 2:24 "[Prophet Elisha] And he turned back, and looked on them, and cursed them in the name of the LORD. And there came forth two she bears out of the wood, and tare forty and two children of them."

3) In Matthew 2:16 "Then Herod, when he saw that he was mocked of the wise men, was exceeding wroth, and sent forth, and slew all the children that were in Bethlehem."

The first two instances are of the Old Testament and the third of New Testament. The basis for the first denoted triangle. In the first verse the focus is on just the sons while the last two verses the plural "children" could include girls also. The basis for the second denoted triangle. Note in Exodus 12:29 children and others died also as it states, "At midnight the LORD struck down all the firstborn in the land of Egypt, from the firstborn of Pharaoh who sat on his throne to the firstborn of the prisoner who was in the dungeon, and all the firstborn of the livestock." This is the tenth plague that was done against the Egyptians.

▽/△ **There are three men who began to reign and/or begin their work assigned to them of God at the age of thirty years old that were not Levites.**

The Levites were those who had to do the service of the Lord from thirty years old to fifty as indicated in Numbers 4. The three men were Joseph in Genesis 41:46, David in 2 Samuel 5:4, and Jesus in Luke 3:23. The first two men are of the Old Testament and who became noted leaders, governor and King, and it is stated that they both were "thirty years old." The third is in the New Testament and at the start of his ministry on earth it is stated "thirty years of age." The first denoted triangle. Jesus is also referred to as "Son of David" in sixteen verses (Matthew 1:1, 20, 9:27, 12:23, 15:22, 20:30, 21:9, 15, 22:42; Mark 10:47, 48, 12:45; Luke 3:31, 18:38-39. In my view this links the last two men of the three. The second denoted triangle. Here are the verses:

1) Genesis 41:46 "And Joseph was thirty years old when he stood before Pharaoh king of Egypt. And Joseph went out from the presence of Pharaoh, and went throughout all the land of Egypt" (governor over Egypt in verse 41:41).

2) 2 Samuel 5:4 "David was thirty years old when he began to reign, and he reigned forty years."

3) Luke 3:23 "And Jesus himself began to be about thirty years of age, being (as was supposed) the son of Joseph, which was the son of Heli" (when he started his ministry as it has been implied).

▽ **There are three men who for forty days and forty nights are mentioned going without food and water or fasting.**

The first is Moses (Exodus 24:18, 34:28-29; Deuteronomy 9:18, 25, 10:10). He is stated doing this activity twice. The second is Elijah (1 Kings 19:8). These two are linked to this activity by being on and/or around Mount Sinai/Horeb. The third is Jesus who fasted in the wilderness (Matthew 4:1-2). This is the basis for the denoted triangle.

▽ **There are three only sons of women who were raised from the dead:**

1) In 1 Kings 17:8-23 the Prophet Elijah raised the only son of a "widow woman" of Zarephath in vs. 21-22 ". . .he stretched himself upon the child three times, and cried unto the LORD,. . .and the soul of the child came into him again, and he revived."

2) In 2 Kings 4:8-37 the Prophet Elisha raised the only son of a "Shunammite woman" after he pronounces that she would have one being barren in verse 32 " . . .when Elisha was come into the house, behold, the child was dead, and laid upon his bed", and in verse 34 ". . .he went up, and lay upon the child, and put his mouth upon his mouth, and his eyes upon his eyes, and his hands upon his hands: and he stretched himself upon the child." In verse 35 "he returned, and walked in the house to and fro; and went up, and

stretched himself upon him: and the child sneezed seven times, and the child opened his eyes."

3) Jesus raised the only son of a widow from Nain in Luke 7:14 "And he said, Young man, I say unto thee, Arise."

The first two of the three are linked in the Old Testament and also Elijah was Elisha's master at one point. This is the basis for the denoted triangle.

▽/▽/▽ **There are three verses where the phrase "twelve years old" is stated.**

The first two verses of the three are almost identical and they refer to Manasseh, the son of King Hezekiah of Judah becoming the new king. The third scripture pertains to Jesus in the Temple in Jerusalem. This is the first denoted triangle. Here are the verses:

1) 2 Kings 21:1 "Manasseh was twelve years old when he began to reign, and reigned fifty and five years in Jerusalem. And his mother's name was Hephzibah."

2) 2 Chronicles 33:1 "Manasseh was twelve years old when he began to reign, and he reigned fifty and five years in Jerusalem."

3) Luke 2:42 "And when he was twelve years old, they went up to Jerusalem after the custom of the feast."

From another perspective there are three children who are mentioned in the Bible who were twelve years old or "twelve years" of age. The first two children are Manasseh and Jesus and the third child is the daughter of Jairus "a ruler of the synagogue" who Jesus raised from the dead. Her age is mentioned in Mark 5:42 and Luke 8:42. Here are those verses:

Mark 5:42 "And straightway the damsel arose, and walked; for she was of the age of twelve years. And they were astonished with a great astonishment."

Luke 8:42 "For he had one only daughter, about twelve years of age, and she lay a dying. But as he went the people thronged him."

Of these three children, the first two are boys, and kings and the third a girl. The second denoted triangle. Of the three children the names of the first two are given. For the third it is not. The third denoted triangle. For the first two children "twelve years old" is stated for them. The third "twelve years of age" is stated. Another identified triangle, ▽.

△ **There are three instances where a multitude of people were fed miraculously**.

1) By the Prophet Elisha in 2 Kings 4:38-44 (100 men)
2) By Jesus in Matthew 14:17-21 (5000 men), Mark 6:38, 44 (5000 men), Luke 9:14-17 (5000 men), John 6:9-13 (5000 men)
3) By Jesus again in Matthew 15:34, 38 (4000), Mark 8:1-9 (4000).

In the Old Testament instance the Prophet Elisha with a "pot of pottage" that was thought to contain "death in the pot" (2 Kings 4:40) and makes it harmless. Note that twenty loaves is also mentioned as being a part of their meal in verse 4:42. In the Old Testament instance one hundred is the number as having been fed while the last two instances mention thousands. In the two references mentioned in the New Testament a very little amount of "loaves and fishes" were used to feed the multitudes. The basis for the denoted triangle. Elisha was involved in one and Jesus the last two.

Another identified triangle,△. A Triangle diagram is shown below for the stated activity:

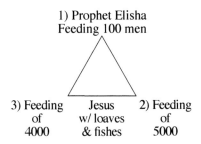

1) Prophet Elisha
Feeding 100 men

3) Feeding
of
4000

Jesus
w/ loaves
& fishes

2) Feeding
of
5000

△/△ **There are three verses that use three words to describe a particular animal that is called a donkey**.

The donkey is referred to and described by the three words of colt, foal, and ass. The first verse is Jacob describing, in part, his fourth son Judah as Jacob is about to die. The last two verses are linked in that the second verse is a prophecy about Jesus and the third verse is the fulfillment of that prophecy telling of how Jesus was riding/sitting on the animal in the city of Jerusalem. This is the basis for the first denoted triangle. The last two verses of the three state ". . .a colt the foal of an ass." The use of the three words together. The second denoted triangle. Here are the verses:

1) Genesis 49:11 "Binding his **foal** unto the vine, and his **ass's colt** unto the choice vine; he washed his garments in wine, and his clothes in the blood of grapes."

2) Zechariah 9:9 "Rejoice greatly, O daughter of Zion; shout, O daughter of Jerusalem: behold, thy King cometh unto thee: he is just, and having salvation; lowly, and riding upon an ass, and upon a **colt the foal of an ass**."

3) Matthew 21:5 "Tell ye the daughter of Sion, Behold, thy King cometh unto thee, meek, and sitting upon an ass, and a **colt the foal of an ass.**"

Also read in John 12:15, "Fear not, daughter of Sion: behold, thy King cometh, sitting on an ass's colt" that states the same prophetic event, but it only uses two of the three words. Of the three verses ". . .daughter of Zion/Sion. . . ." is stated in the last two verses. Another identified triangle,△. Of the three words colt and foal both are used to describe a young animal. Another identified triangle,▽.

△/▽/▽ **Three people in four scriptures mention the title of Messiah/Messias.**
The first person is the angel Gabriel who visits the prophet Daniel, while the last two people are Andrew the brother of Simon Peter and the adulterous woman at the well who tells others. The last two people associate the title with Jesus. This is the basis for the first denoted triangle. Notice that the two men mention the term first and second with a woman being the third person. The basis for the second denoted triangle. The first two are men who are righteous and the third person is a sinner. The third denoted triangle. Of the three people, the last two are mentioned in the same book. Another identified triangle,△. Of the three, the first person is from heaven. Another identified triangle,△. Of the three individuals the names of the first two of them are given. Another denoted triangle,▽. Here are the verses:

1) Daniel 9:25 "Know therefore and understand, that from the going forth of the commandment to restore and to build Jerusalem unto the **Messiah** the Prince shall be seven weeks, and threescore and two weeks: the street shall be built again, and the wall, even in troublous times."

2) Daniel 9:26 "And after threescore and two weeks shall **Messiah** be cut off, but not for himself: and the people of the prince that shall come shall destroy the city and the sanctuary; and the end thereof shall be with a flood, and unto the end of the war desolations are determined."

3) John 1:41 "He first findeth his own brother Simon, and saith unto him, We have found the **Messias**, which is, being interpreted, the Christ."

4) John 4:25 "The woman saith unto him, I know that **Messias** cometh, which is called Christ: when he is come, he will tell us all things."

▽/△/▽/▽ **Three men who displayed unflattering pride.**

1) **Naaman** who was a leper displays his pride when he is told to "[10]. . .Go and wash in Jordan seven times, and thy flesh shall come again to thee, and thou shalt be clean.[11]But Naaman was wroth, and went away, and said, Behold, I thought, He will surely come out to me, and stand, and call on the name of the LORD his God, and strike his hand over the place, and recover the leper. [12]Are not Abana and Pharpar, rivers of Damascus, better than all the waters of Israel? may I not wash in them, and be clean? So he turned and went away in a rage" (2 Kings 5:10-12). Naaman eventually did what he was told and was "cleansed" of his leprosy.

2) **King Uzziah of Judah** who "[16]. . .went into the temple of the LORD to burn incense upon the altar of incense. [18]And they withstood Uzziah the king, and said unto him, It appertaineth not unto thee, Uzziah, to burn incense unto the LORD, but to the priests the sons of Aaron, that are consecrated to burn incense: go out of the sanctuary; for thou hast

trespassed; neither shall it be for thine honour from the LORD God. [19] Then Uzziah was wroth, and had a censer in his hand to burn incense: and while he was wroth with the priests, the leprosy even rose up in his forehead before the priests in the house of the LORD, from beside the incense altar. [20]And Azariah the chief priest, and all the priests, looked upon him, and, behold, he was leprous in his forehead, and they thrust him out from thence; yea, himself hasted also to go out, because the LORD had smitten him. [21] And Uzziah the king was a leper unto the day of his death, and dwelt in a several house, being a leper; for he was cut off from the house of the LORD: and Jotham his son was over the king's house, judging the people of the land" (2 Chronicles 26:16-21).

3) **The Pharisee** of Jesus' parable, "[10]Two men went up into the temple to pray; the one a Pharisee, and the other a publican. [11]The Pharisee stood and prayed thus with himself, God, I thank thee, that I am not as other men are, extortioners, unjust, adulterers, or even as this publican. [12] I fast twice in the week, I give tithes of all that I possess. [13] And the publican, standing afar off, would not lift up so much as his eyes unto heaven, but smote upon his breast, saying, God be merciful to me a sinner. [14] I tell you, this man went down to his house justified rather than the other: for every one that exalteth himself shall be abased; and he that humbleth himself shall be exalted" (Luke 18:10-14).

The first two men are in the Old Testament and the third in the New Testament. The first denoted triangle. The last two men showed their pride in the temple and first man outside. The second denoted triangle. The first two men are recorded as actual events while the third pertains to a parable. The third denoted triangle. Of the three men, the issue of leprosy is mentioned for the first two men. The fourth denoted triangle. There are others who are recorded that displayed a proud heart such as King Saul of 1 Samuel 15, King Hezekiah of Judah in 2 Chronicles 32:25-26, Sennacherib King of Assyria via his servants in 2 Kings 18-19 and Isaiah 37, and Herod in Acts 12:21-23. The three that are mentioned displayed their pride directed towards a unique person, the man of God, Elisha, or in a unique place, the Temple. For these three the stories were short very detailed in my view.

▽/▽ There are three instances where Satan had divine discussions:

1) In Job 1:6-12
2) In Job 2:1-6
3) In the Gospels of Matthew 4:1-11, Mark 1:12-13, and Luke 4:1-13.

The first two instances relate to a discussion between God and Satan about Job, and God allowing Satan to tempt and afflict Job to test his faith. The third instance is in the three Gospels where Satan tries three ways to tempt Jesus. This is the basis for the first denoted triangle. Two of the discussions were held in heaven and the third was held on earth with Jesus. The second denoted triangle.

△ There are three verses where it is stated that "the sun" shall be darken and "the moon" not give her light.

All of The verses relate to God's wrath. Of the three verses the last two verses mentions that "after . . . tribulation" the actions of the sun and moon are done. The basis for the denoted triangle. Here are the verses:

1) Isaiah 13:10 "For the stars of heaven and the constellations thereof shall not give their light: the sun shall

be darkened in his going forth, and the moon shall not cause her light to shine."

2) Matthew 24:29 "Immediately after the tribulation of those days shall the sun be darkened, and the moon shall not give her light, and the stars shall fall from heaven, and the powers of the heavens shall be shaken:"

3) Mark 13:24 "But in those days, after that tribulation, the sun shall be darkened, and the moon shall not give her light,"

Note the verse of Ezekiel 32:7 "And when I shall put thee out, I will cover the heaven, and make the stars thereof dark; I will cover the sun with a cloud, and the moon shall not give her light."

▽ **Read of the three instances, four verses, where it is stated that the kingdom would be given to someone unto ". . .the half of the kingdom".**

There were two instances where it is addressed to queen Esther, twice in the first instance, in the first two verses, and once in the second instance. The third instance it is addressed to Herodias' daughter Salome by King Herod. This is the basis for the denoted triangle. The phrase is stated to two women. Here are the verses:

1) Esther 5:3 "Then said the king unto her, What wilt thou, queen Esther? and what is thy request? it shall be even given thee to the half of the kingdom."

2) Esther 5:6 "And the king said unto Esther at the banquet of wine, What is thy petition? and it shall be granted thee: and what is thy request? even to the half of the kingdom it shall be performed."

3) Esther 7:2 "And the king said again unto Esther on the second day at the banquet of wine, What is thy

petition, queen Esther? and it shall be granted thee: and what is thy request? and it shall be performed, even to the half of the kingdom."

4) Mark 6:23 "And he sware unto her, Whatsoever thou shalt ask of me, I will give it thee, unto the half of my kingdom."

△/△ Read of three very evil wives in the Bible who had people punished without just cause.

The first wife is Potiphar's wife who accuses Joseph falsely in front of her husband of him trying to force himself on her and had him thrown in prison in Genesis 39:7-20. The second wife is Jezebel,queen to king Ahab, who had God's prophets killed in 1Kings 18:4 and who also has a man named Naboth accused falsely to gain his land and had him killed in 1 Kings 21. The third wife is Herodias, married to Herod his brother who was alive, who had John the Baptist killed via Salome her daughter in Matthew 14:6-12, Mark 6:19-28. Of these three women the last two women has someone killed while the first had someone imprisoned. This is the basis for the first denoted triangle. The last two wives of the three are rulers/queens of the land, Israel and Judah/Judea respectively. The second denoted triangle.

△/△ Three times in the Bible it is stated "My God, My God, why hast thou forsaken me?"

Of the three verses the first verse is considered a prophecy. The next verses are the words of Jesus as he is on his cross. The first denoted triangle. The question is made at the end of the last two verses being the translation. The second denoted triangle. Here are the verses:

1) Psalms 22:1 "My God, my God, why hast thou forsaken me? Why art thou so far from helping me, and from the words of my roaring?"

2) Matthew 27:46 "And about the ninth hour Jesus cried with a loud voice, saying, Eli, Eli, lama sabachthani? that is to say, My God, my God, why hast thou forsaken me?"

3) Mark 15:34 "And at the ninth hour Jesus cried with a loud voice, saying, Eloi, Eloi, lama sabachthani? which is, being interpreted, My God, my God, why hast thou forsaken me?"

▽/△ **Three people in the Bible had dream/visions of the "latter days" or what some refer to as the "end times" pertaining to an image or Beasts.**

1) King Nebuchadnezzar and the statue of metals and clay in Daniel 2:1-45

2) Daniel and the four beasts in Daniel 7:2-27

3) John of Patmos, Book of Revelation, and the twenty-one judgments

The first two men of the three have a dream/vision that parallel each other as it relates to interpreted kingdoms represented by metals for King Nebuchadnezzar and beasts for Daniel. The first denoted triangle. The last two men of the three are linked by having visions of "Beasts" coming out of the sea in Daniel 7:3, 6 and Revelation 13:1-2 respectively and both state a beast that is "like . . . a leopard. . . ." The second denoted triangle.

Also the last two men of the three have a vision of the archangel Michael in Daniel 12:1-2, "And at that time shall Michael stand up, the great prince which standeth for the children of thy people: and there shall be a time of trouble, such as never was since there was a nation even to that same time: and at that time thy people shall be delivered, every one that shall be found written in the book. ²And many of them that sleep in the dust of the earth shall awake, some to everlasting life, and some to shame and everlasting contempt." In Revelation 12:7 it states, "And there was war in heaven: Michael and his angels fought against the dragon; and the dragon fought and his angels". Another identified triangle,△.

The first two men of the three are recorded in the same book and existed together with Daniel being a man of God to the King. Another identified triangle,▽. The last two men of the three are men of God. Another identified triangle,△. Of the three men, Daniel and John were told about the "seal" of a "book." "But thou, O Daniel, shut up the words, and seal the book, even to the time of the end" in Daniel 12:4, and John in Revelation 22:10, "And he saith unto me, Seal not the sayings of the prophecy of this book". Another identified triangle,△.

Of the three men, the last two men's visions mention the man called "the Son of man" who will be involved in "end times" in Daniel 7:13, Revelation 1:13, and 14:14. Another identified triangle,△. These last three verses mentioned, the last two are in the same book. Another identified triangle,△. Of the three men, the last two mention in their visions they saw "the books were opened" as it relates to the judgment of God. Another identified triangle,△. Note, the book of Daniel is the twenty-seventh book of the Old Testament and the book of Revelation is the twenty-seventh book of the New Testament.

▽ **There a number of scriptures that refer to getting wisdom, knowledge, and understanding.**[30]

Of these three, understanding is greatest of them. There are those who say Knowledge is intellect and Wisdom is divine. In my view, without understanding neither of the

---

[30]   Exodus 31:3, Exodus 35:31, Proverbs 2:6, Isaiah 11:2, Daniel 1:4, Daniel 1:17, Daniel 2:21, and Colossians 1:9

first two are fruitful. Wisdom and Knowledge both have to be ascertained from someplace. This is the basis for the denoted triangle.

▽ **There are three instances where a person delivered a major list of items to the people that was of divinity.**
The first and second are the ten commandments that were given by God the Father twice to Moses in Exodus 32:19 and 34:1, and recorded two times in Exodus 20:3-17 and Deuteronomy 5:7-21. Note that Moses broke the first stone list.

The third list is the Beatitudes given by Jesus, God the Son, in Matthew 5:1-12/Luke 6:20-26. God the father wrote it twice as stated by Exodus 34:1, and Jesus spoke it once. This is the basis for the denoted triangle.

Note that in reading Deuteronomy 5:22, God the Father also spoke the Ten Commandments to the people, "out of the midst of the fire, of the cloud, and of the thick darkness." Two of the three members of the Holy Trinity, the Father and the Son, were involved with the giving of a major list. Another identified triangle, ▽.

▽ **There are a number of scriptures that mention together the three metals gold, silver, and brass (or bronze) predominately in that order.**[31]
First two metals that are mentioned are precious metals and the third is not. The basis for the denoted triangle. Note that these metals were used as part of the construction of the Tabernacle in Exodus 26-27, 35-38, and 40. Gold was used as part of the construction of Solomon's Temple (1 Kings 6:20-22, 30, 32, 7:50; 2 Kings 18:16; 2 Chronicles 3:4-10,

---

[31]   Exo. 25:3, 31:4, 35:5, 35:32; Num. 31:22; Jos. 6:19, 6:24, 22:8; 2 Sam. 8:10; 1 Chr. 18:10, 22:14, 22:16, 29:2; 2 Chr. 2:7, 2:14; Isa. 60:17; Dan. 2:32, 2:35, 2:45, 5:4, 5:23; Matt. 10:9; Rev. 9:20.

4:22). The use of silver and brass are mentioned as being a part of the materials used for the temple construction in 1 Chronicles 29:4 and 2 Chronicles 4:9 respectively. None of the metals are recorded being used in the construction of the second temple. It is mentioned that "vessels" were made from these three metals also.

▽ Blindness was used as a weapon physically three times by those of God.

The first two verses mention a host of people were made blind, the third mentions a single person. This is the basis for the denoted triangle. The first two instances are in the Old Testament and the third in the New Testament,. Another identified triangle,▽. Of the three instances angles were involved in the act in the first verse. Another identified triangle,△. Here are the verses:

1) Genesis 19:11 "And they [the two angels] smote the men that were at the door of the house with blindness, both small and great: so that they wearied themselves to find the door."

2) 2 Kings 6:18 "And when they came down to him, Elisha prayed unto the LORD, and said, Smite this people, I pray thee, with blindness. And he smote them with blindness according to the word of Elisha."

3) Acts 13:11 "And now, behold, the hand of the Lord is upon thee, and thou shalt be blind, not seeing the sun for a season. And immediately there fell on him a mist and a darkness; and he went about seeking some to lead him by the hand."

Note that in Deuteronomy 28:28 and Zechariah 12:4 there is the threat of it being used, but there is no notable actual follow-up event.

▽/△/▽ **There are three men who were named Saul in the Bible.**

1) The first man is recorded in Genesis 36:37-38 as the sixth King in the land of Edom the descendants of Esau.
2) The second man is King Saul the first king of Israel as recorded in the books 1st and 2nd Samuel and 1st Chronicles. He is also mentioned in Psalms 18:1, 52:1, and 54:1.
3) The third man named Saul of Tarsus, a persecutor of Christians who later had his name changed to Paul and became an apostle of Jesus (Acts 7:58 – Act 26:14).

Of the three men, the first two are kings. The basis for the first denoted triangle. Of the three men, the last two are descendants of Israel. The second denoted triangle. Of the three men, the first two are in the Old Testament. The third denoted triangle.

▽/▽ **There are four Ethiopian men mentioned in the Bible:**

1) "Tirhakah King of Ethiopia" who came and fought for Hezekiah the King of Judah against the Assyrians in 2 Kings 19:9 and Isaiah 37:9.
2) (King) Zerah the Ethiopian who came up against Asa the King of Judah in 2 Chronicles 14:9-12.
3) Ebedmelech the Ethiopian eunuch servant in the house of Zedekiah the king of Judah in Jeremiah 38:7, 10, and 39:16 and it is noted that he is mentioned by some to be an official.
4) "A man of Ethiopia" a eunuch of "great authority" under the queen of the Ethiopians named Candace

who "had come to Jerusalem for to worship" in Acts 8:27.

Of the first three mentioned who are in the Old Testament, the first two are Kings who had hosts of men. The third works for a king. The first denoted triangle. The first three men are named with the third being a eunuch. The second denoted triangle. The first, third, and fourth men were in Judah but not against it, and of these three the last two are eunuchs. Another identified triangle,△. Note the unnamed second wife of Moses in Numbers 12:1 was an Ethiopian.

▽ There are four instances where three individuals came to visit or see a person:

1) "The LORD" and two companions came to see Abraham in Genesis 18:2 "And he lift up his eyes and looked, and, lo, three men stood by him: and when he saw them, he ran to meet them from the tent door, and bowed himself toward the ground."

2) Three friends of Job's came to see him when he was ill and going through his trial in Job 2:11 "Now when Job's three friends heard of all this evil that was come upon him, they came everyone from his own place; Eliphaz the Temanite, and Bildad the Shuhite, and Zophar the Naamathite: for they had made an appointment together to come to mourn with him and to comfort him."

3) Three Magi/wisemen/kings came to see Jesus when he was a baby in Matthew 2:11 ". . .they saw the young child with Mary his mother, and fell down, and worshipped him: and when they had opened their treasures, they presented unto him gifts; gold, and frankincense, and myrrh." The number is not

given, but it is assumed to be three based on tradition and the number of gifts he was given, three.

4) Three men came for Peter as messengers of Cornelius of Caesarea in Acts 10:19-20 "While Peter thought on the vision, the Spirit said unto him, Behold, three men seek thee. Arise therefore, and get thee down, and go with them, doubting nothing: for I have sent them."

In all four instances someone of God is being visited. Of these four instances, the most significant visit of three individuals to a person is the third instance. The three men came to worship someone. The first two instances are in the Old Testament and the third instance being significant in the New Testament. With the third instance being more significant, the first, the third, and fourth who had the three visitors the first two instances of these three the groups came to visit a "friend". This is the basis for the denoted triangle. I noticed that in 1 Corinthians 16:17 Apostle Paul states, regarding three men, "I am glad of the coming of Stephanas and Fortunatus and Achaicus: for that which was lacking on your part they have supplied." There is no mention if these three are coming to see anyone in particular with Paul being in Ephesus as 1 Corinthians 16:8 suggests.

△/▽ There are four verses that state "hath put all things . . .under his feet" implying that God had put all things under someone feet.

Of the four verses the first, second, and fourth verses mention the words "Thou" or "he" implicating God the father as the possessor of the "things" where the last two verses of these three are in the New testament. This is the basis first denoted triangle. Of the four verses, the first verse refers to "man" no one in particular. The last three verses which are in the New Testament pertain to Jesus and what God the father has done for him. The apostle Paul is associated as being the author of the first two verses of the three for certain. The third verse is attributed to him, but there is no evidence recorded to support that notion, it is said. This is the basis for the second denoted triangle. Here are the verses:

1) Psalms 8:6 "Thou madest him to have dominion over the works of thy hands; thou hast put all things under his feet:"
2) 1 Corinthians 15:27 "For he hath put all things under his feet. But when he saith all things are put under him, it is manifest that he is excepted, which did put all things under him."
3) Ephesians 1:22 "And hath put all things under his feet, and gave him to be the head over all things to the church,"
4) Hebrews 2:8 "Thou hast put all things in subjection under his feet. For in that he put all in subjection under him, he left nothing that is not put under him. But now we see not yet all things put under him."

▽ **Three times an array of twelve precious stones is mentioned:**

1) In Exodus 28:15-21
2) In Exodus 39:6-14
3) In Revelation 21:18-20

The first two times, the twelve stones are mentioned as it relates to the Hoshen / breastplate that is worn by the Jewish High Priest and the third time it is stated a "wall of the city were garnished with all manner of precious stones" with these stones listed similar to the breastplate. This is the basis for the denoted triangle. Also the first two times are in the

Old Testament and the third in the New Testament. Another identified triangle,▽.

△ There are three verses relating to a mark/seal on the foreheads of God's people.

1) In Ezekiel 9:4 "a mark upon the foreheads of the men that sigh and that cry for all the abominations that be done in the midst thereof."
2) In Revelation 7:3 "Hurt not the earth,. . .till we have sealed the servants of our God in their foreheads."
3) In Revelation 9:4 ". . .should not hurt the grass of the earth, . . .but those men which have not the seal of God in their foreheads."

The last two of the three are in the same book and relate to the "hurt" of the earth and the seal of God. The basis for the denoted triangle.

▽ There are three references to the number 666 in the Bible in the format of "six hundred . . . threescore and six" relating to a man:

1) In 1 Kings 10:14 "Now the weight of gold that came to Solomon in one year was six hundred threescore and six talents of gold. . . ."
2) In 2 Chronicles 9:13 "Now the weight of gold that came to Solomon in one year was six hundred and threescore and six talents of gold."
3) In Revelation 13:18 "Here is wisdom. Let him that hath understanding count the number of the beast: for it is the number of a man; and his number is Six hundred threescore and six."

The first two verses are in the Old Testament and relate to the weight in talents (1 talent = 75 U.S. pounds/34.3 kilograms or 49,950lbs / 22,843.8kg) of gold "in one year" to King Solomon, and the third is in the New Testament relating to a man, The Beast of the Sea, The Anti-Christ. This is the basis for the denoted triangle. The first two references are in the Old Testament and one in the New Testament. Another identified triangle, ▽.

△/▽ Three verses relate to the sun turning into darkness and the moon into blood.

1) In Joel 2:31 "The sun shall be turned into darkness, and the moon into blood, before the great and the terrible day of the LORD come."
2) In Acts 2:20 "The sun shall be turned into darkness, and the moon into blood, before that great and notable day of the Lord come."
3) In Revelation 6:12 "when he had opened the sixth seal, the sun became black as sackcloth of hair, and the moon became as blood."

All three verses relate to the Day of Judgment. The first one is in the Old Testament and the last two are in the New Testament. The first denoted triangle. Notice also that the first two verses are virtually identical. The third is not. The second denoted triangle.

△ Three beasts in the Bible are stated to have "ten horns."

1) In Daniel 7:7 the Unknown beast, "a fourth beast, dreadful and terrible, and strong exceedingly; and it had great iron teeth: . . . and it had ten horns."

2) In Revelation 12:3 "and behold a great red dragon, having seven heads and ten horns, and seven crowns upon his heads."

3) In Revelation 13:1 "And I stood upon the sand of the sea, and saw a beast rise up out of the sea, having seven heads and ten horns."

The last two of the three beasts are linked to Revelation and in their actions and description. The basis for the denoted triangle. In Daniel 7:24, the fourth beast, and in Revelation 17:12, the second beast, both state that "the ten horns . . .are ten kings."

▽ **Read of the three who sacrificed their one and only child.**

1) In Genesis 22:12 with Abraham and Isaac ". . .for now I know that thou fearest God, seeing thou hast not withheld thy son, thine only son from me."

2) In Judges 11:34-36 with Jephthah and his vow to God and his only daughter ". . .and she was his only child; beside her he had neither son nor daughter. . . . for I have opened my mouth unto the LORD, and I cannot go back."

3) In John 3:16 God's "only begottten son" Jesus.

The first two are of men in the Old Testament and the third is of the Divine in the New Testament. The basis for the denoted triangle.

▽/ △/▽ **There were three people who ascended into heaven in corporeal form.**

The first two did it without dying, Enoch in Genesis 5:22-24/Hebrews 11:5 and the book of Jasher 3:36, and Elijah in 2 Kings 2:11. These two both on chariots with horses of fire in a whirlwind. The third person is Jesus was died first rose from the dead and then ascended in Mark 16:19, Luke 24:50-51, and Acts 1:9-12. This is the basis for the first denoted triangle. Note: Jesus was astral and corporeal at the same time because He is God. The last two ascensions are detailed in the Bible while the first one is not of the three. The second denoted triangle. The first two are men are mentioned in the Old Testament while the third in the New Testament. The third denoted triangle. Note, God used a whirlwind one other time in Job chapters 38-42 to speak. Another identified triangle,$\triangledown$. Over the decades I heard a number of people say, and read in the bible, that three people ascended into heaven Enoch, Elijah, and Jesus. No one in my entire life ever stated how Enoch ascended into heaven until I read it in the Book of Jasher. The last two men I was told about and I read about but I never knew the details of how Enoch did it of the three men. Another identified triangle,$\triangle$. Below is a triangle diagram representing the first triangle:

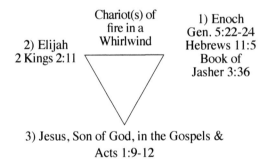

Chariot(s) of fire in a Whirlwind

2) Elijah 2 Kings 2:11

1) Enoch Gen. 5:22-24 Hebrews 11:5 Book of Jasher 3:36

3) Jesus, Son of God, in the Gospels & Acts 1:9-12

$\triangledown/\triangledown$ **There are three verses where it is stated to "put off thy. . ." shoes/shoe ". . .from off thy. . ." feet/foot because "the place. . . thou standest is holy."**

In the first verse God tells Moses in the bush that is burning. In the second verse the angel says it to Joshua as he is near the city of Jericho. In the third scripture Stephen, a deacon, states it in the retelling of the story of Moses in the New Testament. This is the basis for the first denoted triangle. Also the first two men of the three are linked to the events of the Exodus. The second denoted triangle. Here are the verses:

1) Exodus 3:5 "And he said, Draw not nigh hither: put off thy shoes from off thy feet, for the place whereon **thou standest is holy** ground."

2) Joshua 5:15 "And the captain of the LORD'S host said unto Joshua, Loose thy shoe from off thy foot; for the place whereon **thou standest is holy.** And Joshua did so."

3) Acts 7:33 "Then said the Lord to him, Put off thy shoes from thy feet: for the place where **thou standest is holy** ground."

△ **There are three instances where it is explicitly stated that Heaven is God's "throne" and the earth his "footstool."**

1) In Isaiah 66:1 "Thus saith the LORD, The heaven is my throne, and the earth is my footstool."

2) In Matthew 5:34-35 "But I say unto you, Swear not at all; neither by heaven; for it is God's throne: Nor by the earth; for it is his footstool."

3) In Acts 7:49 "Heaven is my throne, and earth is my footstool."

The first scripture is in the Old Testament and the last two scriptures are in the New. This is the basis for the denoted triangle. Note there is the verse that implies that earth is God's footstool in Lamentations 2:1, but Heaven is not mentioned.

▽/△ Three people died after falling some distance.

1) In 1 Samuel 4:11,18 record where the priest Eli falls backwards from his seat and breaks his neck because of the news of the ark of God being taken by the Philistines.
2) In 2 Kings 9:30-33 Queen Jezebel, who is disguised, is thrown out of a window to her death. The word defenestration comes to mind which means "the act of throwing someone or something out of a window."[32]
3) In Acts 20:9-10 "a certain young man named Eutychus" falls from ". . .the third loft, and was taken up dead." Paul then embraced him and he is revived.

Of the three people the last person is revived. The basis for the first denoted triangle. The last two people of the three fall out of a window." The second denoted triangle.

△/△ There are three verses that state the phrase "in the day of the Lord."

The first verse pertains to God the Father while the last two verses relate to God the son, Jesus. The basis for the first denoted triangle. Of these three verses the last two verses are in the New Testament. The first verse is in the Old Testament. The basis for the second denoted triangle. Here are the verses:

1) Ezekiel 13:5 "Ye have not gone up into the gaps, neither made up the hedge for the house of Israel to stand in the battle in the day of the LORD."

---

[32] Source - Wikipedia, Defenestration, 2014, http://en.wikipedia.org/wiki/Defenestration, Retrieved 04.06.2014

2) 1 Corinthians 5:5 "To deliver such an one unto Satan for the destruction of the flesh, that the spirit may be saved in the day of the Lord Jesus."

3) 2 Corinthians 1:14 "As also ye have acknowledged us in part, that we are your rejoicing, even as ye also are ours in the day of the Lord Jesus."

▽/△ **There are three verses that state the phrase "God is one".**

The first two verses of the three state "The LORD our God is one LORD." The first denoted triangle. Of the three, the first verse is in the Old Testament while the last two verses are in the New Testament. The second denoted triangle. Here are the verses

1) Deuteronomy 6:4 "Hear, O Israel: The LORD our God is one LORD."

2) Mark 12:29 "And Jesus answered him, The first of all the commandments is, Hear, O Israel; The Lord our God is one Lord."

3) Galatians 3:20 "Now a mediator is not a mediator of one, but God is one."

Note that the mezuzah, a case that is decorative that is affixed to Jewish homes that contains inscribed verses, has this phrase within it from the first mentioned verse.

▽/▽/△ **Three books, three verses, of the Bible mention as metaphors the use of a breastplate and a helmet.**

The first two instances mention "righteousness as a breastplate" and "breastplate of righteousness" in Isaiah 59:17 and Ephesians 6:14 respectively. The third metaphor is "breastplate of faith and love" in 1 Thessalonians 5:8. The first denoted triangle. The use of the helmet is stated as "helmet of salvation" for the first two books while the third states "for an helmet, the hope of salvation." This is the basis for the second denoted triangle. Of the three verses the first verse is in the Old Testament while the last two verses are in the New Testament. The third denoted triangle. Here are the verses:

1) Isaiah 59:17 "For he put on righteousness as a breast-plate, and an helmet of salvation upon his head."
2) Ephesians 6:14 "and having on the breastplate of righteousness" and Ephesians 6:17 "And take the helmet of salvation."
3) 1 Thessalonians 5:8 "putting on the breastplate of faith and love; and for an helmet, the hope of salvation."

△/▽ The word "silly" is mentioned three times.

1) In Job 5:2 "For wrath killeth the foolish man, and envy slayeth the silly one."
2) In Hosea 7:11 "Ephraim also is like a silly dove without heart: they call to Egypt, they go to Assyria."
3) In 2 Timothy 3:6 "For of this sort are they which creep into houses, and lead captive silly women laden with sins, led away with divers lusts,"

Of the three verses the first verse is directed at no particular individual but the last two verses are directed at particular groups, Ephraim and women. The first denoted triangle. The first two verses are in the Old Testament while last verse is in New Testament. The second denoted triangle.

▽/▽ There are three verses where God is defined as "a consuming fire."

The first two verses state, "the LORD thy God." The third verse states "our God." The first denoted triangle. The first two verses are in the same book in the Old Testament and the third in the New Testament. The second denoted triangle. Here are the verses:

1) Deuteronomy 4:24 "For the LORD thy God is a consuming fire, even a jealous God."
2) Deuteronomy 9:3 "Understand therefore this day, that the LORD thy God is he which goeth over before thee; as a consuming fire he shall destroy them."
3) Hebrews 12:29 "For our God is a consuming fire."

▽/▽ **Three verses state the contents of the Ark of the Covenant.**

Of the three, the third verse states more items in the Ark while the first two scriptures state the same information. The basis for the first denoted triangle. It is mentioned twice in the Old Testament and once in the New Testament. The second denoted triangle. Here are the verses:

1) 1 Kings 8:9 "There was nothing in the ark save the two tables of stone, which Moses put there at Horeb, when the LORD made a covenant with the children of Israel, when they came out of the land of Egypt."
2) 2 Chronicles 5:10 "There was nothing in the ark save the two tables which Moses put therein at Horeb, when the LORD made a covenant with the children of Israel, when they came out of Egypt."
3) Hebrews 9:4 "Which had the golden censer, and the ark of the covenant overlaid roundabout with gold, wherein was the golden pot that had manna, and Aaron's rod that budded, and the tables of the covenant."

△/▽ **There are four verses that state "The just shall live by. . .faith."**

Of the first three verses which state the clause, it is at the end of the three verses with the first verse stating the word "his" within the clause also. The first denoted triangle. The last three state the clause in the New Testament. The clause is stated in the last or fourth verse in the first part of the verse. This is the basis for the second denoted triangle. Here are the verses:

1) Habakkuk 2:4 "Behold, his soul which is lifted up is not upright in him: but the just shall live by his faith."
2) Romans 1:17 "For therein is the righteousness of God revealed from faith to faith: as it is written, The just shall live by faith."
3) Galatians 3:11 "But that no man is justified by the law in the sight of God, it is evident: for, The just shall live by faith."
4) Hebrews 10:38 "Now the just shall live by faith: but if any man draw back, my soul shall have no pleasure in him."

△/△ **Three times the story of the Prophet Elijah/Elias and the time that there was no rain is recorded.**

The last two verses of the three mention the amount of time that there was no rain which was three years and six months. The first verse does not state the time. The first denoted triangle. The last two verses of the three also mention the prophet as Elias in the New Testament and Elijah in the Old Testament. The second denoted triangle. Here are the verses:

1) 1 Kings 17:1 "And Elijah the Tishbite, who was of the inhabitants of Gilead, said unto Ahab, As the LORD God of Israel liveth, before whom I stand, there shall not be dew nor rain these years, but according to my word."
2) Luke 4:25 "But I tell you of a truth, many widows were in Israel in the days of Elias, when the heaven

was shut up three years and six months, when great famine was throughout all the land."

3) James 5:17 "Elias was a man subject to like passions as we are, and he prayed earnestly that it might not rain: and it rained not on the earth by the space of three years and six months."

▽/▽ **There are three verses where it is stated in some fashion "I am the first and the last".**

The first two verses state as part of the verse, "I. . .am" relating to "first" and "last" while the third just states "I am the first and the last." The first denoted triangle. The first two verses are in same book and in the Old Testament of the three. This is the basis for the second triangle. Here are the verses:

1) Isaiah 44:6 "Thus saith the LORD the King of Israel, and his redeemer the LORD of hosts; I am the first, and I am the last; and beside me there is no God."

2) Isaiah 48:12 "Hearken unto me, O Jacob and Israel, my called; I am he; I am the first, I also am the last."

3) Revelation 1:17 "And when I saw him, I fell at his feet as dead. And he laid his right hand upon me, saying unto me, Fear not; I am the first and the last."

Note the verse of Isaiah 41:4 that states also "I the Lord, the first, and with the last; I am he."

△/▽/△ **Read of four "sore judgments" of God that are stated in four instances.**

The four judgments use the sword, famine, pestilence, and "noisome beasts." The first three instances are in the same book and God states he will "send" them. The last two are in the same chapter of the first three. This is the basis for the first denoted triangle. Also the second and third instances of the first three state the judgments "pass through" the person(s) and the land respectively. The second denoted triangle. I focused next on the 2nd, 3rd and 4th instances where the second instance spans four verses and the last two instances are stated similarly, with minor variations, and state the judgments of the sword and famine as the first two judgments. The third denoted triangle. Here are the verses:

1) Ezekiel 5:17 "So will I send upon you famine and evil beasts, and they shall bereave thee; and pestilence and blood shall pass through thee; and I will bring the sword upon thee. I the LORD have spoken it."

2) Ezekiel 14:13, 15, 17, 19 presents the order of the four judgments separately

   1. ". . .and will send famine upon it" in verse 13
   2. "If I cause noisome beasts to pass through the land" in verse 15
   3. "Or if I bring a sword upon that land" in verse 17
   4. "Or if I send a pestilence into that land" in verse 19.

3) Ezekiel 14:21 "For thus saith the Lord GOD; How much more when I send my four sore judgments upon Jerusalem, the sword, and the famine, and the noisome beast, and the pestilence, to cut off from it man and beast?"

4) Revelation 6:8 "And power was given unto them over the fourth part of the earth, to kill with sword, and with hunger, and with death, and with the beasts of the earth."

△/▽ **Three books of the Bible mentions Michael the archangel by name.**

1) In Daniel 10:13, 21, 12:1
2) In Jude 1:9
3) In Revelation 12:7

The first book is in the Old Testament and the next two are in the New Testament. In the first book there is not a reference to "archangel" or angel but it is implied. The last two scriptures of Jude and Revelation state "archangel." The first denoted triangle. In the book of Daniel of the three verses Michael is called "one of the chief princes," "prince," and "great prince" respectively. The last verse of these three relates to the "latter days" or "end times" based on the scripture of Daniel 12:2, "And many of them that sleep in the dust of the earth shall awake, some to everlasting life, and some to shame and everlasting contempt." Daniel 12:1 is the greater of the three verses in my view within the Book of Daniel. The second denoted triangle. Michael's name is mentioned in the Old Testament in the first book, three times, and once each in the last two books which are in the New Testament. Another identified triangle, $\triangle$.

$\nabla/\triangle$ **Three angels of God are mentioned by name in the Bible:**

1) Gabriel in Daniel 8:16, 9:21, and Luke 1:19, 26
2) Michael in Daniel 10:13,21, 12:1, Jude 1:9, and Revelation 12:7
3) Abaddon (Hebrew)/ Apollyon (Greek) "angel of the bottomless pit" in Revelation 9:11

Of these three, the first two are mentioned multiple times and are both mentioned in the book of Daniel. The third is not. The first denoted triangle. The last two angels are mentioned in the book of Revelation while the first is not. The second denoted triangle. Note that the fallen angel (Lucifer, Satan, the Devil, and Beelzebub) is mentioned at least 124 times in the Bible.

△/▽ There are three verses where Satan/Lucifer/Red Dragon fell from Heaven.

The first one is stated in the Old Testament once and twice in New Testament. The first denoted triangle. The first two states the fall ". . .from heaven. . ." while the third is implied. The second denoted triangle. Here are the verses:

1) Isaiah 14:12 "How art thou fallen from heaven, O Lucifer, son of the morning! how art thou cut down to the ground, which didst weaken the nations!"
2) Luke 10:18 "And he said unto them, I beheld Satan as lightning fall from heaven."
3) Revelation 12:4 "And his tail drew the third part of the stars of heaven, and did cast them to the earth" (The Great Red Dragon in verse 3).

▽/△ There are three verses that state and relate to "a time, and times," and a half of a time.

As part of Christian eschatology or the subject relating to "end times," I learned over time there are those who have interpreted this information as to mean 1260 days or 42 months or 3 ½ years. I viewed these verses to establish the triangle pattern. The first two of the three are in the same book and the third is not. The first denoted triangle. The last two verses of the three states a half of a time along with "time" and "times" while the first scripture states "the dividing of time" or dividing of a time i.e. half with "time" and "times." The second denoted triangle. There are other verses such as Revelation 11:3 and 12:6 that mention 1260 days while Revelation 11:2 and 13:5 state "forty and two months." Here are the three mentioned referenced verses:

1) Daniel 7:25 "and they shall be given into his hand until a time and times and the dividing of time."

2) Daniel 12:7 "and sware by him that liveth forever that it shall be for a time, times, and a half."

3) Revelation 12:14 "where she is nourished for a time, and times, and half a time, from the face of the serpent."

▲**Commentary**: The three Roman numeral 10s that were viewed in binary as 101010 totaling 42 or six 7s, I noticed that number has other significance in the Bible. "There are 42 generations (names) in the Gospel of Matthew's version of the Genealogy of Jesus; it is prophesied that for 42 months the Beast will hold dominion over the Earth (Revelation 13:5); 42 men of Beth-azmaveth were counted in the census of men of Israel upon return from exile (Ezra 2:24); God sent bears to maul 42 of the teenage boys who mocked Elisha for his baldness (2 Kings 2:23)" (Wikipedia, 42 (number), 2013, http://en.wikipedia.org/wiki/42_(number), Retrieved 10.11.2013)

▽ **Thirty-three times the three patriarch names of Abraham, Isaac, and Jacob are mentioned together.**[33]

Five times the names Abraham, Isaac, and Israel are mentioned (Exodus 32:13, 1 Kings 18:36, 1 Chronicles 1:34, 29:18, and 2 Chronicles 30:6. Jacob/Israel is the third generation in which he and his offspring are the fulfillment of the promised nation God made. "According to the classic Jewish texts. . .", Jacob, ". . .the third and last patriarch. . ."[34] The triangle is based on Jacob being the fulfillment of God's promise.

---

[33] Gen. 31:53, 32:9, 35:27, 50:24; Exo. 2:24, 3:6, 3:15, 3:16, 4:5, 6:3, 6:8, 33:1; Lev. 26:42; Num. 32:11; Deut. 1:8, 6:10, 9:5, 9:27, 29:13, 30:20, 34:4; 2 Kings 13:23; Jer. 33:26; Matthew 1:2, 8:11, 22:32; Mark 12:26; Luke 3:34, 13:28, 20:37; Acts 3:13, 7:8, 7:32

[34] Source - Wikipedia, Jacob, 2013, http://end.wikipedia.org/wiki/Jacob, Retrieved 03.20.2013

△ **Four times the phrase "third hour" is stated in Matthew 20:3, Mark 15:25, Acts 2:15, and Acts 23:23.**

Of these four, the second mentions Jesus being crucified at that time and the last two state "the third hour of the day/night" respectively. The last two are verses also in the same book. The denoted triangle is based on the last three scriptures, actual events. The first verse in Mark states the time when Jesus was crucified and the next two verses in Acts relate to the eleven Apostles first and Paul next, an Apostle later, respectively. The first verse pertains to a parable that Jesus told of workers being paid a penny for working in the vineyard.

▽ **There are as many as forty-eight references relating to "the third day."**[35]

On the third day something happens while indicating that nothing, in a sense, happened or something different happened on days one and two. This is the basis for the denoted triangle. What is significant is that Jesus stated a number of times that he would rise again on the third day. How come he did not reference the first, second, or fourth or any other day? Read the five scriptures where it states "the third month" in Exodus 19:1, 1 Chronicles 27:5, 2 Chronicles 15:10, 2 Chronicles 31:7, Esther 8:9, and Ezekiel 31:1. Read the thirteen scriptures where it states "the third year."[36] Of these last two listings most of them start off with "In the third. . .". Special note in Deuteronomy 14:28 and

---

[35] Gen. 1:13, 22:4, 31:22, 34:25, 40:20, 42:18; Exo. 19:11-16; Lev. 7:17-18, 19:6-7; Num. 7:24, 19:12-19, 29:20, 31:19; Josh. 9:17; Judg. 20:30; 1 Sam. 20:5, 12, 30:1; 2 Sam. 1:2; 1 Kings 3:18, 12:12; 2 Kings 20:5, 8; 2 Chr. 10:12; Ezra 6:15; Esth. 5:1; Hos. 6:2; Matt. 16:21, 17:23, 20:19, 27:64; Mark 9:31, 10:24; Luke 9:22, 13:32, 18:33, 24:7, 21, 46; John 2:1; Acts 10:40, 27:19; 1 Cor. 15:4.

[36] Deut. 26:12; 1 Kgs 15:28, 33, 18:1, 22:2: 2 Kgs 18:1, 19:29: 2 Chr. 17:7; Esth. 1:3; Isa. 37:30; Dan. 1:1, 8:1,10:1.

Amos 4:4 it is stated that "tithes" were to be given after "three years." Notice that fifty-three scriptures mention the phrase "three days," seventeen scriptures mention the phrase "three months," and forty-one scriptures mention the phrase "three years" but NONE state "three weeks."

Only three verses relate to "three weeks." The phases "three full weeks" and "Three whole weeks" are in Daniel 10:2, 3 respectively. "One and twenty days" is also mentioned in Daniel 10:13. With these three verses a triangle is form, another one, with the first two verses stating weeks and the third stating days, ▽.

▽ There have been those who have researched the Bible to determine that there are three heavens.

I was taught over the years of this fact as well. The first two are ruled by Satan i.e. that which is of the earth or the "firmament of heaven" and outer space. The third heaven is where God's kingdom resides. This is the basis for the denoted triangle.

△ The languages of the Bible's early history revolves around the three: The Hebrew text, the Greek Septuagint (LXX), and the Latin Vulgate.

The first mentioned language is the basis for the other two mentioned. These are also the languages used on Jesus' cross. This is the basis for denoted triangle. The Septuagint is also recognized by three roman numeral characters that fit the pattern. Another identified triangle, △. The first two of these three, Hebrew and Septuagint, were done before the birth of Jesus and the third, the Latin Vulgate, afterwards in time. Another identified triangle,▽. It has been stated "The Bible has been translated into many languages from the biblical languages of Hebrew, Aramaic and Greek." And that "Biblical Aramaic is closely related to Hebrew as both are in the Northwest Semitic language family."[37] Based on this information the first two languages, Hebrew and Aramaic, are linked to the same family of languages of the three. Another identified triangle, $\triangledown$.

$\triangledown$ Finally, Abraham is the patriarch to the three major religions of Judaism ✡, Christianity ☨, and Islam ☾ in the world.

They are also known as the Abrahamic religions which are monotheistic. Judaism and Christianity are closely linked with Christianity being born out of Judaism, and Islam which stands alone among the three. The basis for the denoted triangle.

There is a common figure within the subject of eschatology that which relates to "end times" of the three religions: The coming of the Jewish Messiah, the Second Coming of Christ or the Messiah, and the coming of the Mahdi, the redeemer of Islam, respectively. In Jewish eschatology this man is not known. In Christian eschatology he is Jesus who will be coming a second time. There are those who view him as the man who is the Jewish Messiah as well. In Islamic eschatology there is a man called the Mahdi who will come and he will be assisted by Jesus who is called Isa. In this context Jesus is mentioned in the last two of the three religions pertaining to subject of eschatology. Another identified triangle, $\triangle$.

Of the three eschatological views the last two of them have a stated evil man. In Christianity the character that is described is called Anti-Christ also known as "The Beast." A wolf in lamb's clothing, "Beware of false prophets, which come to you in sheep's clothing, but inwardly they are ravening wolves" (Matthew 7:15). In Islam the man described is called the Masih ad-Dajjal meaning in Arabic "The Deceiver" or a false messiah. Another identified triangle, $\triangle$.

---

[37] Source - Wikipedia, Bible translations, 2013, en.wikipedia.org/wiki/Bible_translations, Retrieved 04.09.2013

Examples of the Divine Pattern in Modern Science

Perhaps it may be asked why should I look into searching for the Divine Pattern within the subject of science? I would respond and state that if God is **omnipotent** – all powerful, **omniscience** – all knowing, and **omnipresent** – present everywhere, then the divine pattern should be exhibited within science as well where two items are linked and one separate but still linked to the other two within a given subject matter. Based on current information that was researched, I did not find anything that showed a common denominator of all the scientific discoveries and activities made over time. I went looking and researching for the consistency of the divine pattern. Here is what was found looking at some of those scientific discoveries while thinking in the form of a triangle.

▼ According to the noted cosmologist Stephen Hawking in a Discovery Channel 2011 documentary called and asked the question "[Grand Design] Did God create the universe?". It was stated in this documentary that there are three ingredients to creating a universe: Matter, Energy, and Space. Based on work done by Albert Einstein, matter and energy are linked as being "two halves of the same coin" with the equation $E=mc^2$ which was stated in the documentary. Space stands alone of the three. This is the basis for the denoted triangle. Another point of view to the Big Bang theory, which tries to explain how the universe was created in that something small exploded and expanded rapidly, is that God indeed created the universe based on His three pattern. Many acknowledge that He is how the birth of the universe or cosmos began according to Genesis chapter 1. "Let all the inhabitants of the world stand in awe of him. For he spake, and it was done; he commanded, and it stood fast." (Psalms 33:8-9) The illustrated divine triangle diagram is below:

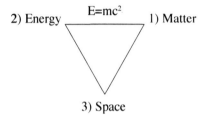

2) Energy $\quad$ $E=mc^2$ $\quad$ 1) Matter

3) Space

▼/▼ Of the three ingredients presented above, I focused on one in particular, matter. An atom is the basic element of anything which is called Matter. The atom consist of a proton, a neutron, and an electron in its most basic form, with the proton and neutron being linked forming the nucleus and the electron rotating around the two of them. The first denoted triangle. Every element has components that are a multiple of these three items, where in a majority of the cases there are more neutrons than protons and electrons except for hydrogen (H) which does not have a neutron. I can say at a minimum there is the same number of all three for each element in only nine of the 118 listed elements. Those elements that have the same number of all three items are: Helium (He) two each of the three, Carbon (C) six each of the three, Nitrogen (N) seven each of the three, Oxygen (O) eight each of the three, Neon (Ne) ten each of the three, Magnesium

(Mg) twelve each of the three, Silicon (Si) fourteen each of the three, Sulfur (S) sixteen each of the three, and Calcium (Ca) twenty each of the three. Ten unique elements of the 118. These and all the other elements comprised the periodic table. I also reviewed each of the elements in the periodic table where there were an equal number of protons and electrons, i.e. a stable or neutral or normal atom, with neutrons being more of the other two items separately based on the atomic structure of an 108 listed elements.[38] The second denoted triangle. The other ten mentioned elements are an exception because they are ten unique elements. The diagrams are shown below:

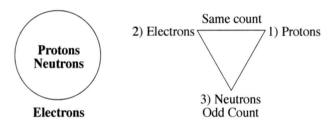

▼/▲/▼ In looking at the components of the atom from a subatomic/particle physics perspective, a proton is composed of three quarks in which two quarks are up and one quark is down. A neutron is also composed of three quarks in which two quarks are down and one quark up. A quark is defined as a "fundamental constituent of matter" and an "elementary particle."[39] This is the basis for the first two denoted triangles. It is said that this subatomic structure for protons and neutrons, quarks, was proposed by physicists Murry Gell-Mann

---

[38]   Source - Periodic Table: Atomic Number, 2012, http://www.chemicalelements.com/show/atomicnumber.html, Retrieved 11.26.12 & Chemicol, 2012, http://www.chemicool.com, Retrieved 11.26.2012

[39]   Source - Wikipedia, Quark , 2011, http://en.wikipedia.org/wiki/Quark, Retrieved 12.14.2011

and George Zweig in 1964. The three combined quarks are called a baryon and they, protons and neutrons, "make up most of the mass of the visible matter in the universe."[40] Again, from a particle perspective the other component of the atom, the electron, is called a lepton another "elementary particle."[41] The two types of subatomic components of the atom are two baryons and one lepton. The basis for the third denoted triangle. The electron component of the atom was discovered in 1897 by British physicist Sir Joseph John "J. J." Thomson, (12.18.1856 – 08.30.1940). In 1919 the proton was discovered by New Zealand-born British chemist and physicist Ernest Rutherford, (08.30.1871 – 10.19.1937). In 1932 the Neutron was discovered by Sir James Chadwick (10.20.1891 – 07.24.1974) a physicist who also worked under Ernest Rutherford in Germany. The triangle diagram shown below is based on subatomic components of the atom, (u =up, d=down):

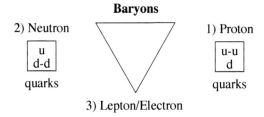

Baryons

2) Neutron

| u |
| d-d |

quarks

1) Proton

| u-u |
| d |

quarks

3) Lepton/Electron

▲/▲ There is something called the Standard Model of particle physics where two of three, three generations of subatomic particles, elementary, comprises visible matter. The first generation of subatomic particles is the three generations of quarks: 1) Up & Down, 2) Strange & Charm, and

---

[40] Source - Wikipedia, Baryon, 2011, http://en.wikipedia.org/wiki/Baryon, Retrieved 12.14.2011

[41] Source - Wikipedia, Lepton, 2011, http://en.wikipedia.org/wiki/Lepton, Retrieved 12.14.2011

3) Top & Bottom. All the visible matter that we see around us is derived from the first generation of quarks while the other two are not used for that purpose. The basis for the first denoted triangle. The second generation of subatomic particles is the three generations of leptons: 1) electronic leptons, electron and electron neutrino, 2) muonic leptons, muon and muon neutrino, and 3) tauonic leptons, tau and tau neutrino. All the visible matter that we see around us is made up in part from the first generation of leptons while the other two are not used for that purpose. The basis for the second denoted triangle. Visible matter seems to fall under two other particle classifications which are hadrons and fermions relating to baryons and leptons. There is another particle classification called bosons, the third, which visible matter does not fall under. I noticed that there are three groups within the Standard Model of elementary particles. The quarks, leptons, and bosons or gauge bosons, or a.k.a. force carriers. Visible matter is within the first two groups of the three. Another identified triangle,▲. Scientists have stated recently that they have found evidence of the long sought after "God particle"/Higgs boson in July 2012 and confirmed in March 2013. It is said to be sought in relationship to one of the quarks in the third generation of quarks. I thought of the discovery and how it was made and thought of 2 Corinthians 12:2 because it alludes to the place where God is, the "third heaven." With the confirmed discovery of the Higgs boson, there are now three named bosons along with the W and Z bosons. These two bosons, W and Z, together are called weak bosons, of the Standard Model of particle physics. Another identified triangle,▼.

▼ Water (H_2O), the molecule essential for all life on planet Earth, is made up of two parts of the hydrogen atom and one part of the oxygen atom, the three atoms that it contains. It is what some call a "triatomic molecule" i.e. a molecule that is made up of three atoms only. This is the basis for the denoted triangle. There are those who say that the adult human body is made up of about 66 percent water. Also there are those who say that about 66 percent or 2/3s of the Earth is covered by water. Other triatomic molecules are ozone (O_3) and nitrogen dioxide (NO_2). Diagram of the water molecule is shown below:

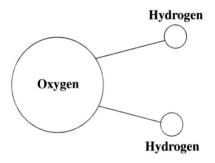

▲/▼ Reviewed the molecule, another "triatomic molecule", that is essential to plant life on the planet called Carbon dioxide (CO_2). It is comprised of one carbon atom and two oxygen atoms. The first denoted triangle. It is said that as part of the cycle known as photosynthesis most plant life absorbs carbon dioxide, light, and water to produce oxygen as a waste by-product. Of the three items needed for photosynthesis, water is the tangible item. The second denoted triangle.

▲ Reviewed the molecular formula of Vitamin C, an ascorbic acid which is a needed nutrient for human life. Its formula make up is as such $C_6H_8O_6$ i.e. eight hydrogen atoms with six carbon atoms and six oxygen atoms. This is the basis for the denoted triangle. I could call this make up a complex triatomic formula/molecule where there are three atoms in multiples that have been combined. The C was chosen being that it is the third letter in the English alphabet.

▼ Reviewed the element symbols on the periodic table of the three major metals of the Bible gold, silver, and brass. The element symbol for gold is Au. The element symbol for silver is Ag. There is no element symbol for brass because it is a mixture of the elements of copper (Cu) and Zinc (Zn) and perhaps other metals as well. In biblical times it is said that brass was a combination of copper, the base for the metal, and tin. Of the three biblical metals mentioned, the first two are stated on the periodic table as an element. The third is not. This is the basis for the denoted triangle.

▲ Reviewed the three most commonly known states of matter, that which is for the most part is visible, which is derived from the atom. The three normal states are solid, liquid, and gas. Matter that is in a Solid or Liquid states are linked in that they are more tangible than a gas or gaseous state. This is the basis for the denoted triangle. The triangle diagram is as follows:

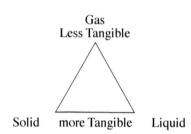

Gas
Less Tangible

Solid   more Tangible   Liquid

▼/▲/▼ I looked at the first three planets in our Solar system. Of the planetary symbols of Mercury ☿, Venus ♀, and Earth ⊕, notice that the first two symbols are similar of these three. The first denoted triangle. Focused next on the time it takes the planets of Mercury 88 days, Venus 225 days, and Earth 365 days to complete a revolution around the Sun. The last two planets of the three take hundreds of days to complete one revolution around the Sun. The second denoted triangle. The average number of days of the three is 226. Of the first three planets Earth, the third planet from the Sun, is the only planet in this Solar system that has sustaining life on it. The third denoted triangle. Of the three planets, Earth is the first to have a moon. Another identified triangle,▼. Also of the three, Venus and Earth generate weather patterns while Mercury does not. Another identified triangle,▲. For the earth, it takes twenty-four hours to complete one revolution of itself which is called a day. The twenty-four hours can be broken up into three eights. The time designation of the three eights are morning, afternoon, and evening. Of the three the daylight is dimmest during sunrise, the morning, and sunset, the evening. Another identified triangle,▲. Of the first two planets that have moons, Earth and Mars, there are three moons between them. Earth with one moon and Mars with two moons. Another identified triangle,▲.

Since the focus has been about triangles one wonders how often do the three planets form a triangle around or in front of the Sun or some linear alignment where Mercury and Venus and together in front of or around the Sun with the Earth alone positioned in front of the three, Mercury, Venus and the Sun? Or all three planets being aligned in front of the Sun? Here are the triangle diagrams of the three planetary symbols:

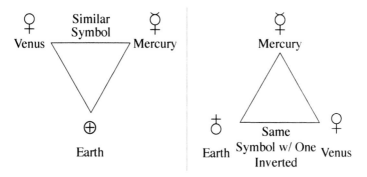

Symbols Source: http://en.wikipedia.org/wiki/Astronomical_symbols

Note that for decades we learned that there were ten major celestial bodies within our solar system the Sun, Mercury, Venus, Earth, Mars, Jupiter, Saturn, Uranus, Neptune, and Pluto. In 2006 it is said that Pluto was declared not to be a planet anymore. There are still some who disagree with the new classification. Of the ten the Sun, is the only stationary body with the other rotating around it.

▼ Reviewed the three major celestial bodies that greatly effects all humanity and life as we know it. First the Earth the celestial body we exist on and the second is earth's Moon. The major effect that the moon has is that it is involved in the periodic movements of bodies of waters based on the gravitational pull on the earth called tides. The third celestial body is the sun which provides a source of light, heat, and energy. The earth and the moon are linked based on proximity of the three. This is the basis for the denoted triangle.

▼/▼/▼ In biology reviewed some of the external body orifices of human and mammalian species on the planet. There are three facial orifices in a typical human and mammalian body that are used for breathing. They are the two nostrils of the nose and the mouth. The first denoted triangle. Of these three, two are constantly open. The second denoted triangle. A closer look at the three major functions of the mouth in that it used for sustenance and breathing in which both of these are linked to the intake of something, nourishment and air, and the output that is produced from it is vocalization. For humans it is speech. The basis for the third denoted triangle. It is said that we as humans spend a third of our lives sleeping. This would suggest that the other two-thirds of our lives is spent doing other activities. Another identified triangle,▲. Also reviewed the three orifices used in human sexual practices within human female which are the "Va-Jay-Jay" and rectum which both are below the abdomen, and the mouth which is above the abdomen. Another identified triangle,▼. Two of the orifices are in the front of the body and the third is in the rear. Another identified triangle,▼.

▼ It is said, and based on observation, that the human head, along with some other animals, has three pairs of external cavities which are two eyes, two nostrils, and two ears. Of the three pairs, two pair are located in the front of the human head the eyes and nostrils, with the other pair on the sides of the human head. This is the basis for the denoted triangle.

▼ As corporeal beings, our survival depends on three essentials things which are food, water, and air or oxygen to be specific. Food and water are linked closely in that they are items that have to be acquired while air/oxygen, mostly, is given from our environment. The basis for the denoted triangle.

▲ Reviewed the three parts of one Sigmund Freud's conceptualization of the human psyche relating to psychology: 1) Id, 2) Ego, and, 3) Super Ego. It relates to the basic human instincts/needs while ego and super ego, in my view, are related to conscious awareness. This is the basis for the denoted triangle.

▲ Cosmologists such as Stephen Hawking, and other space enthusiasts, as part of their research about the universe, worked to provide proof mathematically that for most black holes, being stable, they are described as having three measured properties. The first is mass, a star's collapse at its life's end, second "angular momentum" or its rotation rate, and third an electrical charge. Based on the description I can say that without a collapsed mass, momentum and electric charge cannot exist for any of type of black holes in space. The last two items are by-products of the first event. This is the basis for the denoted triangle. The most common form of black holes, it is said, with these characteristics are Kerr-Newman or those that rotate.

▼/▲ I read of the Three Ages of the Dinosaurs or geological periods: Triassic, Jurassic, and Cretaceous. The first two are linked by the major "Triassic–Jurassic extinction event via climate change or asteroid impact or massive volcanic eruptions."[42] The first denoted triangle. Beginning in the Jurassic period, the supercontinent called Pangaea had begun breaking into two land masses. The north called Laurasia and to the south called Gondwana.[43] "During the Cretaceous period . . . the supercontinent of Pangaea completed its tectonic breakup into present day continents, although their positions were substantially different at the time."[44] The last two periods of the three are linked by the movement of the "Pangaean super-continent." The second denoted triangle. Interestingly, in my view, there are seven identified continents in the world today.

▲ There were three nuclear weapons detonated in the year of 1945 which were the first three in the world. The first one was called, oddly, Trinity which was used as a test in New Mexico on 07.16.1945. The other two were used on the Japanese cities of Hiroshima on 8.6.1945 and Nagasaki on 8.9.1945. The names of the nuclear weapons were "Little Boy" and "Fat Man" respectively. The last two are linked to being used on the nation of Japan three days apart and three

---

[42] Source - Wikipedia, Triassic–Jurassic extinction event, 2012, http://en.wikipedia.org/wiki/Triassic%E2%80%93Jurassic_extinction_event, Retrieved 12.26.2012

[43] Source - Wikipedia, Jurassic, 2012, http://en.wikipedia.org/wiki/Jurassic, Retrieved 12.26.2012

[44] Source - Wikipedia, Cretaceous Paleography, 2012, http://en.wikipedia.org/wiki/Cretaceous#Paleogeography, Retrieved 12.26.2012

weeks apart from the first nuclear detonation in New Mexico. The first weapon was used as a test and the last two were used in combat. This is the basis for the denoted triangle.

▲/▼ With the talk of the Mayan calendar and its end, I reviewed its design. "The Maya calendar uses three different dating systems in parallel, the Long Count, the Tzolkin (divine calendar), and the Haab (civil calendar). Of these, only the Haab has a direct relationship to the length of the year."[45] This is the basis for the first denoted triangle. The order of the three is the Haab, Tzolkin, and Long Count. The Haab is stated to have eighteen months which are twenty days in length plus five additional days, called Wayab. This is very close to the modern Western/Gregorian calendar of 365 days with twelve months. "A Calendar Round date is a date that gives both the Tzolkin and Haab."[46] Because of a shortcoming of the "Calendar Round" in dating, fifty-two years in length, the Long Count system/calendar was devised to provide a dating method that was more accurate. This is the basis for the second denoted triangle. Much of the world's attention has been focused on the Long Count which ends on Friday, 12.21.2012 in the Gregorian calendar and 13.0.0.0.0 in the Mayan. Many believed that this date was end of the world. I have concluded that the Mayan sense of time also revolves around the three pattern.

▼/▼ As part of political science, I reviewed the three, separate but equal, branches of government, i.e. U.S., the legislative, executive, and judicial, where the pattern is also

---

[45] Source - The Mayan Calendar, 2008, http://www.webexhibits.org/calendars/calendar-mayan.html, Retrieved 12.20.2012

[46] Source - Wikipedia, Maya Calendar Round, 2012, http://en.wikipedia.org/wiki/Maya_calendar#Calendar_Round, Retrieved 12.20.2012

displayed. The legislative branch and the executive branch are connected in that they are both elected directly by the citizenry. The judiciary is not. This is the first denoted triangle. The biggest responsibility of the legislative and executive branches is to pass legislation that effects the citizenry. Note also that the Vice President of the United States is a member of both the executive and legislative branches as President of the Senate. The responsibility of the Judicial branch is to participate in court cases that challenge or require some interpretation of the legislation that has been passed by the two other government branches. This is the second denoted triangle. The Executive and Legislative branches are in consultation with each other more than they are with the Judicial Branch. Of the three branches there are acronyms associated with the Executive and Judicial branches. P.O.T.U.S. standing for the "President of the United States" and S.C.O.T.U.S. standing for the "Supreme Court of the United States". The acronyms for these ten individuals, the President and the nine Justices. There is no stated acronym for the Legislative branch at least not akin to these. Another identified triangle,▼. It is said that in parliamentary systems, those of and in other counties, the legislative and executive branches are connected/linked and the judiciary branch is often independent of the other two branches.

There are those who say that the government of the United. States was based on the scriptures of which one is Isaiah 33:22 which states, "For the LORD is our judge, the LORD is our lawgiver, the Lord is our king; he will save us." Of the three items that "the LORD is," the third item listed is the greatest, "our King". Another identified triangle, ▽. The three items are associated with the branches of government in order based on what is stated as the Judicial, "judge," Legislative, "lawgiver," and "king," Executive. Note this pattern of the three branches also extends down to lower levels of government such as the state and local municipalities here in the United States.

▲ "In United States politics, the **iron triangle** comprises the policy-making relationship among the congressional committees, the bureaucracy, and (special/private) interest groups."[47] Of the three mentioned, the last two are linked by the bureaucracy, and (special/private) interest groups in that the interest groups have to deal more with the bureaucracy in my view. The basis for the denoted triangle.

▲ As part of the science of Criminology, I have read and heard of the three things profilers look at as it relates to serial crimes, Victimology, Modus operandi, and signature. The first is "Victim ology - it tells us who the victims were, their health and personal history, social habits and personality, but also provides ideas as to why they were chosen as victims." Victimology is "the study of victims: an examination of every facet of their lifestyle, background, health, and physical characteristics."[48] The second, "Modus operandi - someone's habits or manner of working, their method of operating or functioning (Mode of Operation)."[49] And third, "The Signature Aspect (Calling Card) - conduct that is a unique and integral part of the offender's behavior and goes beyond the actions needed to commit the crime."[50] Of the

47   Source - Wikipedia, Iron triangle, 2014, http://en.wikipedia.org/wiki/Iron_triangle_(US_politics) 04.21.2014

48   Source - TruTV.com, 2011, VICTIMOLOGY: THE STUDY OF VICTIMS IN CRIMINAL INVESTIGATIONS, http://www.trutv.com/library/crime/criminal_mind/profiling/victimology/1.html, Retrieved 11.21.2011

49   Source - Wikipedia, Modus Operandi, 2011, http://en.wikipedia.org/wiki/Modus_operandi, Retrieved 11.21.2011

50   Source - Crime & Clues, 2011, http://www.crimeandclues.com/index.php/criminal-investigation/, Retrieved 11.21.2011

three the last two items are more linked to perpetrators of crimes in my view. This is the basis for the denoted triangle.

▼ In ethnomusicology, i.e. the study of music, it is said that one Alan P. Merriam states "there are three aspects always present in musical activity: concept, behavior, and sound."[51] Of these three, the greatest is sound for without it what is the point of music in my view. The basis for the denoted triangle. "In music, a trio (an Italian word) is a method of instrumentation or vocalization by three different sounds or voices to make a melodious music or song. . . . Common forms of such trios include the 'piano trio' — piano, violin and cello — and the 'string trio' — violin, viola and cello."[52] Also, there is a musical instrument called the triangle, ▲.

▲/▼ Reviewed the three major components of a desktop computer/Personal Computer (PC), relating to some of the early history of them in computer science, which are the monitor, the cpu/system unit, and the keyboard. The CPU or system unit was considered the main essential item of the three since it is the "brains" and you could not do much of anything without it. The other two items could be considered peripherals. This is the basis for the first denoted triangle. Of these three components, the monitor and the system unit needed electrical power supplied to them separately. The second denoted triangle.

▼ Reviewed the electric three color traffic light created in the early 1900s that is used in North America and in other parts of the world. The standard colors used as lights, predominately,

---

51   Source - Wikipedia, Aspect of music, 2013, http://en.wikipedia.org/wiki/Aspect_of_music, Retrieved 04.15.2013

52   Source - Wikipedia, Trio (music), 2013, http://en.wikipedia.org/wiki/Trio_(music), Retrieved 06.03.2013

are red, yellow, and green. From one perspective the first two colors, red and yellow, are primary colors of the three while green is a combination of yellow and blue, the third primary color. The basis for the denoted triangle. From another perspective the colors of red and green are illuminated longer than the yellow during the proper operation of the three color traffic light. Another identified triangle, ▼.

▲ In electrical engineering there is what is called "three-phase electric power." "In a three-phase system, three circuit conductors carry three alternating currents (of the same frequency) which reach their instantaneous peak values at one third of a cycle from each other. Taking one current as the reference, the other two currents are delayed in time by one third and two thirds of one cycle of the electric current. This delay between phases has the effect of giving constant power transfer over each cycle of the current and also makes it possible to produce a rotating magnetic field in an electric motor." "A three-phase system is usually more economical than an equivalent single-phase or two-phase system at the same voltage because it uses less conductor material to transmit electrical power."[53] From one perspective, and in my view, once one of the three starts there is a measured time delay for the other two after the first one based on the information. The basis for the denoted triangle.

▼ "A third rail is a method of providing electric power to a railway train, through a semi-continuous rigid conductor placed alongside or between the rails of a railway track. It is used typically in a mass transit or rapid transit system, which has alignments in its own corridors, fully or almost fully seg-regated from the outside environment. In most cases, third

---

[53] Source - Wikipedia, Three phrase electric power, 2013, http://en. wikipedia.org/wiki/Three-phase_electric_power, Retrieved 03.07.2013

rail systems supply direct current electricity."[54] The first two rails are used for the track of the transit/train rail cars and the third rail is used to power those transit/train cars. This is the basis for the denoted triangle. This Third Rail is also used as part of another subject matter. "The third rail of a nation's politics is a metaphor for any issue so controversial that it is "charged" and "untouchable;" any politician or public official who dares to broach the subject will invariably suffer politically. The term is most commonly used in North America. The "third rail of American politics" is often said to be cutting Social Security; the "third rail" of Canadian politics is said to be health care."[55]

▼/▲/▲ In the measuring of time a device called a three-hand clock or wall clock, devices large and small that are similar, are used around the world. The hands are the second hand, minute hand, and the hour hand. Of the three, the hour hand is the shortest and slower of the three. The first denoted triangle. From another perspective the second hand moves faster around the clock that the other two hands. The second denoted triangle. In some instances, perhaps many, the second hand is a different color that the other two hands. The third denoted triangle.

▲ In statistics, reviewed what is called "The Monty Hall problem" which is a puzzle of probability where it relates in short to, "Suppose you're on a game show, and you're given the choice of three doors: Behind one door is a car; behind

---

[54] Source - Wikipedia, Third rail, 2013, http://en.wikipedia.org/wiki/
      Third_rail, Retrieved 12.17.2013

[55] Source - Wikipedia, Third rail of politics, 2013, http://en.wikipedia.
      org/wiki/Third_rail_of_politics, Retrieved 12.17.2013

the others, goats."[56] A simple way of looking at the problem is that you are given a one in three chance of winning a car behind a door with a two in three chance of not winning the prize. The denoted triangle is based on what is behind the three doors.

▼/▲ I recalled the three elements of fire, that which was taught to me when he was young, which are heat, oxygen, and fuel. Without enough heat and oxygen it cannot be started nor be sustained. The first denoted triangle. With continued fuel it cannot be stopped. The second denoted triangle.

▼ Reviewed the first three prime numbers. For many years I and others were taught in school that the first three prime numbers were 1, 3, and 5. Some time ago, 2 replaced one as the first prime number. With this change the number 5 still remained the third prime number. (Note: A prime number is a number that can only be divided by itself and one.) Think of the Pentateuch/Torah the first five books of the Bible. Another math fact is that the number five is also the third factorial prime number. "A factorial prime is a prime number that is one less or one more than a factorial (all factorials > 1 are even)."[57] The first few factorial primes are: 2, 3, 5, and 7 – "2 (0! + 1 or 1! + 1), 3 (2! + 1), 5 (3! – 1), 7 (3! + 1)." The number five is also the second pernicious number. "In number theory, a pernicious number is a positive integer that has a number of 1s in its binary representation which is a prime number. Equivalently, the sum of the digits of a pernicious number, when represented

56   Source - Wikipedia, Monty Hall problem, 2013, http://en.wikipedia. org/wiki/Monty_Hall_problem, Retrieved 04.29.2013

57   Source - Wikipedia, Factorial prime, 2013, http://en.wikipedia.org/ wiki/Factorial_prime, Retrieved 06.21.2013

in base 2, is a prime."[58] The first pernicious number is three. Finally, the number five is first safe prime number. "A safe prime is a prime number of the form 2p + 1, where p is also a prime. (Conversely, the prime p is a Sophie Germain prime.)"[59] The first few safe primes are: 5, 7, and 11. The denoted triangle is based on the fact that the addition of the first two prime numbers equals the third prime number, 2 + 3 = 5.

▲/▲/▲ It is noted that in Roman numerals for the number 777 it is expressed as DCC=700, LXX=70, VII=7 where each number is expressed by three character and two of which are the same for each number. Each number is the basis for a denoted triangle.

▼ "In mathematics, the Pythagorean theorem — or Pythagoras' theorem — is a relation in Euclidean geometry among the three sides of a right triangle. It states that the square of the hypotenuse (the side opposite the right angle) is equal to the sum of the squares of the other two sides. The theorem can be written as an equation relating the lengths of the sides a, b and c, often called the Pythagorean equation: $a^2 + b^2 = c^2$ where c represents the length of the hypotenuse, and a and b represent the lengths of the other two sides."[60] It is also called a triangle formula. The denoted triangle is based on the configuration of the three variables of the formula with the first two being linked and the third being the result of the first two variables.

---

[58] Source - Wikipedia, Pernicious number, 2013, http://en.wikipedia. org/wiki/Pernicious_number, Retrieved 06.21.2013

[59] Source - Wikipedia, Safe prime, 2013, http://en.wikipedia.org/wiki/ Safe_prime, Retrieved 06.21.2013

[60] Source - Wikipedia, Pythagorean theorem, 2013, http://en.wikipedia. org/wiki/Pythagorean_theorem, Retrieved 12.02.2013

▼ Trigonometry, "Mathematical discipline dealing with the relationships between the sides and angles of triangles. Literally, it means triangle measurement, though its applications extend far beyond geometry."[61] Reviewed the six functions that are used as part of trigonometry which are sine (sin), cosine (cos) and tangent (tan/tg), cotangent (cot/cotg), secant (sec), and cosecant (csc/cosec). The two function pairs of sin/cos and sec/csc of the six, or two-thirds, are linked to the term hypotenuse which is "the longest side of a right-angled triangle, the side opposite the right angle."[62] This is the basis for the denoted triangle.

▲ As I grew up, I recall going through the Philadelphia, Pennsylvania public educational school system that was divided into three levels or stages. The first level/stage was elementary school, or what some may call primary education, where I went through grades first to sixth. The next level/stage was middle school, or what is also called junior high or secondary schooling, where I was in grades seventh to ninth. The final level was High school, or what some may call secondary college, where I was in grades ten to twelve. Of these three level/stages the last two are linked to being three years in length. The basis for the denoted triangle. I learned that in other countries around the world they have followed this pattern of schooling also as in Mexico, China, South Korea, and Israel perhaps with some minor adjustments. Other areas in the United States also, perhaps with some adjustment, follow this pattern.

---

[61] Source - Merriam-Webster, Trigonometry, 2013, http://www.merriam-webster.com/dictionary/trigonometry, Retrieved 02.27.2013

[62] Source - Wikipedia, Hypotenuse, http://en.wikipedia.org/wiki/Hypotenuse, Retrieved 03.03.2013

▼/▲ Reviewed the elements of "The three Rs" which "refers to the foundations of a basic skills-orientated education program within schools: **reading, writing and arithmetic**. The original phrase 'the Three Rs' came from a previous speech made by Sir William Curtis in 1795."[63] In the performance of the reading and arithmetic the functioning of an individual's hand may or may not be required but the use of the hand, or in some cases mouth or feet, is required for writing. This is the basis for the first denoted triangle. Of these three Rs the last two are proceeded by another letter, w and a respectively. The second denoted triangle.

▼ Reviewed the telephone number format that is use in the U.S. and Canada and other parts of North America for tele-communications. In part, the area code, it is said was rolled out in 1947 and part of the North American Numbering Plan (NANP)."The NANP number format can be summarized in the notation NPA-NXX-xxxx" where "NPA" is the "Numbering Plan Area Code", "Nxx" is the "Central Office (exchange) code", and the "xxxx" is the "Subscriber Number"[64] The format consists of three digits for the area code, three digits for the exchange code, and four digits for subscriber or "station number," ten digits in all. Of these three the first two are three digits and the third four digits. This is the basis for the denoted triangle. In 1995 it became mandatory to use this format when communicating with a particular party via a telephone. There is another number used which is 1 as the prefix. This is not mentioned because it

---

[63]   Source - Wikipedia, The three Rs, 2014, http://en.wikipedia.org/wiki/The_three_Rs, Retrieved 01.28.2014

[64]   Source - Wikipedia, North American Numbering Plan, 2014, http://en.wikipedia.org/wiki/North_American_Numbering_Plan, Retrieved 03.04.2014

has become commonly understood that it must be used when calling a telephone number noted as 1+areacode+number.

▼ I read the statement, "Actuarial science is the discipline that applies mathematical and statistical methods to assess risk in insurance, finance and other industries and professions."[65] In short, in my view based on the definition, assessed risk is determined by "mathematical and statistical methods." This is the basis for the denoted triangle.

▲ It is said, "The triangle to be one of the basic shapes of geometry: a polygon with three corners or vertices and three sides or edges which are line segments." There are seven types of Triangles:

1) Equilateral – All sides equal and all three angles are 60 degrees
2) Isosceles – Two of the sides equal along with two of the angles are equal
3) Scalene – No sides equal along with none of the angles being equal
4) Right Triangle – Only one of the three angles is 90 degrees
5) Obtuse – Only one of the three angles is greater than 90 degrees
6) Acute – All three of the angles are less than 90 degrees
7) An oblique – All of the three angles are more or less than 90 degrees.[66]

---

[65] Source - Wikipedia, Actuarial science, 2014, http://en.wikipedia.org/wiki/Actuarial_science, Retrieved 03.07.2014

[66] Source - Wikipedia, Types of triangles, 2012, http://en.wikipedia.org/wiki/Triangle#Types_of_triangles, Retrieved 12.20.2012

"The sum of the lengths of any two sides of a triangle always exceeds the length of the third side, a principle known as the triangle inequality."[67]

▼ Reviewed the subject of a triangular number in which objects are counted and stacked upon each other to form of an equilateral triangle. Such numbers include 3, 6, 10, 15, 21, and 66. An example using the number 21 is given below. Note that four of the six rows or 2/3s are numbered. This is the basis for the denoted triangle:

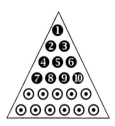

The number one is the first triangular number as shown in the example above but it is also noted that, "Three is the second triangular number and it is the only prime triangular number." It is said that Ten is the third Centered Triangular Number after the numbers one and four. "A centered (or centred) triangular number is a centered figurate number that represents a triangle with a dot in the center and all other dots surrounding the center in successive triangular layers. Each centered triangular number from ten onwards is the sum of three consecutive regular triangular numbers."[68]

---

[67] Source - Wikipedia, 2013, Triangle, http://en.wikipedia.org/wiki/ Triangle, Retrieved 01.30.2013

[68] Source - Wikipedia, Centered triangular number, 2013, http://en.wikipedia.org/wiki/Centered_triangular_number Retrieved 4.02.2014

One final note I will state is "The phrase 'Third time's the charm' refers to the superstition that after two failures in any endeavor, a third attempt is more likely to succeed."[69] Superstition? In my view it seems to be more of a reality than what has been stated. Besides, this seems to be more in line with the new "Law/Rule of Threes" that I have identified.

Of the seven types of triangles presented the preferred triangle of the divine is the equilateral which signifies the equality of each in the Holy Trinity. "TRIANGULAR (Equilateral) – This halo was developed intentionally to separate the Father from the Son and Holy Spirit. It is used only to represent a person of the Trinity, typically God the Father. The triangular halo was not instituted until the 11th century A.D. After the 16th century A.D., the image of God the Father ceased being used. Instead, His name in Hebrew (YHWH) is found inside the triangle."[70] It is said that there is halo that is associated with the divine. "TRI-RADIANT – This halo consists of three bars contained in a circle. It is to be used to represent only a member of the Trinity, usually Jesus."[70] The image of the triangle with the name of God (YHWH) within it in Hebrew is shown below:

Source of image:
http://www.phoenixmasonry.org/masonicmuseum/glossary/images/
sacred_tetractys_1.jpg

[69] Source - Wikipedia, 3(number), 2013, http://en.wikipedia.org/wiki/3_(number), Retrieved 12.04.13

[70] Source - Halos, 2013, http://www.christiansymbols.net/halos_4.php, Retrieved 01.07.2014

○ Conclusion

B ased on my beliefs, and research, I can say that 6,000 years not specifically knowing of God's divine pattern has come to an end. It is very eye opening. The three main areas of focus for this work were Judaism of the Old Testament of the Bible, Christianity of the New Testament of the Bible, and Science. A downward triangle of its own,▼. Over 1,900 years ago, the apostle John wrote of the vision he was given on the Isle of Patmos for the book of Revelation in what is called the "Cave of the Apocalypse" with no idea that there was logic at work that he was not allowed to see and understand. I think of how perhaps a monument should be erected near the site to honor his work and the discovery of the logic that was behind his vision.

Perhaps there are those who can view some of the analysis presented as trivial, but no analysis such as this has ever has been done on the Bible. Besides as Zechariah 4:10 suggests, it is unwise to "despise the day of small things." This was an in-depth comprehensive look at the number three in that is said is the perfect number of divinity. The in the introduction of this book it is stated, "All scripture is given by inspiration of God" in 2 Timothy 3:16. Based on the information that has been discovered and presented this has been proven to be true.

As opposed to the analysis done by others, I looked at the entire Bible as a system focusing on the number three and the triangle pattern as its core or base. I had to think in triangles. You could say I am thinking like a computer hacker, hack the Bible. I have to think that the probability of finding the divine pattern is astronomical after studying all the researched information. For if ancient scholars had a more in-depth knowledge and understanding of looking for patterns or profiling in the writings of the Bible, perhaps this pattern could have be found sooner.

With various writers of the Bible, there was not a whole lot of collaboration, if any, between the writers which is an indication to me that the Bible had to be inspired by divinity. The signature of the divinity within the Bible is this three, triangular, pattern which has been hiding in plain sight all this time.

It has been stated that the hexagram could have started to be used as part of the Jewish identity as a symbol perhaps in the 11th century. From 1008, to be exact, to 2010 when its origin was discovered. Just over a 1,000 years. It is also said that the hexagram was on a ring given to him, the Michael the Archangel, as a seal, the "seal of Solomon." Whatever the history of the hexagram as a symbol on earth, it does have its beginnings from the divine in my view. From my perspective no more will the origin of the symbol be unknown as others have stated. I have a sense of how the 13th-century Spanish Rabbi Bachya ben Asher and the early 20th-century Slovak Rabbi Michael Ber Weissmandl may have felt as they worked as some of the first on what is known now as the Bible Codes, (ELS), during their times, and later revisited by Dr. Rips and his team later in the 20th century.

The King James version of the Bible, the version that does not contain the fourteen books relating to what is called the Apocrypha, was used for this book since it is stated to be the third official translated Bible into English sanctioned by the Church of England under the British Monarchy. The other two were, the first was the *Great Bible* commissioned by the Church of England during the reign of King Henry VIII, and the second was the *Bishops' Bible* under Queen Elizabeth, produced by the authority of the Church of England. The King James Version is significant since it has stood the test of time being 400 years old (1611-2011) and has been reference across the world during that time. What better way to commemorate its publication than with this sort of a project.

I can say for certain that Jesus definitely was the Son of God because he followed in the footsteps of his Father based on the pattern. A good son will follow after the pattern of his father. A good father will create a pattern that he would want his son to follow. Jesus followed after the pattern of his Father, God, as indicated in the Gospels. "For verily I say unto you, That many prophets and righteous men have desired to see those things which ye see, and have not seen them; and to hear those things which ye hear, and have not heard them" (Matthew 13:17). Over time there have been billions of people who have passed through the earth since the origin of man and none were given the revelation or have proved with solid evidence, in my view, of the Almighty God's MASTER plan/ pattern such as this. This is part of the Almighty's Master plan or perhaps just the TIP of His plan. It is akin to finding a DNA match where the match is 100 percent.

"For centuries, science and faith have been polarized on some of the most fundamental questions in the universe, sometimes with deadly consequences." One of those questions in my view is, "the ultimate question – whether God exists. . . . From the far reaches of the cosmos to the inner working of the human mind, scientists and believers around the world are using science to open new frontiers in this ultimate quest."[71] The History Channel aired a show

---

[71] Source - The History Channel 2 TV Show Schedule, Proving God (mouse over caption), 2013, http://www.history.com/schedule/

on 12.13.2011 called *"Proving God"* which, in my view, attempted to provide some guidance in answering that question, "whether God exists." There are those religious leaders over time had stated, "Science is from the pit of Hell." Such leaders in my view should complement those involved in science for proving that there is a God and he has a plan and a design. There have not been any reports that I know of where scientists have paid homage to graven images or demonic entities requesting assistance in their research. Also there are those who mock those who believe in the "Supreme being" in the realm of science and believe in an arrogant manner, in my view, with making such statements as presented in a 2011*"Proving God"* documentary, "As science has gotten better and better, God has had less and less to do" with no insight into his plan. I think of those who are proponents of evolution and their view of how man came to be a being. How come or why has it not been recorded over the few millennia where apes, chimps, and orangutans that have been captive displayed the phenomenon of transforming into men. I would think that some record of such events back in ancient times should exist. "Evolution Created Life From Lifeless 'Primordial Soup,' Scientists Suggest"[72] One strongly agrees with the notion, based on what has been discovered and revealed, as stated **"Science without Religion is Lame, Religion without Science is blind" (Albert Einstein, 1941)**. "The fool hath said in his heart, There is no God." (Psalms 14:1 and 53:1) The link/union between Religion and Science has been found and for me it is an embrace of reason and revelation. This is a

---

h2/3/31/2013?view=day&tz=CT, Retrieved 05.19.2013

[72] Source - Huffingtonpost.com, 2012, "Evolution Created Life From Lifeless 'Primordial Soup', Scientists Suggest", http://www. huffingtonpost.com/2012/02/21/evolution-may-have-created-life_n_1290810.html, Retrieved 02.21.2012

breakthrough. One thinks how the three pattern has brought to light the introduction of religion and science united. It is said that the two are diametrically opposing views that cannot be reconciled. Based on the evidence presented here, they were never mutually exclusive to each other.

Could I have discovered and proven the true "theory of EVERYTHING (ToE)" i.e. the synergy of all the physical phenomenon that is known? Discovering the true link between religion and science including the true "Law/ Rule of Threes?" The missing link? "When the solution is simple, God is answering." (Albert Einstein)

For me the debate between the science of the Theory of Evolution and the theory of Intelligent Design has been settled. It is Intelligent Design that revolves around the form of a triangle, God's three pattern. Creation Science/ Intelligent Design today has a true place in the marketplace of ideas being revamped, reshaped, and redefined based on God's pattern which is evident from both the religious and scientific perspectives. In my view, the Bible and the universe that we know has the Creator's trademark stamped all over them. Those involved in curriculum and coursework for Creation Science and Master of Divinity degrees may want to include my findings as part of their programs. I can say that those dubbed "Nontrinitarians" who focus only on Jesus, based on their assumption, cannot make the link between religion and science with their view.

On 06.05.2012 it was stated in a headline that "46% Americans Believe In Creationism According To Latest Gallup Poll."[73] On 08.12.2013 I read an article that stated, "Religious people are less intelligent than atheists, study

---

[73] Source - Huffingtonpost.com, 2012, Huffingtonpost.com/2012/06/ 05/americans-believe-in-creationism_n_1571127.html, Retrieved on 06.05.12

finds. Religious people are less intelligent than non-believers, according to a new review of 63 scientific studies stretching back over decades. A team led by Miron Zuckerman of the University of Rochester found 'a reliable negative relation between intelligence and religiosity' in 53 out of 63 studies."[74] During the first quarter of this year a study was released entitled "The State of the Bible 2013" that was done for the American Bible Society. It stated that of those surveyed, 88 percent of them "own a Bible," 80 percent of them thought "the Bible was sacred," and 61 percent of them "wish they read the Bible more." It was also stated that "77% believe the values and morals of America are declining,"[75] Perhaps that number will improve based on what has been discovered. I could say it has been almost 6,000 years in the making, and discovered in 21st century based on the Gregorian calendar. At some point in time, this analysis should be presented to the International Association for Pattern Recognition (IAPR) for their consideration. I think of the saying that mentions three items "Hitting two birds with one stone" is applicable.

Discovering that the divine pattern is well established, I looked further into the word apocalypse. Many associate the meaning of the word with the destruction of the world, doom and gloom, but there is another which many tend to forget or overlook. The word comes from the Greek literally meaning "lifting of the veil" or to uncover or disclose. The latter meaning in this case is the appropriate definition to use, a revelation of the divine pattern. Many thought Friday, 12.21.2012 was going to be the end of the world based on the Mayan calendar date of 13.0.0.0.0. Based on what has been discovered the latter

---

[74] Source - Yahoo News, 2013, http://news.yahoo.com/religious-people-are-less-intelligent-than-atheists—study-finds—113350723.html#upCr476, Retrieved 08.12.2013

[75] Source - American Bible Society: The State of the Bible 2013, 2013, http://www.americanBible.org/state-Bible, Retrieved 04.05.2013

definition of the word would have been applicable for the date. With so many examples of the three pattern identified in and out of the Bible I had to think of eschatology, that part of theology that focuses on the end of mankind and/or the end of the world or a state in the future, as it relates to the divine pattern.

I discovered the God-head was seen three times in all their glory on Earth. In Exodus 33:18, 22-23 God the Father came to earth and Moses saw his terrestrial back parts in his glory. The four Gospels state that God the Son came to earth and was seen in his terrestrial glory by many people twice during the transfiguration and after his resurrection. Here is the triangle diagram of what I have stated (saved the best for last):

Three Glorious Appearances of God the Father & Son on Earth
(1) God the Father / Jehovah
Seen by Moses (Exodus 33:18,21-23)
Exodus33:18 ". . . I beseech thee, shew me thy glory."

3) After his Resurrection God the Son   **(2) The Transfiguration**
    Seen by many   **Jesus**   **Seen by three (Peter, James & John)**
    (Matthew 28:3,9-10,16   **(Matthew 17:1-9, Mark 9:2-8, and**
    Mark 16:10-12,   **Luke 9:28-36) — Matthew 17:2**
    Luke Chapter 24,   **". . .and his face did shine**
    John 20:17-26,   **as the sun, and his raiment**
    Acts 1:1-10)   **was white as the light."**

Matthew 28:2-3 states, "And, behold, there was a great earthquake: for the angel of the Lord descended from heaven, and came and rolled back the stone from the door, and sat upon it. His countenance was like lightning, and his raiment white as snow."

Luke 24:4 states, "And it came to pass, as they were much perplexed thereabout, behold, two men stood by them in shining garments."

John 20:12 states, "And seeth two angels in white sitting, the one at the head, and the other at the feet, where the body of Jesus had lain."

Based on the description of the angels mentioned, Jesus' appearance should have been similar after his resurrection even though it is not stated of the three appearances. The three glorious appearances of the divine was reviewed again, but this time with a focus on the time they occurred using, for the sake of argument, the date of 1491 B.C.E as a point of reference to revise the triangle. Along with the revision of the triangle, the subject of the Second Coming of Jesus is mentioned. It is noted that there have been other dates to consider as it relates to the Exodus of the children of Israel from Egypt in various Bibles, but in the King James Version this date has been used. The revised triangle diagram is as follows:

Three Glorious Appearances on Earth
(1) God the Father
Exo. 33:18,21-23
(Seen by one person, Moses, in his Glory)
(2500 years from Adam or 1500 B.C.E)
≅1500 years earlier
Before Jesus

Second	God the son	First
Coming	Jesus	Coming
????	2000+	The Gospels
(3)	Years	(2)

Jesus' third glorious appearance to be seen again by many (Matthew 24:30/ Revelation 19:11-16)

(seen by three first at the transfiguration in his glory then by many after his death in Matthew 17:1-9, Mark 9:2-8, Luke 9:28-36; and Matthew 28:3,9-10,16, John 20:17-18; Mark 16:12, Luke 24. 4000 years from Adam.)

The time between God the Father's appearance to Moses 2500 from Adam, and Jesus' ascension into heaven seems to be about 1,500 years later. It has been 2,000+ years since the ascension of Jesus. Jesus' third appearance will be the third time he will have been seen in all his glory, and the God head will have come to earth three times. In Acts 1:11 two angels in white tell the apostles that Jesus will return in all his glory. In Hebrews 9:28 it states, "So Christ . . .shall he appear the second time without sin unto salvation." I read scriptures where three heavenly individuals mention Jesus coming back in Matthew 24:44, 25:13; Mark 13:34-35; Luke 12:40, 18:8; John 14:3, 28 and Acts 1:10. The first person to state and/or allude to his return is Jesus himself in the scriptures related to the four gospels. The last scripture relates to two angels who tell Jesus' disciples that he is coming back. Another identified triangle,$\triangle$. He "shall so come in like manner as ye have seen him go into heaven" (Acts 1:11).

In Matthew 24:36-39 it states, "But of that day and hour knoweth no man, no, not the angels of heaven, but my Father only. [37] But as the days of Noah were, so shall also the coming of the Son of man be. [38] For as in the days that were before the flood they were eating and drinking, marrying and giving in marriage, until the day that Noah entered into the ark, [39]And knew not until the flood came, and took them all away; so shall also the coming of the Son of man be."

In Matthew 8:29 it states even the demons, devils, know that there is "that day" of the Lord, "And, behold, they cried out, saying, What have we to do with thee, Jesus, thou Son of God? art thou come hither to torment us before the time?" In 1 Thessalonians 5:2 it states, "For yourselves know perfectly that the day of the Lord so cometh as a thief in the night." There have been many over time in history who have tried and have been trying to predict when Jesus would come back. This is impossible for men to try and predict. I find it interesting that not many, if any, looked at the day of the week relating to eschatology as a beginning. There are only seven days and the chances are 1 in 7 or 0.142857142857142857, statistically speaking a 14 percent chance that he is going to return on one of the days of the week. I know the odds increase as those unlikely days of the week are eliminated, Monday-Thursday, Saturday and Sunday.

I focused on one particular day of the week. I thought of Matthew 27:29-53 and in the other Gospels, where it states, "[51]And, behold, the veil of the temple was rent in twain from the top to the bottom; and the earth did quake, and the rocks rent; . . .[52] the saints which slept arose, and came out of the graves after his resurrection, and went into the holy city, [Jerusalem] and appeared unto many." It is called Good Friday by many but I call the day the corruption of God's Friday because of that day's events that grieved him again. It is stated in Genesis 6:6, "And it repented the LORD that he had made man on the earth, and it grieved him at his heart." I thought about the account of human origin as stated in Genesis 1: 27 and 31, "So God created man in his own image, in the image of God created he him; male and female created he them. . . . [31]And God saw everything that he had made, and, behold, it was very good. And the evening and the morning were the sixth day." The verse of interest that leads me to think that God would return and/or past judgment on a Friday is Zephaniah 1:3 where it states, "I will consume man and beast; I will consume the fowls of the heaven, and the fishes of the sea." The order in which creatures are to be consumed is the opposite order of how all creatures were created as recorded in Genesis 1:20-27. By focusing on Friday, God would be reclaiming that day of the week that grieved him, thus coming full circle. It is noted that the Mayan calendar end date of 12.21.2012 fell on a Friday. ANY GIVEN FRIDAY!

Analyzing further relating to Good Friday, I thought of the number of hours Christ was dead from being on the cross to his resurrection. It is roughly thirty-nine hours from giving up the "ghost" at 3 pm (Luke 23:44, 46) to his rise on Sunday about 6 am (Matthew 28, Mark 16:2). Under Jewish custom any part of the day, however small, is included as part of or considered a full day. This could lead to controversy, in my view, in some circles.

I thought of how scientists would suggest that somewhere in the universe there is a celestial object either a planetoid, comet, asteroid, or even the same star of Bethlehem that herald Jesus' birth as stated in Matthew 2:2 that can rotate approximately every thirteen hours. This can be considered a day in God's eyes thus leading to the three thirteen hour days, 39/3. God does not have to focus on three Earth days. Who's to say that the star that herald Jesus' birth could have been viewed also as part of his departure? This, in my view, would satisfy the three day notion that some biblical scholars are concerned about. I thought further of how there are only 24 hours, 8 times 3, in the day and when Jesus returns he will return in one of those 24 hours, a 0.041667 percent or a 4 percent chance on a given Friday. I read in 1 Corinthians 15:52 which states, "In a moment, in the twinkling of an eye, at the last trump: for the trumpet shall sound, and the dead shall be raised incorruptible, and we shall be changed." There are 86,400 seconds in a 24 hour day. I wonder how many seconds or perhaps milliseconds are in a "twinkling of an eye"?

There is a name of a kingdom and area in the Old Testament that is used in the New Testament to characterize the future state of the world. Revelation 14:8 states, "Babylon is fallen, is fallen, that great city, because she made all nations drink of the wine of the wrath of her fornication," and Revelation 18:10 states, "Alas, alas, that great city Babylon, that mighty city! for in one hour is thy judgment come." I thought of how it is stated four times in the Old Testament the phrase "in the land of Shinar" in Genesis 10:10, 11:2, Daniel 1:2, and Zechariah 5:11, a place referred by some as Babylonia within the geographical area called Mesopotamia.

Note: the word "Shinar" is mentioned seven times: Genesis 10:10, 11:2, 14:1, 14:9; Isaiah 11:11; Daniel 1:2; Zechariah 5:11. There is a man mentioned by the name of "Nimrod" in Genesis 10:9-10, a mighty man that has a kingdom in Shinar. Jasher 7:45 states, "And all nations and tongues heard of his fame, and they gathered themselves to him, and they bowed down to the earth, and they brought him offerings, and he became their lord and king, and they all dwelt with him in the city at Shinar, and Nimrod reigned in the earth over all the sons of Noah, and they were all under his power and counsel." "Nimrod: he began to be mighty upon the earth" (1 Chronicles 1:10). In Genesis 11:1 it states, "And the whole earth was of one language, and of one speech." Also in the book of Jasher 7:46 it states, "And all the earth was of one tongue and words of union." The narrative goes on to suggest that under Nimrod a tower was built in the city of Babel "whose top may reach unto heaven" (Genesis 11:4, 9). In the book of Jasher 8:21 it states, "And all the princes of Nimrod and his great men took counsel together; . . . and they said to each other, Come let us build ourselves a city and in it a strong tower, and its top reaching heaven." As Revelation chapter 13 suggests, a person called the Beast, the Anti-Christ, will have control over all political, religious, commercial, and social environments on the earth which is akin to what the Nimrod had in Genesis and in the Book of Jasher.

With the Babylonia in the Mesopotamia (Iraq, Iran, etc.) area being mentioned in Genesis and Revelation, I thought of a coming of a full circle where God intervened and disrupted the plans of Nimrod "in the land Shinar" and as he is stated to do the same with the Anti-Christ, as defined in the book of Revelation, with his seemingly figurative environment called "Babylon" that encompassed the whole world. Scholars say that Mesopotamia is the "cradle of civilization." According to these two biblical accounts, in this case it seems history will repeat itself. The past is prologue. I read in Acts 7:2 which states, "The God of glory appeared unto our father Abraham, when he was in Mesopotamia, before he dwelt in Charran." Charran/Haran was a place Abraham went to before getting to the Land of Canaan in Genesis 11:31. "And the great city was divided into three parts, and the cities of the nations fell: and great Babylon came in remembrance before God, to give unto her the cup of the wine of the fierceness of his wrath" (Revelation 16:19).

A shepherd can lead a herd of sheep if he has control of the lead sheep. The Beast called the False Prophet has the characteristic of a sheep "two horns like a lamb" (Revelation 13:11). He is a leader of sheep. The Antichrist will be able to lead that "flock" being the shepherd in this case. It is stated that the earliest known battle in human history that was documented was at "The Mount of Megiddo" or Armageddon for the Egyptian Pharaoh Thutmose III using the technology of that day. I would think that the final battle will be more documented using various technologies to record that event. It is noted that the word "Babylon" is mentioned six times in the book of Revelation (14:8, 16:19, 17:5, 18:2, 10, and 21). Revelation 13:18 states the identity of "The Beast," "Here is wisdom. Let him that hath understanding count the number of the beast: for it is the number of a man; and his number is Six hundred threescore and six" or 666. I noticed that there are seven characters in the Roman numeral system. Their values are as follows, I=1, V=5, X=10, L=50, C=100, D=500, and M=1000. When adding and using the first six symbols, DCLXVI, in descending order it calculates to the number 666. I looked also at the three Greek symbols that total 666 as well chi X=600, xi ξ=60, and stigma ς=6. In continuing to think of how things coming full circle, I thought of how in Luke chapter 2 Jesus was in Jerusalem as a baby and in chapter 23 returned to Jerusalem to be judged just before his death. I read in Luke 3:23-38 of how the genealogy of Jesus is listed starting with him, the Son of God, and going backwards all the way back to Adam "which was the son of God." In Luke 5:1-11 Jesus, as part of his recruitment of some of his disciples, found them fishing in the Lake of Gennesaret a.k.a. Sea of Galilee, "Simon answering said unto him, Master, we have toiled all the night, and have taken nothing: nevertheless at thy word I will let down the net." When they did as he told them they caught "a great multitude of fishes." Peter and the two sons of Zebedee are mentioned and were astonished at the miracle. In John 21:1-14, after Jesus' resurrection and before his ascension into heaven, he finds his disciples fishing at the sea of Tiberias, a.k.a the Sea of Galilee, and says, "Children, have ye any meat? They answered him, No. And he said unto them, Cast the net on the right side of the ship, and ye shall find. They cast therefore, and now they were not able to draw it for the multitude of fishes." In this instance they caught and brought in "an hundred and fifty and three" fishes. Peter and the two sons of Zebedee are mentioned and were again astonished at the miracle. Jesus ended with his disciples where he began with them, fishing based on the mentioned verses.

In Genesis chapter 19 two angels are involved with the destruction of the cities of Sodom and Gomorrah, those who were viewed as wicked in God's eyesight. In Revelation chapter 11, God's "two witnesses" are also involved in God's judgment of the wicked. In the first and last books of the Bible, two of God's individuals are involved in the judgment of men on earth. Men displayed wickedness towards the two mentioned in the book of Genesis and it is also the case for the two of the book of Revelation.

One other subject researched was the Prophecy of the Popes which is said to be a list of Popes, with the last Pope named Petrus Romanus or Peter the Roman, one who is in

the "ministry of Bishop of Rome, Successor of Saint Peter
... the See of Rome, the See of Saint Peter" (Quote stated by
Pope Benedict XVI, 02.11.2013). It is said that this prediction was put forth in the 12th century by an Irish archbishop
Malachy O' Mongair later called St. Malachy. The name of
the last Pope makes me think of the one called the first Pope,
Simon Peter, the disciple of Jesus and how it is stated in
Matthew 16:18, "And I say also unto thee, That thou art Peter,
and upon this rock I will build my church; and the gates of
hell shall not prevail against it." Based on the Gospels, Peter
was either the first or the third disciple chosen of Jesus. It is
something to think about.

With this latest information and since it has been proven
that the Bible comes full circle relating to the beasts, truly
things do go in circles. The moon has revolved around the
earth for millennia. The earth has revolved around the Sun
for millennia. Other celestial objects, as well as the entire
universe have been revolving for millennia. It is said that the
earth wobbles like a gyroscope spinning on its axis taking
26,600 years to complete a precession or rotation. How can
we humans, being infinitesimal in this grand universe, think
we are going to escape this phenomenon of things going in
circles? WE DON'T! It behooves us to learn from the past. "It
is he that sitteth upon the circle of the earth" (Isaiah 40:22).

According to Jewish legend, there is a secret name of
God that is supposed to be the formula for all of creation
and if that name is pronounced backwards it is supposed to
annihilate all of creation. Could that name be encoded within
the biblical triangle pattern? I thought that since there are 66
books of the Bible it is 2/3s of a whole. What or where is the
other 1/3? Sixty-six is also a triangular number. Can I view
the Old Testament containing 39 books/ (13x3) and the New
Testament containing 27 books/ (9x3) as being two of three
books and the third book written divinely amongst the two
i.e. the compilation of the discovered divine triangles into a

book? Those involved in the Bible code, ELS, activities were only looking for hidden messages. Perhaps I know now that there should be the search for the hidden book. Six days God worked during creation for two triangles so why not three books/Testaments or a triangle of them? Something that is "born" out of the two testaments. I took a quick look at how the Tanakh or Hebrew Bible was compiled with the three books consisting of the Torah, Nevi'im, and Ketuvim. The Torah or first five books of the Christian Bible stands alone. The Nevi'im is the book of the Prophets. The Ketuvim is the book of the Writings. I viewed this compilation in a form of a triangle, where from a Christian perspective, I saw that the last two books contained information relating to the prophets Daniel, and what appears to be a combination of Ezra and Nehemiah, into a single body of work called Ezra-Nehemiah, another identified triangle, △. There are three separate books of prophets considered and mentioned within the Christian Bible that is among the Ketuvim or "Writings" book of the Hebrew Bible. The triangle of the Tanakh is as follows:

The Tanakh
1) Torah
The Law / Teaching

3
Books
of the
Tanakh

3) Ketuvim/   prophets   2) Nevi'im
Kethubhim   Nebhiim
(The Writings)   (the Prophets)

"Where is the promise of his coming? . . . all things continue as they were from the beginning of the creation" (2 Peter 3:4). Based on the 04.03.1968 Martin Luther King, Jr. statement from the Battle Hymn of the Republic hymnal, "Mine eyes have seen the glory of the coming of the Lord" in my view is truer today than ever before. In order to understand God's glory we must understand His story. He specializes in triangles. I have learned some of the psychology of the Divine. For me the revelation of the Three/triangle pattern is the TIP of the iceberg or more accurately the "flagship" as to whom he/they and what he/they are. Based on the information that has been discovered for one the true Final destination and Final Frontier is to see the Holy Trinity in all their GLORY!

A good portion of this work was done referencing information that was presented on the internet as the reference section indicates. This had to be done. It is said that we are in the information age. Newly discovered information presented in this book needed to be shown as incorporating the use of new technology. There are those who say "God is in the details." This pattern of the divine should be found also in the work of one Nostradamus amongst his quatrains, those four line poems or stanzas. I can only image what I could find in the ancient text, biblical and other religious documents, in other countries around the world in which those texts as well can be examined for the divine triangular pattern. I read in Romans 5:12-18 how by "one man" death entered into the world via sin and by faith in "one man" leads to life eternal the "free gift." I now know that the cracking of the Bible will lead to the cracking of the sky and Jesus' return one day.

"Learn as if you were to live forever" (Mahatma Gandhi)
"Thy word is a lamp unto my feet,
and a light unto my path." (Psalms 119:105)
"And he said, Unto you it is given to know
the mysteries of the kingdom of God." (Luke 8:10)
Now, the seal has been broken.

Appendix: TOP 12+ Major Biblical . . . Patterns

(IMPORTANT: READ ALL TRIANGLE SHAPES FROM RIGHT TO LEFT)

△/▽ **1)** The Three built Houses of God:

1. The Tabernacle of the Congregation under Moses in Exodus 25-31
2. The First Temple under King Solomon in 1 Kings 6:1-38, 1 Kings Chapter 7 and Chapter 8
3. The Second Temple in the book of Ezra, a prophet and under foreign rule in 2 Chronicles 36:22-23, Ezra 1:1-4, and Ezra 5.

The second temple was started by either Zerubbabel in Zechariah 4:9, "The hands of Zerubbabel have laid the foundation of this house" or Sheshbazzar in Ezra 5:16, "Then came the same Sheshbazzar, and laid the foundation of the house of God which is in Jerusalem." In Ezra 2:2 Zerubbabel is stated to be some of the first to return to Jerusalem from Babylon. The first house was mobile and the other two houses were stationary. This is the basis for first denoted triangle. The Ark of the Covenant only occupied the first two of the three houses of God. The second denoted triangle. Also the configuration of the three had a place called the Holy of Holies in the midst of them. The third future Jewish temple is called by some the visionary Temple of Ezekiel because it is describe in the Book of Ezekiel starting in chapter 40. The three temples, the two of the past and the one of the future is the basis for another identified triangle,▽. The second Jewish temple was recorded to have been destroyed in 70 A.D. by the Romans. A major remnant of this Temple was left standing which is called today the "Western Wall." One would think that whenever the third Jewish temple is built there will be some type of incorporation of this remnant linking the Second Jewish Temple to the Third one of the three. Another identified triangle,△.

▽ 2) The finger of God wrote on stone three times. The first two times relates to the Ten Commandments on stone tablets in Exodus 20:3-16 and Deuteronomy 5:6-21 that were given to Moses twice. The third time is in Daniel 5:25-28 on the wall. This is the basis for the denoted triangle. The third time God writes it is out of anger with the written four words of which two of them were the same against King Belshazzar's. Three of the words written on the wall are related to the judgment of the Kingdom of King Belshazzar, the first, second, and the fourth and of these three the last word is changed. Another identified triangle,▽. The first two times of the three when God writes he is calm. Another identified triangle,▽. In essence God used and wrote three words for his message against the king Belshazzar and the last word was changed in Daniel's interpretation of the writing. Another identified triangle,▽

△/▽ **3)** Read of the three single angelic birth announcements:

1. In Judges 13:3 by unnamed angel as stated in Judges 13:18 "And the angel of the LORD said unto him, Why askest thou thus after my name, seeing it is secret?" This is relating to the birth of Samson.
2. In Luke 1:5-25 by Gabriel and the birth of John, the Baptist, to Zacharias
3. In Luke 1:26-38 by Gabriel to Mary of the birth of Jesus.

The first denoted triangle is based on the fact that Gabriel makes the last two announcements of the three and they are linked where the parents/sons are cousins as well as being in the New Testament. First two men were Nazarites unto God, linked, in that the angel mentions statements ". . .drink no wine nor strong drink. . ." in Judges 13:7, ". . .shall drink neither wine nor strong drink" in Luke 1:15 before they are born. This is an attribute of a Nazarite. The last son Jesus was not a Nazarite. This is the basis for the second denoted triangle. The first son was strong physically and the last two sons are strong spiritually. Another identified triangle,△. The "Holy Ghost" was involved with the last two births as stated in Luke 1:15 and 1:35, also in Matthew 1:21, respectively. Of the three sons the last two names are given by the angel Gabriel, John and Jesus in Luke 1:13 and Luke 1:31 respectively. Another identified triangle,△ (Note: In Genesis 18:10 "The Lord", with two others, provided the first birth announcement with the fore-telling of Isaac.) A triangle diagram is shown below for the three mentioned sons:

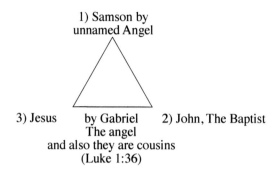

1) Samson by
unnamed Angel

3) Jesus   by Gabriel   2) John, The Baptist
The angel
and also they are cousins
(Luke 1:36)

△ **4)** Read of the three glorious appearances of the Godhead on earth:

1. God the Father Jehovah seen by Moses in Exodus 33:18, 21-23. Exodus 33:18 ". . . I beseech thee, shew me thy glory."
2. The first by God the Son Jesus during the Transfiguration where he was seen by his three disciples Peter, James and John in Matthew 17:1-9, Mark 9:2- 8, Luke 9:28-36. Matthew 17:2 ". . .and his face did shine as the sun, and his raiment was white as the light."
3. Jesus, God the Son, again after his resurrection he was seen by many in Matthew 28:3, 9-10,16; Mark 16:10-12, Luke Chapter 24, John 20:17-26 and Acts 1:1-10.

Since the angel mentioned in Matthew 28:3 ". . .His countenance was like lightning, and his raiment white as snow" Jesus' appearance should have been similar after his resurrection. Based on scriptures such as Matthew 24:30 "And then shall appear the sign of the Son of man in heaven: and then shall all the tribes of the earth mourn, and they shall see the Son of man coming in the clouds of heaven with power and great glory" and Revelation 19:11-16 Jesus has a third glorious appearance to make and he will be seen again by many, practically by everyone this time. The basis for the denoted triangle is God the Father was seen once and God the Son twice on earth in their glory.

▽/△ **5)** The HOLY Trinity, as it is said to be and mean "three in one." Read in Matthew 28:19 after his resurrection Jesus states to his disciples, "Go ye therefore, and teach all nations, baptizing them in the name of the Father, and of the Son, and of the Holy Ghost." Some call it the Great Commission and used in the Trinitarian formula. Two of the three names have been given. God the Father's name which is given is JEHOVAH mentioned in three books, four verses, in Exodus 6:3, Psalm 83:18, Isaiah 12:2, and Isaiah 26:4. A previously identified triangle,▽, within the three books, God the Son, Jesus, Matthew 1:25 ". . . and he called his name JESUS." The name of the Holy Ghost/ Spirit we don't know as of yet of the three. This is the first denoted triangle. Also notice how beginning in the book of Matthew we are introduced to the existence of Jesus and of the "Holy Ghost," or Holy Spirit, the second and third members of the Holy Trinity. These two are not mentioned at all in the Old Testament, at least not as we know them in the New Testament. God the Father is of and in the Old Testament and Jesus and the Holy Ghost is in and of the New Testament predominantly. This is the basis for the second denoted triangle. Of the three Jesus is the only one to have been born into this world. Another identified triangle,△. The name of God and his son both begin with the letter J in English, in Latin I, and Hebrew Y. One would think that the name of the Holy Ghost/Spirit would begin with the letter J as well.

△ **6)** Read of how three calves of gold were made by the Children of Israel in Exodus 32:3-4/Deuteronomy 9:16

when they were out of Egypt near Mount Sinai, Exodus 32:4-8, and in 1 Kings 12:28-29 in the Northern Kingdom of Israel where King Jeroboam had two built in the cities of Bethel and Dan. This is the basis for the denoted triangle. After the three were built it was stated that ". . . thy gods, O Israel, which brought thee up out of the land of Egypt." The first created calf is also mentioned in Psalm 106:19, Nehemiah 9:18, and Acts 7:41. Of these three verses two verses are in the O.T. and one in N.T. Another identified triangle,▽.

▽/△/▽ 7) According to the Bible there have been three people who have ascended into heaven in corporeal form. Two of which are in the Old Testament and they did it without dying. Enoch, Jude 1:14 "And Enoch also, the seventh from Adam, in Genesis 5:22-24)/Hebrews 11:5/Book of Jasher 3:36, ". . .and it was upon the seventh day that Enoch ascended into heaven in a whirlwind, with horses and chariots of fire". Elijah, 2 Kings 2:11 "And it came to pass, as they still went on, and talked, that, behold, there appeared a chariot of fire, and horses of fire, and parted them both asunder; and Elijah went up by a whirlwind into heaven". These two both on chariots with horses of fire in a whirlwind. The third person to ascend into heaven is in the New Testament with Jesus, after his death and resurrection, in Mark 16:19, Luke 24:50-51, and Acts 1:9-12. This is the basis for the first denoted triangle. (Note: Jesus was astral and corporeal at the same time because He is GOD). The last two ascensions are detailed in the Bible while the first one is not. The second denoted triangle. The first two men did not see death but the third person did. The third denoted triangle. Note, with God using a whirlwind with Enoch and Elijah, God used a whirlwind one other time in Job 38-42 to speak. Another identified triangle,▽. Over the decades I heard a number of people say, and read in the bible, that three people ascended into heaven Enoch, Elijah, and Jesus. No one in my entire life ever stated how Enoch ascended into heaven until I read it in the Book of Jasher. The last two men I was told about and I read about but I never knew the details of how Enoch did it of the three men. Another identified triangle,△. Below is a triangle diagram representing the first denoted triangle:

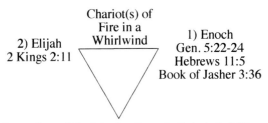

Chariot(s) of
Fire in a
Whirlwind

2) Elijah
2 Kings 2:11

1) Enoch
Gen. 5:22-24
Hebrews 11:5
Book of Jasher 3:36

3) Jesus, Son of God, in the Gospels & Acts 1:9-12

▽ **8)** Read of the three instances where a person delivered a major list of items to the people that was of divinity. The first and second are the ten commandments that were given by God the Father twice to Moses (Exodus 32:19, 34:1) and recorded two times in Exodus 20:3-17 and Deuteronomy 5:7-21. Note Moses broke the first stone list. The third are the Beatitudes given by Jesus, God the Son, in Matthew 5:1-12/Luke 6:20-26. God the father wrote it, twice as stated in Exodus 34:1 and Jesus spoke it once. This is the basis for the denoted triangle. Note that in reading Deuteronomy 5:22 God the Father also spoke the Ten Commandments to the people ". . .out of the midst of the fire, of the cloud, and of the thick darkness." Two of the three members of the Trinity were involved with the giving of a major list. Another identified triangle, ▽.

▽/△ **9)** Read Revelation Chapters 6-16 and the 21 judgments. The first two groups of 7s, the seven seals and the seven trumpets, are linked via the seventh seal being opened and releasing the seven trumpets. The seven vials/bowls are mentioned separately. "And when he had opened the seventh seal, there was silence in heaven about the space of half an hour [30 minutes]. ²And I saw the seven angels which stood before God; and to them were given seven trumpets" (Rev. 8:1-2). The seven vials/bowls are mentioned separately starting in chapter 16. The first denoted triangle. One can also view how the first group of 7 is handled by the Lamb of God and the last two groups of 7s are handled by two groups of seven angels. The second denoted triangle. One notes that these 21 judgments are preceded by sevens messages to seven churches in Revelation chapters 2 and 3. The two triangle diagrams of the two views of 21 judgments are shown below:

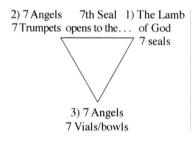

▽ **10) Read in Revelation of the three who are killed and are resurrected from the dead. In Revelation 11:3-12, the "two witnesses" of God who are killed by Satan, "the beast that ascendeth out of the bottomless pit" and are resurrected ". . .after three days and an half the Spirit of life from God entered into them." In Revelation 13:3 and 17:8 the Antichrist is ". . .wounded to death; and his deadly wound was healed" and ". . .which had the wound by a sword, and did live" (Revelation 13:14). Satan resurrects him by indwelling in him as interpreted by some via the scriptures of Revelation 17:8-13. This is the basis for the denoted triangle. To one this would**

make since in that Jesus was raised from the dead so why would not The Beast/Antichrist via Satan. Based on all of the referenced scriptures here Satan is involved in some way with all three. The death of God's two and the resurrection of his man the Antichrist. Another identified triangle,▽.

△/△ 11) Read of the three particular men mentioned and described who were or will be human individuals in the New Testament who ended or will end up in Hell/lake of fire.

First, the parable of the "certain rich man" in Luke 16:22-23 ". . .the rich man also died, and was buried; ²³ And in hell he lift up his eyes, being in torments, and seeth Abraham afar off, and Lazarus in his bosom." The second and third persons are The Beast and the False Prophet in Revelation 19:20, "And the beast was taken, and with him the false prophet that wrought miracles before him, with which he deceived them that had received the mark of the beast, and them that worshipped his image. These both were cast alive into a lake of fire burning with brimstone." In Revelation 20:10 the two are also stated as being there. This is the basis for the first denoted triangle. Of the three men the first man is part of a parable and the last two men are of a vision. The second denoted triangle. Read of others there who are in the place as stated in 2 Peter 2:4, "For if God spared not the angels that sinned, but cast them down to hell, and delivered them into chains of darkness, to be reserved unto judgment." Also read in Revelation 20:13 of those that are there, "And the sea gave up the dead which were in it; and death and hell delivered up the dead which were in them: and they were judged every man according to their works." Along with the mentioned, others in Rev. 21:8 lists the types of people that joins them, ". . .the fearful, and unbelieving, and the abominable, and murderers, . . . and all liars, shall have their part in the lake which burneth with fire and brimstone:" Note: Read of the specific scriptures in Matthew 5:22 and Luke 10:15, Matthew 11:23, 23:15, 33 of those that are in danger or risk of going into hell. Read in three books, four other notable scriptures, relating to the subject of Hell and its purpose in Psalms, Proverbs, and Isaiah:

Psalms 9:17 "The wicked shall be turned into hell, and all the nations that forget God."

Proverbs 27:20 "Hell and destruction are never full; so the eyes of man are never satisfied."

Isaiah 5:14 "Therefore hell hath enlarged herself, and opened her mouth without measure: and their glory, and their multitude, and their pomp, and he that rejoiceth, shall descend into it."

Isaiah 28:15 "Because ye have said, We have made a covenant with death, and with hell are we at agreement; when the overflowing scourge shall pass through, it shall not come unto us: for we have made lies our refuge, and under falsehood have we hid ourselves."

Of the first three verses the second and third are linked relating to the size of Hell. An identified triangle,△. Of the last three verses the fourth verse implies some level of comfort with it in my view. Of the three books the last book has two verses while the first two books have one verse each. Another identified triangle,▽.

△/△/▽/▽ **12)** The three beasts of the triumvirate, The unholy trinity, Satan, a.k.a. Beelzebub, The Anti-Christ (A.C.), and The False Prophet (F.P.).

1. Beast of the Air, Ephesians 2:2 ". . .the prince of the power of the air. . .", - Great Red Dragon who ". . .having seven heads and ten horns, and seven crowns upon his heads" in Revelation 12:3.
2. Beast of the Sea, evil fisher of men, - ". . .having seven heads and ten horns, and upon his horns ten crowns, and upon his heads the name of blasphemy" in Revelation 13:1.
3. Beast of the Earth/Field - who ". . .he had two horns like a lamb, and he spake as a dragon" in Revelation 13:11.

The first beast is not stated as a beast but is described as one, a dragon. Also the last two "Beasts" are recorded as "Beasts" being of the Sea and Earth. The first denoted triangle. The last two, The Anti-Christ and False Prophet are linked as being human. Satan is not in either case. The second denoted triangle. The first two beasts, of the air and sea, are connected based on the described characteristics, 7 heads/10 Horns/7 or 10 crowns. The third denoted triangle. Since animals are consider beasts one thinks of Genesis 1:20-25 and the creation of beasts on Days 5 (sea and air) and 6 (earth/field) and makes the correlation that the beasts of Revelation are a mirror image and a dark opposite of the beasts of Creation. It is as if the Bible has come "full circle." The fourth denoted triangle is based on the two days for the beasts of creation. In the order and in the three areas where beasts were created man was given ". . .dominion over the fish of the sea, and over the fowl of the air, and over the cattle, and over all the earth, . . ." as stated in Genesis 1:26. The unholy trinity is the direct opposite of the Holy Trinity. Here are the triangle diagrams below:

1) Great Red Dragon
Satan
(Beast of the Air)

3) Beast   Human   2) Beast
of the   Rev. 12:3, 13:1, 11   of the
Earth   Sea
(F.P.)   (A.C.)

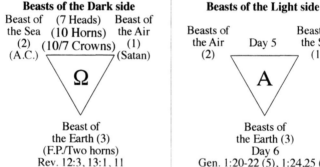

Beasts of the Dark side

Beast of   (7 Heads)   Beast of
the Sea   (10 Horns)   the Air
(2)   (10/7 Crowns)   (1)
(A.C.)   (Satan)

Ω

Beast of
the Earth (3)
(F.P./Two horns)
Rev. 12:3, 13:1, 11

Beasts of the Light side

Beasts of   Beasts of
the Air   Day 5   the Sea
(2)   (1)

A

Beasts of
the Earth (3)
Day 6
Gen. 1:20-22 (5), 1:24,25 (6)

I am Alpha and Omega
(Rev. 1:11)

*** Bonus of Three more ***

+1)△/▽/▽ Read of the three instances where an angel is seen with his sword. The first instance is by the prophet Balaam in Numbers 22:31, "Then the LORD opened the eyes of Balaam, and he saw the angel of the LORD standing in the way, and **his sword drawn in his hand**." The second instance is by Joshua in Joshua 5:13,15, ". . .Joshua was by Jericho, that he lifted up his eyes and looked, and, behold, there stood a man over against him with **his sword drawn in his hand:** " (verse 13) ". . .the captain of the LORD'S host said unto Joshua, Loose thy shoe from off thy foot; for the place whereon thou standest is holy" (verse 15). The third instance is by King David and "the elders of Israel" in 1 Chronicles 21:16, "And David lifted up his eyes, and saw the angel of the LORD stand between the earth and the heaven, **having a drawn sword in his hand** stretched out over Jerusalem. Then David and the elders of Israel, who were clothed in sackcloth, fell upon their faces." The first man had to have his eyes opened before he saw the angel. The other two sighting this was not done. This is the first denoted triangle. In the first two instances the angel is on the ground and no one is injured. In the third instance the angel is in the air and 70,000 men die relating to his presence in 1 Chronicles 21:14. This is the second denoted triangle. Of the three instances, in the first two only one man saw the angel and in the third a number of men. This is the basis for the third denoted triangle. Note also the phrase ". . .his sword drawn in his hand" is stated in the first two instances but not in the third. Another identified triangle, ∇. Also the first two instances are connected to the Exodus of the children of Israel from Egypt some time afterwards, the third is not. Another identified triangle, ∇. Of the three instances the last angel does something else also as recorded in 1 Chronicles 21:27, "And the LORD commanded the angel; and he put up his sword again into the sheath thereof". Another identified triangle, ∇.

Note: Genesis 3:24 states, ". . .he placed at the east of the garden of Eden Cherubim, and a flaming sword which turned every way, to keep the way of the tree of life". There is no mention or record of anyone seeing them. Also note in Psalm 104:4 it states, "Who maketh his angels spirits; his ministers a flaming fire."

+2) △/▽/▽ Read of the three people in four scriptures where they mention the title of Messiah/Messias in Daniel 9:25, 26, John 1:41, and John 4:25. The first person who mentions the title is the angel Gabriel who visits the prophet Daniel while the last two people of the three are Andrew the brother of Peter and the adulterous woman at the well who tells others. The last two people of the three associates the title with Jesus. This is the basis for the first denoted triangle. Notice that the two men mention the term being the first and the second with a woman mentioning it being the third person. The basis for the second denoted triangle. The first two are men who are righteous and the third person is a sinner. The third denoted triangle. Of the three people the last two of them are mentioned in the same book △. Of the three the first person is from heaven. Another identified triangle, △. Of the three individuals the names of two of them are given. Another identified triangle,▽. Here are the scriptures:

> Daniel 9:25 "Know therefore and understand, that from the going forth of the commandment to restore and to build Jerusalem unto the Messiah the Prince shall be seven weeks, and threescore and two weeks: the street shall be built again, and the wall, even in troublous times."

> Daniel 9:26 "And after threescore and two weeks shall Messiah be cut off, but not for himself: and the people of the prince that shall come shall destroy the city and the sanctuary; and the end thereof shall be with a flood, and unto the end of the war desolations are determined."

John 1:41 "He first findeth his own brother Simon, and saith unto him, We have found the Messias, which is, being interpreted, the Christ."

John 4:25 "The woman saith unto him, I know that Messias cometh, which is called Christ: when he is come, he will tell us all things."

+3)▽/▽ Read of the three Roman emperors recorded in the New Testament of the Bible with the title "Caesar". The first Gaius Julius Caesar Augustus was the first ever Roman Emperor of the Roman Empire ". . .Caesar Augustus. . ." in St. Luke 2:1. The second Tiberius Julius Caesar Augustus was the second Roman Emperor ". . .Tiberius Caesar. . ." in St. Luke 3:1. The third mentioned Roman emperor is Tiberius Claudius Caesar Augustus Germanicus the fourth Roman Emperor in Acts 11:28,". . . Claudius Caesar" and 18:2. The first two Roman emperors mentioned lived during Jesus' life of the three. The first denoted triangle. Of the three mentioned emperors the first two are also named in the same book of Luke. The second denoted triangle. Notice also that the title of Caesar is after the names of Tiberius and Claudius and not Augustus. Another identified triangle,△. All three emperors are a part of the Julio-Claudian Dynasty. The third Roman emperor Caligula is not recorded at all in the text. It is said that Caligula, as the third Roman emperor viewed himself as deity and had ". . .ordered the erection of a statue of himself in the Jewish Temple of Jerusalem. . .". (Wikipedia, Caligula, 2013, http://en.wikipedia.org/wiki/Caligula, Retrieved 01.02.2013) An act that should exclude an individual from being mentioned in the text in my view.

References / Resources / Web links, Computer programs, and Books

The Bible code – http://en.wikipedia.org/wiki/Bible_code

Torah Bible Codes | Bible codes | Torah Codes - http://www.realBiblecodes.com

Online Parallel Bible - www.Biblehub.com/

The Bible Gateway - www.Biblegateway.com

HOLY BIBLE: Text Files - http://atschool.eduweb.co.uk/sbs777/Bible/text/

Authorized King James Version - http://en.wikipedia.org/wiki/Authorized_King_James_Version

Meaning of Numbers in the Bible for # 3 - http://www.Biblestudy.org/Bibleref/meaning-of-numbers-in-Bible/3.html

The Symbolism and Spiritual Significance of the Number Three - http://www.greatdreams.com/three/three.htm

Meaning of Numbers in the Bible for # 4 - http://www.Biblestudy.org/Bibleref/meaning-of-numbers-in-Bible/4.html

Meaning of Numbers in the Bible for # 7 - http://www.Biblestudy.org/Bibleref/meaning-of-numbers-in-Bible/7.html

Meaning of Numbers in the Bible for # 8 - http://www. Biblestudy.org/Bibleref/meaning-of-numbers-in-Bible/8.html

Meaning of Numbers in the Bible for # 9 - http://www. Biblestudy.org/Bibleref/meaning-of-numbers-in-Bible/9.html

Meaning of Numbers in the Bible for # 10 - http://www. Biblestudy.org/Bibleref/meaning-of-numbers-in-Bible/10.html

Meaning of Numbers in the Bible for # 20 - http://www. Biblestudy.org/Bibleref/meaning-of-numbers-in-Bible/20.html

Sigil - http://en.wikipedia.org/wiki/Sigil_(magic)

Trinity (Holy) - http://en.wikipedia.org/wiki/Trinity

Use of three in the Bible - http://Bible.org/seriespage/use-three-Bible

Bovid (Bovidae Family) – http://en.wikipedia.org/wiki/Bovid

List of Pharaohs - http://en.wikipedia.org/wiki/List_of_pharaohs

Twelve tribes of Israel - http://catholic-resources.org/Bible/History-12Tribes.htm

The 12 Tribes of Israel - http://www.israel-a-history-of.com/12-tribes-of-israel.html

Feast of Unleavened Bread – Feasts of Israel - http://www.christcenteredmall.com/teachings/feasts/unleavened-bread.htm

The Feast of Weeks – Pentecost (Shavuot) - http://www3.telus.net/public/kstam/en/temple/details/pentecost.htm

Old Testament – The Five Offerings - http://www3.telus.net/public/kstam/en/tabernacle/details/offerings.htm

Topical Bible: Caul – biblehub.com/topical/c/caul.htm

The History of Israel: From Ancient Jerusalem to the Present - http://www.israel-a-history-of.com/

List of pharaohs - http://en.wikipedia.org/wiki/List_of_
pharaohs

Moses - From Prince of Egypt to Servant of God - http://
www.ptm.org/99PT/JanFeb/Moses.htm

Three Altars at Bethel - http://pratonix.hubpages.com/
hub/The-Altar-at-Bethel

The Tabernacle - http://en.wikipedia.org/wiki/Tabernacle

Schematic Plan of the Temple (Herod's) - http://www.
Bible-history.com/jewishtemple/JEWISH_TEMPLE
Schematic_Plan_of_the_Temple.htm

The curtain Coverings - http://www.Bible-history.com/
tabernacle/TAB4The_Curtain_Coverings.htm

BRASS;   BRAZEN   -   http://www.Bible-history.com/
isbe/B/BRASS%3B+BRAZEN/

Cassia - http://en.wikipedia.org/wiki/Cassia

Three Entrances: Gate, Door, Vail - http://www.livingBi-
blestudies.org/study/JT13/057.html

Book of Judges - http://en.wikipedia.org/wiki/Book_of_
Judges

Nazarite   -   http://christiananswers.net/dictionary/naz-
arite.html

Star of David – http://en.wikipedia.org/wiki/Star_of_
David

Seal of Solomon – http://en.wikipedia.org/wiki/Seal_of_
Solomon

The Two Kingdoms - http://www.jewishvirtuallibrary.
org/jsource/History/Kingdoms1.html

Chart of Israel's Kings and Prophets – www.thebook-
wurm.com/kingchrt.htm

Shadrach, Meshach, and Abednego - http://en.wikipedia.
org/wiki/Shadrach,_Meshach,_and_Abednego

Baby Name – Baby Name Meanings - http://www.think-
babynames.com/

History of the Book of Psalms - http://psalms.jesusan-
swers.com/

Book of Isaiah - http://en.wikipedia.org/wiki/Book_of_
Isaiah

Book of Isaiah: Introduction to the Book of Isaiah - http://
agards-Bible-timeline.com/blog/isaiah-prophet-
of-the-old-testament/

Book of Ezekiel - http://en.wikipedia.org/wiki/Book_of_
Ezekiel

Fulfillment of Ezekiel's Prophecy of the Wheels - http://
www.Biblewheel.com//Wheel/Ezekiel_Wheels.php

ANE History: Judah in Exile – www.theology.edu/
lec23.htm

The Return to Zion - http://en.wikipedia.org/wiki/The_
Return_to_Zion

The Commandment to Restore and to Build Jerusalem -
http://www.patmospapers.com/daniel/457.htm

The Tanakh - http://en.wikipedia.org/wiki/Tanakh

The Mezuzah - http://en.wikipedia.org/wiki/Mezuzah

Biblical Magi - http://en.wikipedia.org/wiki/Biblical_Magi

Synoptic Gospels - http://en.wikipedia.org/wiki/Synoptic_
Gospels

Synoptic Gospel Parallels – Synoptic Gospels Comparison
- http://www.gospelparallels.com/

Gospel Harmony - http://en.wikipedia.org/wiki/Gospel_
harmony

Cleaning of the Temple - http://en.wikipedia.org/wiki/
Cleansing_of_the_Temple

The Order of the Triple Tradition in the Synoptic Gospels -
http://www.abu.nb.ca/courses/ntintro/OrderTriple.htm

Julius Caesar - http://en.wikipedia.org/wiki/Julius_
Caesar

List of Roman emperors - http://en.wikipedia.org/wiki/
List_of_Roman_emperors

List of Hasmonean and Herodian rulers - http://
en.wikipedia.org/wiki/List_of_Kings_of_Judea#
Roman_Prefects

Rulers in Israel during the Roman Era - http://catholic-resources.org/Bible/History-RomanEra.htm

The Holy Utterances - http://www.stempublishing.com/authors/hughes/HOLYUTTR.html

(Roman god) Jupiter - http://en.wikipedia.org/wiki/Jupiter_(mythology)

(Roman god) Mercury - http://en.wikipedia.org/wiki/Mercury_(mythology)

(Roman goddess) Diana - http://en.wikipedia.org/wiki/Diana_(mythology)

Caiaphas - http://en.wikipedia.org/wiki/Caiaphas

The Three Marys - http://en.wikipedia.org/wiki/The_Three_Marys

An Overview of the Book Of Revelation - http://www.christianinconnect.com/revelation.htm

Revelation: The Seals, the Trumpets, the Woes, and the Bowls - http://www.scribd.com/doc/23141765/Revelation-The-Seals-the-Trumpets-the-Woes-and-the-Bowls

Cave of the Apocalypse - http://en.wikipedia.org/wiki/Cave_of_the_Apocalypse

THE FALSE PROPHET AND IMAGE OF THE BEAST OF REVELATION - http://Biblelight.net/false.htm

The Destruction of the Second Temple - http://www.templemount.org/destruct2.html

Truth for the World - http://www.tftw.org/HTML/BCC/courses/bcc_ots_l18.html

Trefoil - http://en.wikipedia.org/wiki/Trefoil

Borromean Rings - http://en.wikipedia.org/wiki/Borromean_rings

The Whore of Babylon - http://en.wikipedia.org/wiki/Whore_of_Babylon

The Third Woe – www.gideonstrumpet.org/thirdwoe.asp?article=thirdwoe

Battle of Megiddo - http://en.wikipedia.org/wiki/Battle_of_Megiddo_(15th_century_BC)

The Mayan Calendar - http://www.webexhibits.org/calendars/calendar-mayan.html

Jewish eschatology - http://en.wikipedia.org/wiki/Jewish_eschatology

Christian eschatology - http://en.wikipedia.org/wiki/Christian_eschatology

Islamic eschatology - http://en.wikipedia.org/wiki/Islamic_eschatology

Prophecy of the Popes - http://en.wikipedia.org/wiki/Prophecy_of_the_Popes

The King James Code - http://www.Biblebelievers.com/Hoggard_KJV_Code.html

Prophecies Jesus Fulfilled: 44 Prophecies of the Messiah Fulfilled in Jesus Christ - http://christianity.about.com/od/Biblefactsandlists/a/Prophecies-Jesus.htm

The Significance of The Number Three - http://www.betemunah.org/three.html

Nuclear physics – http:// en.wikipedia.org/wiki/Nuclear_physics

Proton - http:// en.wikipedia.org/wiki/Proton

Standard Model (particle physics) - http://en.wikipedia.org/wiki/Standard_Model

Carbon Dioxide – http://en.wikipedia.org/wiki/Carbon_dioxide

Vitamin C - http://en.wikipedia.org/wiki/Vitamin_C

Triatomic molecule - http://en.wikipedia.org/wiki/Triatomic_molecule

Nuclear weapon - http://en.wikipedia.org/wiki/Nuclear_weapon

Scientific symbol for the atom - http://www.thealmightyguru.com/OldNews/2009-02.html

Body Orifice - http://en.wikipedia.org/wiki/Body_orifice

Id, Ego, Super-Ego – http://en.wikipedia.org/wiki/Id,_ego_and_super-ego

Sleep | Brain Rules – http://brainrules.net/sleep

Solar System - http://en.wikipedia.org/wiki/Solar_System

Black Hole - http://en.wikipedia.org/wiki/Black_hole

Axial precession - http://en.wikipedia.org/wiki/Axial_precession

Theory of everything - http://en.wikipedia.org/wiki/Theory_of_everything

Triangular Number - http://en.wikipedia.org/wiki/Triangular _number

Traffic light - http://en.wikipedia.org/wiki/Traffic_light

Area code history - http://www.area-codes.com/area-code-history.asp

Forever 21 - http://en.wikipedia.org/wiki/Forever_21

History of the creation–evolution controversy - http://en.wikipedia.org/wiki/History_of_the_creation evolution_controversy#The_current_controversy

Secrets of the Bible Code Revealed (Documentary) 1998, Grizzly Adams Productions, Inc – http://www.youtube.com/watch?v=6teFSLWG7zE (part 1) and http://www.youtube.com/watch?v=MGgWCkgExG8 (part 2)

Proving God (Documentary), 2011, Karga Seven Pictures for History, A&E Television Networks, LLC – www.youtube.com/watch?v=5_a0oFcomog

Stephen Hawking, "Did God create the universe?", 2011, Darlow Smithson Productions Ltd for Discovery Channel - http://www.youtube.com/watch?v=JOk0fGYf5g4

The American Bible Challenge, 2012-2014, RelativityREAL, Embassy Row, Sony Pictures Television, GSN (Game Show Network) Originals production companies - http://gsntv.com/shows/the-american-Bible-challenge/

Triangle (instrument) - http://en.wikipedia.org/wiki/Triangle(instrument)

Theopolis 3 Bible program for Windows, Rich Meyers, 1997-2004, King James Version

eSword 7.1 Bible program for Windows, Ivan Jurik, 2000-2004, King James Version

Bible+ 3.00 for Palm PDA, (Personal Digital Assistant), Contributing Programmers, King James Version

Book of Jasher, J.H. Parry & Co. Salt Lake City, Utah: 1887

Holy Bible of 1886, Globe Bible Publishing Co., 1886, King James Version

The Thompson Chain-Reference Bible, 1964, B.B. Kirk Bride Bible Co. Inc., King James Version

The Holy Bible, 1990, Thomas Nelson Inc., King James Version

The Holy Bible, 2003, Nelson Inc., King James Version

Complete Jewish Bible, 1998, Jewish New Testament Publications Inc., David H. Stern

The Life of Christ (American Bible Society) 1/20/2012 magazine, Time Inc. Specials

777 and other Qabalistic writings of Aleister Crowley, 1996, Samuel Weiser Inc., Samuel Weiser

The Book of the Angel Raziel, Sefer Raziel HaMalakh, Hebrew version, date unknown, author unknown.

345

CPSIA information can be obtained at www.ICGtesting.com
Printed in the USA
LVOW10s0827060416

482319LV00013B/53/P